AN OLD GATE OF ENGLAND

RYE, ROMNEY MARSH, AND THE WESTERN CINQUE PORTS

By

A. G. BRADLEY

Author of "Highways and Byways in the Lake District," "The Gateway of Scotland," "The March and Borderland of Wales," "Round about Wiltshire," etc.

WITH ILLUSTRATIONS BY
MARIAN E. G. BRADLEY

Copyright © 2018 Read Books Ltd.
This book is copyright and may not be
reproduced or copied in any way without
the express permission of the publisher in writing

British Library Cataloguing-in-Publication Data
A catalogue record for this book is available from
the British Library

PREFACE

I TAKE this opportunity of thanking the many friends who have assisted me towards the accomplishment of this little work. I should mention more particularly my indebtedness to Mr. H. P. Burra for the use of his valuable collection of local works in the library at Springfield; to Mr. Thomas Parkin, F.S.A., of High Wickham, Hastings, for similar help from his well-stored shelves and unrivalled knowledge of his native town and district; to Mr. Arthur Finn, of Westbroke; the Rev. A. Frewen Aylward, Rector of Northiam; and Mr. Walter Dawes, town clerk of Rye, for kind assistance in various ways; and finally to Mr. G. H. J. Tayleur for valuable help in revision of the proof sheets.

It seems advisable, too, to state here that the selection of subjects for illustration was in part curtailed by the war regulations and restrictions affecting certain portions of the sea board and other spots, while the artist's work was in progress.

ARTHUR GRANVILLE BRADLEY.

RED COTTAGE, RYE.

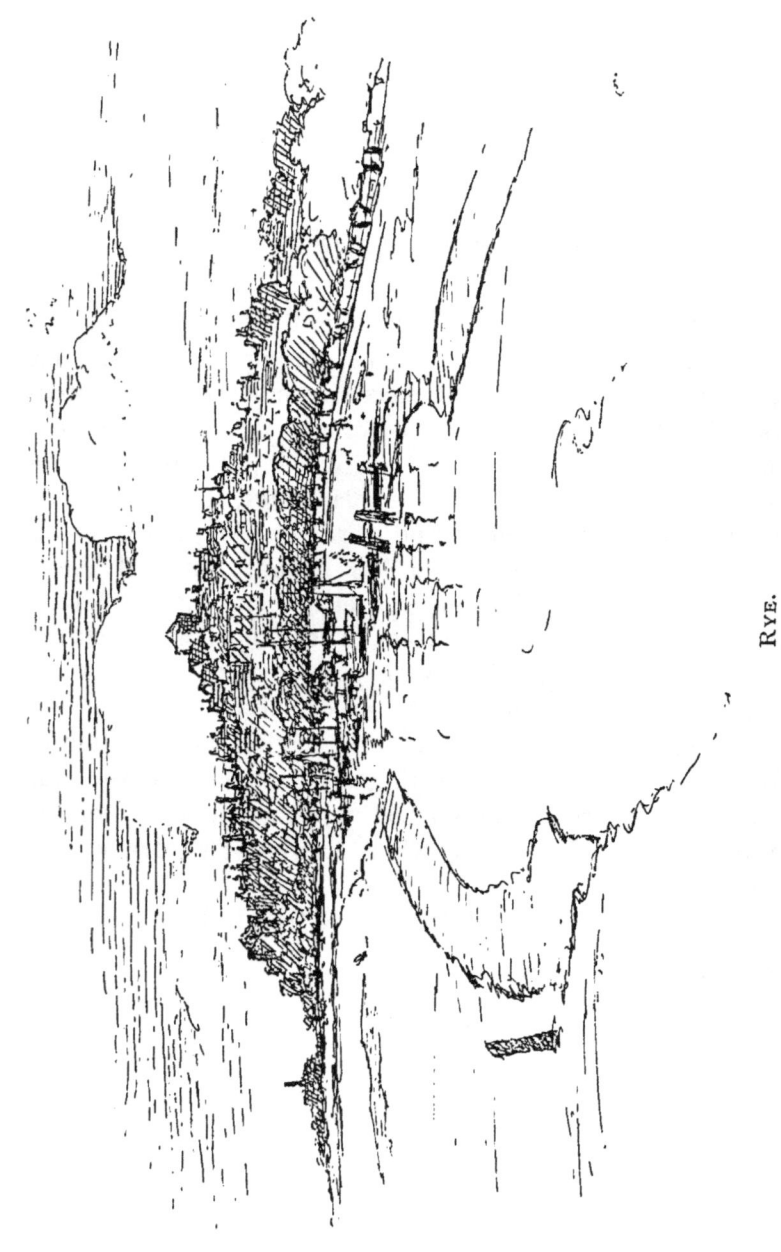
RYE.

CONTENTS

PREFACE

CHAP.		PAGE
I	THE CINQUE PORTS	1
II	RYE	19
III	RYE (*continued*)	65
IV	RYE TO WINCHELSEA	98
V	WINCHELSEA TO HASTINGS	140
VI	HASTINGS TO BREDE AND NORTHIAM	185
VII	NORTHIAM TO RYE	225
VIII	RYE TO BROOKLAND AND LYDD	249
IX	NEW ROMNEY	285
X	DYMCHURCH—BY LYMPNE—TO BILSINGTON	316
XI	RUCKINGE TO RYE	346

LIST OF ILLUSTRATIONS

	PAGE
Rye	*Frontispiece*
Landgate, Rye	3
Interior, Oxenbridge	7
Horne Place	11
Old Ferry House, Rye	16
Rye, from Tillingham Valley	18
Rye, from Wood Rising	19
The Needles, Rye	21
Traders' Passage	24
Landgate, Rye	26
Ypres Tower, Rye	28
Tillingham River and Wall, Rye	30
Rye: Corner of Watchbell Street	33
Old Roofs, Rye	36
Old Cottages, West Street, Rye	38
In Watchbell Street, Rye	42
Watchbell Street, Rye	44
Ship and Anchor, Rye	47
Warehouses, Rye	50
Rye Church, North Door	53
Monastery, Rye	56
Lamb House, from the Garden	58
" "	60
Garden Room, Lamb House	62
Rye, from Camber	63
Mermaid Street, Rye	65
Old Hospital, Rye	67
Rye: Ancient Vicarage	69
Mermaid Inn, Rye	71
Pump Street, Rye	73
Cliff Gardens, Rye	75
The Strand, Rye	77
An Interior, Church Square	81
Interior, Church Square	83

LIST OF ILLUSTRATIONS

	PAGE
Carved Doorway, Rye	84
Camber Castle	97
Winchelsea, from the Marsh	104
Strand Gate, Winchelsea	111
Court Hall, Winchelsea	113
Winchelsea Church: Transept Ruins	115
Winchelsea, from Military Road	117
Street in Winchelsea	123
Winchelsea Church, West Front	130
Winchelsea, from the Shore Road	133
Toll House, Military Road, Winchelsea	139
Fairlight Cliffs	143
Old *Harbour Inn*	147
Between Fairlight and Pett	160
Torfield House, Old Hastings	162
Shovel House, Harding	165
Hastings House	167
East Cliffs, Hastings	169
Old Hastings, Fishing Sheds	171
Hastings, Home of Titus Oates	172
In Old Hastings	174
All Saints Street, Old Hastings	176
Old Hastings Beach	179
Tillingham Valley, from Rye	185
Knellstone, back view	194
Interior, Knellstone	196
Knellstone, from the Front	198
Box Mangle, Knellstone	199
On the Way to Northiam	207
Brickwall	209
Carrier's Farm	212
Church House, Northiam	214
Bodiam Castle	221
Beckley	225
Beckley Church	227
Oxenbridge	230
Peasmarsh, *The Cock Inn*	232
Wittersham Levels	233
,, from the Rother	234
,, A restoration	235
In Wittersham Village	236
Windmill at Wittersham	238
Wittersham, where the Rother meets the Marsh	239
Cross-Roads at Stocks	241
Oxenbridge	243
Oast-Houses, Iden	245

LIST OF ILLUSTRATIONS

	PAGE
Near Iden	248
At Wittersham	248
Rye, from near Winchelsea	250
On the Marsh	253
Guldeford Church, from the Village	255
Guldeford Church on the Marsh	260
On the way to Brookland	262
Between Rye and Brookland	264
The Woolpack Inn	265
Brookland Church	266
,, Bell Tower	268
Lydd	270
,,	273
On the Marsh	284
Old Romney	288
Ivychurch	291
,,	292
New Romney Church	302
The Military Canal	316
The Bridge, Warehorne	322
Roman Walls	326
Lympne and Roman Remains	328
Old Court Lodge, Udimore	340
Ruckinge	346
,, West Door of Church	348
Orlestone	349
Warehorne	357
,,	359
Appledore	362
,,	364
Stone Church	366
,, ,,	367
Marsh, from Cemetery Hill	368
Map of the Western Cinque Ports	369

AN OLD GATE OF ENGLAND

CHAPTER THE FIRST
The Cinque Ports

HASTINGS, Winchelsea, Rye, New Romney, Hythe, Dover and Sandwich, passing from West to East in the order named, constitute the seven Cinque Ports that in the Middle Ages were responsible for the sea defence of England and were the nucleus out of which has grown the British Navy. Most of them are supposed to have been more or less concerned with policing the seas in the Roman-British period under the Count of the Saxon Shore, while during the Saxon era their services both against the Danes and when under their brief rule comes into definite history. But it will suffice here to begin with William the Norman, who crystallized a system which Edward the Confessor had extended and improved from that existing in some form or other under Canute the Dane. We may well ignore all these earlier complications, for the subject is one of such intricacy that in a brief work which is not intended to consist mainly of potted history, its elaboration is out of the quesion. Samuel Jeakes, a learned seventeenth-century Town Clerk of Rye, has achieved a well-merited immortality by publishing the successive charters to the Cinque Ports with copious notes of his own, while the late Professor Burrows, who combined the earlier career of a naval officer with the later distinction of the Oxford chair of modern history, aptly signalized his double qualification by writing an illuminating work upon them. The Ports too are individually fortunate in having found zealous local chroniclers, while the Historical MSS. Commission have published many collections of records of the various towns.

The system which these early Norman Kings developed from the cruder Saxon machinery for the protection of their realm was ingenious, economical and effective. For their war service this group of towns lying on the coast nearest to a foreign shore, and therefore most liable to attack, were given charters, frequently renewed, containing certain privileges, the most valuable of which were immunity from outside taxation and the freedom of all English markets. "They are to be quit," so runs a Rye charter, "on both sides of the sea throughout our whole land of tallage, passage, carriage, rivage, spondage, wreck, re-setting and all customs," and to be answerable at law to none but the King's Constable at Dover. He was the predecessor of that ornamental functionary, the Lord Warden, who to-day in his own person represents about all there is left of the collective glory of the Cinque Ports. In return for all this, each Port was to provide for the King's service when called upon a specified number of ships; these were generally allotted to the said Ports in proportion to their existing circumstances, which were constantly fluctuating; they were expected to serve for fifteen days without charge, receiving payment for longer periods.

The Ports virtually held their charter as a Territorial baron held his lands on military service; they were free corporate towns, somewhat on the Continental model. Those which had been under Lords—Rye for instance, had been made over by the Francophile Edward the Confessor to the Norman Abbey of Fécamp—were eventually resumed by the Crown. They became, in short, communities of free burgesses, quite outside Feudalism or shire jurisdiction, with a Mayor or bailiff, councillors or jurats, generally twelve in number, while every freeman, whether by birth or election, bore the resounding title of "Baron of the Cinque Ports." The very occasional Ryer, or Romneyite, who walked the streets of London in those days must surely have carried himself bravely! Perhaps, however, the true inwardness of the term, peculiar after the twelfth century to the Cinque Ports alone, was understood abroad and discounted! The town, in short, was equivalent to a Barony, so the freeman was literally one fiftieth part, say,

LANDGATE, RYE.

of a baron! Its court had the full right of administering justice, even to the death penalty, though there was an appeal in certain cases to the Lord Warden. For more than a century after the Norman Conquest the Cinque-Ports were not seriously called upon for service. With the Angevin kings powerful on both sides of the Channel, the latter remained, says Burrows, "to all intents and purposes an Anglo-Norman lake." It was not till it became the dividing line between two hostile countries that the bad times for the coast population on either side began, and this dates from the close of the twelfth century and the reign of that reprobate, King John.

It was technically then, but actually a little earlier, that Rye and Winchelsea were included in the " Brotherhood of the Ports," the official title of which was henceforth the Cinque Ports (named in order) "and the ancient towns of Rye and Winchelsea." This by no means implied that the two last were mere appendages, for they were adopted into full partnership, but merely it seems from a natural reluctance to destroy a familiar and historic title, and adopt that of the "Seven Ports." Though all of these last were united by the strongest ties of formal union and a common jealousy for the preservation of their invaluable corporate rights, the three Sussex towns had certain affiliations and were known informally as "the Western Ports," with Hastings the most important for a time, but subsequently yielding consequence to Winchelsea and Rye. The two latter, both as regards the old Winchelsea, destroyed by the sea in 1287, or the one immediately rebuilt that still confronts Rye, two miles across the Marsh, were linked together by the physical fact of their situation on the same sheet of water. Winchelsea for some time was stronger than Rye. But as the number of ships demanded of the several Ports was the chief evidence of their prosperity at the moment, and was constantly fluctuating, such detail, like many others vital to serious study of Cinque Port history, would be only confusing to the reader, who will doubtless be more than satisfied with a brief outline of the system.

From the beginning of the twelfth century " The Ports," as they were often styled for short, had to fight all the King's enemies, regular and irregular, which soon began to swarm in the Channel, to police the home-seas against pirates and to convey the King's troops to all points where warlike enterprises might lead him. East-Anglia and South-West England, regions so associated in our minds with ancient naval achievements, contributed nothing definite as yet to the national offence or defence. It appears that they would have required cash down, while the Ports took payment in charter privileges. In the thirteenth century to "The Royal Navy of the Cinque Ports," the full official title, the Western Ports contributed twenty-one ships, Hastings six, Winchelsea ten, and Rye five, the Eastern Ports thirty-six, Dover twenty-one, Hythe, Sandwich and Romney five apiece. What like of ships they were, most of us have some sort of notion from old seals and illustrations. Twenty to thirty tons seems to have been the normal size of a warship, which after all was merely the usual fishing or coasting vessel fitted up for war. Rounded and curved upward at both ends with a single mast in the centre, one seems familiar with their fantastic shape, further emphasized as it was by the towering forecastle and "after castle" rigged up at either end, with a smaller one at the mast head when prepared for war. A single square-sail was the rig, while an oar did duty for the rudder of later days. Each ship when in commission carried twenty-one men and a boy. So meagre then was our sea vocabulary that the boy was called a *groom*, the master *rector*, and the boatswain *constable!*

Sea fights, however, we may fairly assume, were little more than land fights transferred to an inconvenient arena. We were not yet a naval nation in the true sense of the word; our sailors were hardly more than coasters, neither better nor worse than the French or Flemish. Naval enterprise and prestige in pre-Elizabethan times belonged to the Portuguese, Genoese and Spaniards. The greatest contributing factor to England's rise as a colonial sea power was not, it must be admitted, the Cinque-Port sailors, but the fleet of small ships that from the Tudor period onwards crossed the Atlantic from the ports of Dorset, Devon and Cornwall for the Newfoundland fisheries. The business of the Cinque-Port sailors was simply to protect the country against all and sundry by offence and defence; their great days were those of the bow and arrow.

When guns came into use at sea with larger vessels, the resources of the Ports could no longer meet the occasion, and the King had to provide his own war vessels from the revenue. But the Ports continued to do what they were able to justify their charters and contributed a few ships to the attack on the Spanish Armada. Even during the four preceding centuries which were essentially theirs, the King frequently strengthened the Ports' navy with other subsidized ships, in addition to certain large rowing-galleys that were a regular part of the Royal naval armament. But the Ports really began to decline in the long French wars of Edward the Third. It was not so much that he introduced larger, two-masted ships, known as cogs, for war purposes, but that the shallow harbours of their ever-shifting coast-line were giving constant trouble. From now onward the subsidized vessels from London, East Anglia and the West, were more largely used.

There was no love lost between these other sailors and those of the Ports, who would not have been human had they failed to put on airs. All outside vessels too were expected to dip their flag to a Cinque Port on passing or entering it, and a failure to salute brought, when feasible, an unpleasant reminder. Sometimes, however, it was otherwise, for a Cornish historian relates how a Fowey ship passing Rye refused thus to demean itself, and how the enraged Ryers put out to chastise the impudent Cornishmen " but met with so hearty an entertainment that they were glad to forsake patch without saying farewell." Conspicuous among the strictly professional services of the Ports, which became more urgent after John's expulsion from Normandy and the internationalizing as it were of the Channel, was the Great Victory of Damme (1215) on the Flemish coast, so well remembered in that now landlocked neighbourhood to this day. Soon afterwards the Dauphin Lewis, who had recently come to London to assist the barons, heard with dismay that the French fleet which was following him and consisted of a hundred strongly equipped ships, had been attacked at the mouth of the Thames by a small Cinque-Ports fleet and utterly destroyed, partly by ramming and partly by boarding. Not one ship was left. The "unprofessional" adventures of the Ports, numerous and inevitable in the long and turbulent reign of the weak Henry the Third, which filled so much of the thirteenth century,

INTERIOR, OXENBRIDGE (p. 242).

their victories and disasters, make a tangled and tempestuous story. Left to look after themselves, they suffered much from the vengeance of the French, though getting in at times some resounding counter-strokes. Sympathizing with Simon de Montfort they incurred thereby the wrath of the Pope, who included the Ports' Barons in a Papal Ban, but they showed their opinion of His Holiness by seizing his ship, tearing the sacred papers into fragments and flinging them into the sea.

Edward the First, the antithesis of his foolish father, cultivated the good-will of the Ports and used them as the naval support of all his wars. Their fleet went twice with him to North Wales in his final conquest and settlement of that country, and as many times to Scotland. In the first Welsh war, 1277, they were only used as supply ships, but in the final conquest of the country they took a more active part, bridging with boats the Menai Straits under considerable opposition, and burning the crops upon the island of Anglesey, the fertile granary of North Wales. They were in the Solway with Edward when untimely fate struck down the great warrior statesman King, and changed in a moment what was meant to lead, and quite possibly might have led in his hands, to union and peace, into three centuries of war and hatred. For their services in Wales the King confirmed their charters with amplifications, giving them the only privilege apparently still withheld, that of freedom from "heir and wardship"—an intolerable Norman hardship by which women and minors with property were virtually disposed of by the Crown for cash.

But even Edward failed to strike awe into the Ports or control their ofttimes most excusable irregularities, for his long periods of absence in Wales and Scotland had given the French every encouragement to repeat the liberties which seventy previous years of feeble or chaotic English government had encouraged. Edward's policy was first to settle Scotland, and during the effort to bear everything short of actual outrage from France, and then turn upon that kingdom. King Philip, however, fully grasped the situation and winked with much complacency, if not encouragement, at the unfriendly performances of his Norman and other maritime subjects. Actual assault the English could better have put up with, but when the Norman ships began to swagger past the Ports with Englishmen and dogs hanging alternately from their yards, it was more than they could stand, whether in peace or war, and fierce reprisals were made, culminating in a mutual arrangement to fight it out in strength on April 14, 1293, at a standard hoisted on an empty ship off St. Mahé. The appointment was duly kept by both Norman and Cinque-Port fleets, each supported by vessels of other groups and nationalities. The battle was fought in a high gale and resulted in such a crushing victory for the English that the Normans, according to an English chronicler, " alle that were durst not be seen for fear."

At a later date when Edward sailed for Flanders to settle matters with Philip of France, the Ports fleet which accompanied him, suddenly, before the landing was completed, fell upon the Yarmouth contingent, towards whom they cherished a chronic animosity, burned twenty ships and killed nearly all the crews under the very eyes of the enraged King. In the feeble Edward the Second's journeys to France and in his futile campaign, upon his dead father's tracks in Scotland, which ended in Bannockburn, the Ports fleet assisted, but on the next trip to the north they seem to have declined to follow so inept a monarch. Under the first Edward they had been led by the Alards of Winchelsea, whose beautiful canopied tombs may be seen in its ancient church to-day, the greatest mediaeval sea-captains ever produced in a Cinque Port. Under his weak son and his unworthy favourites the Ports navy lost vigour and unity and were reduced to watching from their harbours the French ships defiantly sweeping the Channel.

With the third Edward and his long triumphant French wars their turn came again, but the national demands were now so great that the Ports vessels ceased to form the bulk of the active fleet. But that was no fault of the portsmen; for with harbours continually deteriorating they maintained their total complement of ships and recovered their ancient spirit. They provided about fifty of the two hundred ships which under the King himself gained the splendid victory over the French at Sluys. At the siege of Calais, they furnished but a seventh of the immense flotilla of seven hundred and ten ships that the chroniclers tell us Edward had collected and that Sandwich alone of Cinque-Port harbours was capable of containing. But in spite of this the chief command of the national fleet was confided to the Warden of the Cinque Ports and their forces regarded as its nucleus, the " regulars," as it were, of the large array gathered between Yarmouth and the Lands End. Doubtless too, many of the King's own ships were manned by Ports men. But their great days really ended in the gloom that clouded the close of Edward the Third's long reign. For after the victory off Rye Bay over the Spaniards, so inimitably described by Froissart, in which the King and his personal following played so heroic a part, the zenith of English mediaeval sea power had been reached; with the failures in France of Edward's closing years, English maritime ascendancy collapsed. French and Spaniards ravaged our shores: almost every Port was burned and sacked, some twice, like Winchelsea, to say nothing of more westerly or East Anglian coast-towns which do not concern us here. But in Richard's youth the French in turn over-reached themselves, and in a gigantic attempt to invade and conquer England lost nearly all the vast fleet and equipment they had collected for the purpose, owing to the ceaseless " nibbling " of English vessels, largely from the much-gutted Cinque Ports, whose sailors captured, it was said, enough wine to float their ships. Both heretofore and subsequently, as the resources of this or that Cinque Port showed signs of being too greatly strained by the demands made on them, certain neighbouring towns or villages were attached to them and endowed with practically all their privileges. These were known as " members or limbs." Hastings, for instance, had Pevensey and Seaford. Rye had Tenterden, which though eleven miles inland had access to tidal water. Romney had Broomhill and Lydd. Dover had Faversham and Folkestone. To Sandwich were united Deal and Fordwich, while Winchelsea and Hythe appear to have had no supports. Besides these " corporate " members, less important places were attached as " non-corporate," with fewer privileges.

Rye, hitherto but weakly fortified, had learnt one lesson by its misfortunes and surrounded itself on the land side with substantial walls and gateways still in part standing. Winchelsea, Hastings and Hythe never recovered. France and England, exhausted with their respective periods of naval triumphs, lay gasping at one another across the channel in a formal peace, while privateers of either one or other of the

HORNE PLACE (p. 364).

nations continued to make the narrow seas a perilous track for any but the strongly armed. Henry the Fourth, however, was far too much worried by troubles at home, including the long revolt of Wales under Glyndwr, to concern himself with France. The last great fighting sailor the Ports produced Henry Pay of Faversham, seems to have come to the fore at this time and laid about him lustily in home waters. He is credited with destroying the French fleet in the act of conveying a considerable army to Milford Haven in support of Owen Glyndwr, a curious blunder, as the whole French force, four thousand strong, were safely landed there, marched nearly to

Worcester and back with the Welsh and spent several unprofitable months in Wales. However he actually did, a little later, with his Ports ships make the surprising haul of 120 enemy vessels laden with iron, salt and wine.

Henry the Fifth, with his sound judgment and vaulting ambition, re-organized the navy under the conviction that the decaying harbours of the Cinque Ports were no longer suitable headquarters for an English fleet in war time, and incidentally that the declining strength of the Ports themselves pointed to a change ; so the chief naval base shifted to Southampton. Many more Royal ships, and of much larger size, were built for the King's French wars, and the great days of the Cinque Ports were over. It was Henry the Eighth, however, who introduced the changes which gradually made England a sea power in our sense of the word, by founding schools of navigation, and thus converting skilful coasting sailors and hardy seafighters into men of a different and wider outlook ready to follow the Portuguese and Spaniards, the boldest navigators of that day, upon their ocean trails. The Ports, however, still kept their charters and their privileges, with the liabilities entailed thereby, for long after this, but the latter became relatively unimportant. Dover from its unique position was virtually taken in hand by the Crown ; Rye with its always considerable population and its still ample harbour retained a modified activity, but the rest were unable to withstand the tremendous drifts of shingle and sand that were driven by the strong tides running up the Channel from the west, which either blocked their harbours, as at Hythe and Hastings, or, assisted by other causes, cut them off completely from the sea, as at Romney, Winchelsea and Sandwich.

So much in brief for the martial side of the Ports' services. But they had other purposes to serve, only less important, and concerning one of them a few words must be said. It is not easy now to realize how vital were its fisheries in old days to the life and support of the nation. Dried or salted herrings

THE CINQUE PORTS

formed the greater bulk of the fish food, and the demand for these, as well as for other fish, increased owing to the numerous fast-days of the Church when meat was banned. The Ports, being nearest to London, were the chief source of this supply, whilst the first obligation of Rye in Tudor and Stuart times was to furnish the Royal household daily with fresh fish; an easy matter no doubt with trains of nimble packhorses. But that is a detail, for it was in the great autumn herring catch, a national event, that the Ports played their official part according to charter. For then as now the herring shoals drifted southward along the north-east coast and then, as to some extent even yet, Yarmouth was the temporary base of operations for all the herring fleets. It had been so from quite early times before there was a single house on the Yarmouth shore. The Cinque-Ports men went there to meet the herrings, and temporarily occupied the site for drying their nets and curing their fish. A great herring fair, at which buyers from London and all parts, even from France and Flanders, attended, had originated on the island, as it then was, at the mouth of the Yare, and even before the Conquest a small town had sprung up. It belonged by overlordship to the Cinque Ports, whose first and oft repeated charters granted them perpetual rights to "den and strond" [dunes and shore]. Even when it grew into a town of East Anglian fishermen, the proprietary and administrative rights of the Ports continued, but with inevitably growing friction.

After Henry the First had given Yarmouth the appointment of its own Provost, the power of the Ports during the autumn visit of their fleets and officials was virtually confined to sharing the magisterial bench and appointing officers to assist the locals in arresting the many ill-doers that such a crowded occasion naturally produced. This temporary coalition in local government was accompanied by most minute observations of etiquette and simply bristled with causes of grievance and offence. Yet it lasted with slight changes for centuries, and caused constant friction, and even bloodshed—witness the pitched battle already told of under the very eyes of Edward the First ! The Yarmouth men and the Ports men hated one another right heartily, though the officials, with their gowns and maces, rubbing shoulders on the high seats of Church, law-court or banquet, had generally if reluctantly to observe the proprieties. There are some humorous accounts of the disputes even in later and more civilized times between the haughty Barons of the Ports and the touchy Yarmouth bigwigs in all their pride of local possession.

It was John who first recognized Yarmouth as a borough, but Edward the First seems to have reduced the everlasting quarrel to at any rate a legal understanding. Having witnessed, as related, a sea fight to the death under his own and his enemies' nose between these two groups of North Sea fishermen, the anomaly of the situation must have been forcibly borne in upon him. He could not end the matter, but he mended it. He gave in short the borough of Yarmouth a final and clear title to its own soil and the management of its own affairs. But the rights of the Ports during the forty days' fair could not be so easily disposed of, and Edward had eventually to compromise with them. The quaint but no doubt necessary rights of " Rogue Justice " were confirmed by this *Dite*, as Edward's compromise was termed. Certain representatives, barons of the Ports, that is to say, sat on the bench with the Yarmouth Justices during the fair, and four Sergeants, one bearing the Port's banner, another the brazen horn (now at New Romney), and the other two more purposeful rods, helped to arrest the many offenders in such a motley seafaring crowd. The prison was under the joint charge of the Yarmouth Mayor and the Barons of the Ports, usually four in number. The ports had hitherto taken the whole of the customs ($4d.$ a ship) levied on other than their own or Yarmouth ships, estimated by Burrows at three hundred and sixty. This was now commuted for a lump sum.

THE CINQUE PORTS

Even with such ameliorations it will be plain enough that material remained and to spare for very pretty rows, and rows there were, and betimes very heated ones. The delegate barons for Yarmouth were chosen at the Brodhull or Brotherhood, the Representative Assembly of the Ports which sat annually for this purpose, and as often as required for others, either at New Romney, that being the most central, or at other Ports in rotation, and transacted all joint business of the Confederation. This last was considerable, as the Ports were intensely jealous of their rights, and though they had their internal disagreements, were as one in maintaining their privileges, the Lord Warden at Dover being in a sense their chief and advocate on such occasions. If, peradventure, some Londoners in absent-minded or malicious mood charged a visiting Baron of the Ports 2s. 6d. market dues on a small transaction, or some unsophisticated official of a Lincolnshire harbour demanded the customary entrance fee, there was a great to-do at the next Brotherhood and formal complaints laid in the offending quarter. They were moreover extremely sensitive in matters of dignity and ritual.

From remote times till quite recent days they had enjoyed the exclusive privilege of bearing the Royal canopy at coronations. It was once disputed by the Barons of the Welsh Marches, and they were Barons indeed! That the Cinque Ports defeated the claim of a set of men who were accustomed to snap their fingers at Kings and sometimes to shift them is significant. The bravery of attire too in which the Cinque-Ports canopy-bearers, about thirty-two in number for King and Queen, ruffled on such occasions was a matter of insistence and pride with the various towns concerned. So also in the much less gorgeous function of the Yarmouth Herring Fair, the Barons delegated by the Brotherhood were provided, not perhaps with finer raiment than their own accustomed scarlet robes, but with cash to entertain handsomely and rather more than return the hospitalities which in spite of bickerings and jealousies were extended to them by the Yarmouth notables.

During the seventeenth century, with the vast changes in the conditions of trade and the country, legalized intrusion of the Ports into Yarmouth affairs came gradually to an end. The machinery of the Fair had apparently outlived its uses. The appearance of two Port Barons with their officers became from a practical standpoint a farce, so their claims to equal leadership in the ornamental part of the business came to be resented. They were not maltreated in the days of Charles the

OLD FERRY HOUSE, RYE.

Second as they probably would have been in those of the Plantagenets under like conditions, but they were quietly snubbed, denied all conspicuous seats and even jostled. So like wise men, they came no more, or rather the Brotherhood in one of those Sessions, which were always held after the Yarmouth Fair to hear the reports, decided to close all accounts with the uncivil Norfolk town. Indirectly the latter suffered by the removal of the old machinery, out of date though it may well have seemed; for the burgesses gradually reduced themselves like those of most other towns into a small, greedy, corrupt group and so conducted affairs as to drive off alien fishermen, to the damage of the town's interest and even to the advantage, it is said, of those of the Cinque Ports.

To return, however, for a moment to the fighting days of the Cinque Ports. Whether England ruled the waves of the comparatively narrow waters then traversed by her little ships seems rather a futile as well as a foolish speculation, since it is so obvious that sometimes she did and sometimes she didn't. I do not think any particular claim to be supreme on that element was part of the national faith. In later centuries when a patriotic Midlander, who had never even seen the sea, lifted up his voice in the chorus of James Thomson's patriotic ode, he felt he was justified merely as an Englishman in identifying himself with his country's sea-going proclivities and triumphs. But it is quite certain that a Warwickshire or Wiltshire yeoman in the time of the three Edwards would have been prodigiously surprised to hear, even in metaphor, that his path was on the ocean wave, or that his home was on the deep! Our Viking blood again is frequently invoked in picturesque periods as the germ of our naval prowess. But is this so? Surely the Norseman when he had flung his family armchair overboard and beached his long black boat on the edge of a good bit of farming country was quite contented, if he could, to stay there indefinitely as an industrious agricultural or pastoral land-lubber. His passion for the sea *quâ* sea seems to have evaporated pretty thoroughly, as the Saxon folk among whom he had thrust himself had good cause to know.

Moreover, if the Cinque Ports were the cradle of the British Navy, as was undoubtedly the case, and their people the best sailors, or at least the best sea-fighters in the England of their day, as they most certainly were, it is not in Kent and Sussex that one looks for the conspicuous Norse strains in the English race; still less to Devon and Cornwall, whose people in their perfervid moments never seem to have heard of the Cinque Ports and are apt to regard British naval supremacy, to say nothing of our oversea Empire, as of their particular creation. But these things are matters of degree and speculation. That the Cinque Ports provided the Royal Navy for centuries, and formed the recognized maritime arm of defence and offence is a matter of fact, and there we will leave it. Its ships were small, its methods perhaps primitive, its range limited when compared with that of the Portuguese and Spaniards. Our ships were rarely seen, I think, even in the Mediterranean. As already related, that otherwise objectionable Blue-beard Henry the Eighth gave the impetus, which through the glorious days of his successors gradually changed all this. And it is a significant reflection that in the strange, floating republic of alien fleets of codfishers on the Banks of Newfoundland, which for generations by a code of unwritten laws kept quite tolerable order among themselves, the English gradually came out top. So much so indeed that they eventually annexed the island in the teeth not merely of the French, Spanish, Portuguese, Flemish and Danish brother-fishermen but of their own Government, which strongly backed up the common tradition that its soil was unattachable except for the drying of nets and curing of fish. But Newfoundland was not Norfolk! Still the great cod fishery with its elected "Fishing Admirals," who were always English, had certain affinities to the Herring Festival of forty days. Both at any rate were of immense import to English, and indeed to European trade, and both were fine training grounds for English seamen: the one for the limited scope of the Middle Ages, the other for the ocean rangers and colonizers of the Tudor and Jacobean period.

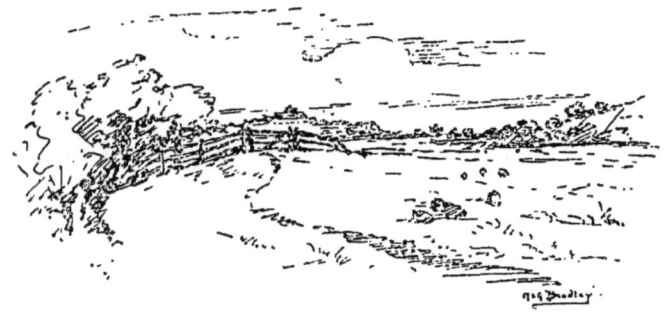

RYE, FROM TILLINGHAM VALLEY.

CHAPTER THE SECOND

Rye

RYE is unique. There is no doubt whatever about that. The better you know your England the more obvious becomes this simple fact. All visitors to Rye do not know their England in the sense here implied. Probably very few of them are thus equipped, but, whether or no, they uniformly admit with their hand on their hearts that they have never

RYE, FROM WOOD RISING.

seen anything at all like Rye. And this is natural enough, as there is nothing in all England in the least like the ancient town. Some people exclaim, "How foreign!" but that is nonsense, no English town is really in the least like a foreign one on a near acquaintance. The contrast hits you instantly in the eye if you have got one, and moreover Rye, though unique, is essentially English. There are other towns as striking, perhaps even more so, and it is my privilege to know all in this country that have any serious claim to aesthetic distinction, and to know most of them very well.

But all such as rank in the same class as Rye, unless Sandwich may be thus reckoned, lie in quite distant parts of the kingdom amid totally different scenes, surroundings and traditions. Comparison would be as absurd as it is proverbially odious. Berwick, red-roofed and up-lifted like a larger Rye, enveloped in its vast Tudor fortifications and crumbling Edwardian walls, looks down upon the Tweed rushing into the North Sea, with features, character and story all its own. Dour little Conway, overshadowed by its vast Edwardian castle and squeezed within the circuit of its own high embattled walls, looks from without like a picture straight out of Froissart, and there is an end of it. Richmond again, its grey old streets climbing to the be-castled height which looks down upon the Swale chafing between woody banks far below, reigns supreme between Tweed and Trent. To the west midlands and the Welsh Marches, with their Cotswold stone, and decorative half-timber dwellings blending so felicitously with castle, abbey or river, or all combined, we must turn for country towns of the rank to which Rye belongs, though all so utterly different. Ludlow, Tewkesbury, and Bridgnorth, probably in the order named, would spring first to the mind of any one unhampered by local prepossessions. Ludlow and Rye indeed might fairly be taken as apposites and yet in a sense complements of one another. Ludlow, essentially feudal, martial and aristocratic in air and tradition; spacious in its thoroughfares, as in the tall half-timbered often stately houses that stand so thick upon them. The Marcher Baron, the Elizabethan grandee, the Cavalier Squire are written all over it from the grey towers of its immense castle, to the uttermost foot of its steep, wide-open streets.

To this and its many kindred types, Rye offers a profound contrast. You see it is a burgher's town at a glance. Its story is obviously that of its people, and it has nothing suggestive in its quaint streets and homely little houses, of Feudalism in any shape or form. Moreover it is essentially of the south, of the sea, of the sand and of a lower-pitched England; another country altogether from these others, and more intensely English if one may venture to say so, for a greater number of successive centuries than they. Its enemies have always been the foreign foes of England and her Kings. It has had little to do with the racial and local wars that have occupied so much of the past over most of the island, as the reader will have already gathered. But the physical surprise in store for the stranger is partly due to the almost exotic character of its site. One does not look for a miniature Gibraltar, or a Mont St. Michel, on this generally mild-mannered coast. But here we have an insulated sandstone rock rising sharply out of a green coast strip, that for twenty miles is as flat as a billiard table, and actually below the level of the sea, which breaks behind it upon interminable barriers of shingle or on low waving ranges of sand dunes.

THE NEEDLES, RYE.

Clustering upon the aforesaid rock, and covering all but its three more or less precipitous sides, one sees the ancient town as a pyramid of red roofs climbing gently to an apex clearly defined by one of the noblest churches in Sussex. From any direction, near or far, and at almost any angle, infinitely varied in tone and colouring by the changing skies and shifting lights, such is the picture Rye presents to the eye of the stranger, as well as to those of its familiars, who never weary of it. The levels out of which it seems so inconsequently to spring, are those of the famous Romney Marsh. Marsh no longer in the vulgar sense, but twenty odd miles in length, by three to eight in depth, of dyked, sheep-flecked, pasture land, thinly sprinkled with ancient churches and villages, that were founded in remote centuries by the monks of Canterbury and their dependents, as they slowly and laboriously pushed back the sea. And all along in rear of the Marsh, from Hythe to the back of Rye, and from Rye on westward to the great Hastings barrier of Fairlight and its sea-beaten cliffs, the old Kent and Sussex coast line, with its bays and promontories, rises high above the levels and proclaims conspicuously the changes of a thousand years. Rye, then, stands near the western and narrower end of the Marsh. Formerly an island, the old coast line rises but a short half-mile behind it to the north, while to the south spread out beneath its precipitous face, two miles or so of level marsh land stretch to the sea which in comparatively recent times beat against its base.

Three tidal rivers meet below the rock of Rye, the greater Rother from the east, and the lesser waters of Brede and Tillingham from the west, hence flowing in one channel seaward through the green levels to the present harbour upon the sea front. Two miles to the westward, confronting Rye over meadows that in the palmy days of the two ancient towns were fleet-ridden waters, stands what is left of Winchelsea, nearly as far from the sea as its neighbour, but unlike the latter, dead for ages, both as a port and as a town. Rye is a still living town, and very much so, while its older and once greater and more powerful vis-à-vis is but a sleepy village, aesthetically delectable beyond a doubt, but of that anon.

Rye is, I suppose, the most painted town in England, both inside and out! For it is not merely as the central feature in a landscape that it so seizes and retains the fancy, but its interior lives up to the expectations thus aroused. Artists revel in its quaint old cobbled streets, and rave over its distant effects under the magic lights for which the atmosphere of Romney Marsh, salubrious though it now be, gets some general credit. In the summer season they sit betimes in serried rows in the by-streets and plant their easels unconcernedly on the pavement of the main thoroughfares. No one notices them in Rye; even the urchins, the artist's bugbear in some famous places, regard them with indifferent eyes as mere common objects of the wayside. Grass is popularly supposed to grow in the streets of Rye, and rumour for once is justified, for the simple reason that in cobbled streets where there is small occasion for wheel traffic, grass always does grow. Hastings folk have been heard to accuse the Rye Corporation of top-dressing it every spring to keep up the aesthetic reputation of their town. As a matter of fact Rye to-day is not in the least a side-tracked somniferous place. It is quite prosperous in those lines of traffic that promote neither dirt, nor smoke, nor slums, nor hideous fabrics. It did not decay like some other Cinque-Ports, when the sea receded, because it had obvious uses as a market town for a very considerable slice of country and its obvious mission as a great smuggling centre. And furthermore it maintained by its navigable river a fair amount of sea-going business and has never ceased to build a few small ships every year. Twenty-five years ago according to credible testimony it did display a much more out-of-the-world air. Strangers were rarely seen in its streets and its population was wholly indigenous.

But many things have happened in the last two decades since Rye was "discovered," if the word is permissible, by the outside world; not harmful things, because there is little space on the crowded rock which carries the old town for builders to work their wild will, though here and there they have tried, and it must be admitted have done their worst. But these offenders have as a rule been natives. Most of the strangers who have taken up their abode in the town have possessed themselves of one or other of its many alluring little old houses, Tudor, Jacobean or Georgian, and have naturally done their best to preserve, not only the structure but the

C

character of the building, since in most cases it was the atmosphere of the place that attracted them. Others again who demanded more elbow-room have perched upon the hill above Rye, the original sea cliff, where in pictures not so very old a lone windmill whirls its sails in solitude. Here many pleasant abodes, now surrounded by delightful gardens, arose during the nineties, commanding an outlook over Rye, Winchelsea,

TRADERS PASSAGE.

the Marsh and the channel unsurpassed on the south coast. But this delectable quarter has nothing to do with the Rye that people come to see, unless they are fortunate enough to have friends up there and so enjoy at their leisure the wonderful prospect from their windows or grounds. That Rye should entirely escape those disfiguring accessories common to every country town that was not quite standing still in the later nineteenth century, would be altogether too much to expect. Without the line of the old walls, or in other words along the flats immediately around the rock, its surplus population has been provided for with that general disregard for effect and harmony that is quite inevitable to sporadic local enterprise.

Perhaps it would be unreasonable to expect anything else. The result in this case is partially to encircle the upstanding old town with a belt of more or less new habitations of a modest and frankly utilitarian type. We were seriously threatened of late on the north side by something very much worse, as well as entirely superfluous, a catastrophe which the war averted. Few indeed know what a narrow escape the town had from a real disaster in the way of bricks and mortar. As one of the most interesting monuments of a stirring past in all England the place is tolerably safe, I think, now for a generation, and for obvious reasons, but I fear those alone, since there is no protection against superfluous vandalism in this country and in all probability never will be.

That Rye was at one time an island is plain to see. When the channel upon its north side towards the old cliff actually came under reclamation nobody quite knows. But by Edward the Third's time it was undoubtedly in part meadow land, and the "Wall," still called by that name, upon its western side, was already in existence as a protection against the waters which surrounded the other three. At any rate there was dry communication with the interior high land before that date.

The origin of Rye is obscure, and it is not for us here to discuss the various theories, for they are nothing more, of local antiquaries. It was an irresistible site for a fishing station, and that should be enough. No particular interest attaches to the place till the Norman period, for the excellent reason that we know little about it, till it appears with Winchelsea as one of the Cinque-Port towns. It was sufficiently important, however, in the time of Edward the Confessor, as already told, to be bestowed by that pro-Norman monarch on a foreign Abbey, that of Fécamp. Richard the First gave the town its first charter, which has been discovered, but enough was said in the last chapter about the charters and the obligations of the Ports generally. It is sufficient that Rye, from its earliest recorded existence, was one of those vital spots of the kingdom where foreign attack was most expected and from which like aggression on our part could be most

LANDGATE, RYE.

readily initiated and launched. It must always, however, have been associated with Winchelsea, though the first place of that name, it must be again remarked, was not the one noticed just now as confronting us across the meadows, which Edward the First built, but another which has lain ever since that day at the bottom of the sea, somewhere off the mouth of Rye harbour. Rye was apparently neither so large nor quite so important as its neighbour, whether the first one that sank into the sea, or its successor raised immediately after its destruction upon the hill two miles away. The population through most of the Middle Ages was probably a fluctuating three thousand, which every one upon any terms with mediaeval statistics will recognize as indicating a quite important town. Both Rye and Winchelsea, however, had increased, we are told, considerably by the end of the thirteenth century.

By Richard the First's time it would seem that the men of Rye had discovered, either prophetically or by bitter experience, that their natural defences and their own stout arms were not sufficient protection against their enemies, who in those days could sail right up to the town. For the King granted leave to " our well-beloved Barons, the Mayor and commonalty of the town of Rye, to enclose and strengthen our said town with a wall of lime and stone." This was accompanied by the customary remission of dues for a certain period to help defray the expenses. These defences, however, seem to have been quite inadequate—for it would be treason to suggest this of the men behind them—since Lewis of France, in his attempt to seat himself upon the English throne, captured Rye and held it for some time. If Rye had shared in the triumphs of the third Edward's reign, it also received some pretty hard knocks. Probably the defences of 1205 were not up to the specifications set forth in Richard's charter. Probably too they had fallen into disrepair. But above all, the north Marsh, the channel on the landward side, as before mentioned, had been " inned," giving access to the town on that quarter and destroying its island character. It was during the reign of Edward the Third that Rye was provided with those substantial walls on its vulnerable side that survive in part to-day, together with two noble, embattled gateways: one at the western extremity, destroyed by the Corporation, as in a ruinous condition, a century ago; and the imposing Landgate, which happily has escaped ravage and to-day admits the London road into the town.

Hitherto, discounting the value of Richard's walls, the Ypres tower, still standing finely up-lifted on the south-eastern point of the town looking seaward, had been regarded as a Keep, a citadel of refuge to Rye's defenders in extremity, though what precise service it actually rendered we do not know. It was built in 1135, according to tradition by William of Ypres, a Norman Earl of Kent (including Sussex), though there seems to be no truth in this or in the position of the said William. But these doughty walls and portcullised gateways of later date seem positively to have tempted the French.

YPRES TOWER, RYE.

For the great misfortune which overtook Rye in the, locally, ever-memorable year 1378, when Richard the Second was a child, was according to a grievous petition framed by the citizens, but the worst of several previous raids. But if one has to dwell at this time rather on the injuries received than the hard blows delivered on the opposite coast by the men of Rye, one must remember the Black Death and the ravages it had made in their fighting strength.

It was in 1378, after vast preparations, that the King of France, in alliance with the Scots and Spaniards, burst in force upon England with serious designs of conquest, and Rye had to bear the first shock. The town was taken, sacked and burnt. Many were killed and those worth a ransom carried to France. That is all we know, except that after this catastrophe several Rye notables, apparently on their return from France, were hung, drawn and quartered for the unsuccessful defence of the town—a cheerful welcome to the returning exiles! The church was badly injured and the bells, according to tradition, carried off to Dieppe, but afterwards rescued by a Rye squadron and brought back again. Poor Rye! its quite harrowing petition, after all these troubles, for funds to repair its defences is eloquent not only of fears for the town and for the kingdom, to which its safety was so vital, but for the necks of the petitioners in case of another failure!

A hundred years before this, Rye and Winchelsea had been relieved of their connexion with the Abbot and monks of Fécamp. For Henry the Third, partial though he was to foreigners, had sense enough to see that a House of French monks was not a desirable overlord for one of the keys of England, and in exchange he gave them lands in Gloucester and Lincolnshire, where presumably they would be harmless. In 1448, *temp.* Henry the Sixth, Rye was captured, plundered and burnt again, and even more thoroughly gutted than on the former occasion, particularly the church. A certain measure of retributive justice must be admitted in the sad afflictions all these coast towns had now to endure. For the harrying of France through the Hundred-Years War, had so filled England with spoil and treasure as to raise the very standard of living and requirements among the higher classes. It was not quite fair, perhaps, that the chief gainers in all this ravage should enjoy the snug shelter of their inland castles, while the burghers of Rye, whose share must have been a relatively modest one, should be left to withstand the constant hammerings of the avengers!

It was the year after the above disaster that Henry the Sixth incorporated Tenterden with Rye for Cinque-Port purposes, and thus states his reasons: "The town of Rye, one of the most ancient towns of the Cinque-Ports (and bordering on the sea where the invasion of our enemies and rebels into our Kingdom of England may very soon be observed) by the burnings hereof made by such our enemies hath fallen into devastation, destruction and waste and impoverishment, not only of land and tenements, but also of inhabitants there. That the said town and the Barons and good men of the same are

TILLINGHAM RIVER AND WALL, RYE.

unable out of their estate without insupportable expenses, to find for us and our heirs, the portion of the Navy contingent to the said town, as they are bound to do." But the attaching of Tenterden, whose business it was to supply and man a ship or two when the Royal Navy was called out, though it helped the King, did not go far towards restoring Rye's prosperity. A further disaster, too, fell upon its sorely smitten people in the next reign, namely the loss of their Bordeaux wine fleet, whether by tempest or an enemy seems uncertain.

In short their great days were over. With a regular Navy gradually in formation, the contributions of Rye became of less and less importance. The Rye men, we are told, built ships for the King, a few of which were always stationed there, and they also helped to man them. But as a Cinque-Port its importance was gone, though it sent a quota to fight the Armada, for which good service tradition says that Queen Elizabeth presented the town with six brass guns engraved with the Spanish arms. But Holloway, who wrote a six-hundred page history of Rye seventy years ago, denies it. The virulent pestilences of the Tudor and Stuart periods found a rare opportunity in the cramped quarters and narrow streets of Rye, so different from the spacious American-like avenues and squares in which Edward the First had laid out its neighbour, Winchelsea. But though smitten on so many sides the Rye men had not lost their vigilance and energy, for I find in a letter from Queen Catherine (Parr) (1544), while acting as Regent to Henry the Eighth, then in France, a notable instance of high service rendered by " certain fishermen of Rye." They captured a Scottish ship bearing some Frenchmen and Scots entrusted with a great number of important letters to the King of France, and others including some from the " dowager " Mary of Guise herself. These were forwarded to Henry so that he might understand " the crafty dealing and juggling of that nation."

Queen Elizabeth shed the light of her countenance on Rye in the year 1573, and knighted four gentlemen of the town. Jeake, who is the only gossip that speaks to us from old Rye days, though his own were those of the seventeenth century, mentions that the Queen was so gratified by the noble entertainment and fervid loyalty of the citizens that she named the place " Rye Royal." But on a similar trip, it may be noted, she had the nerve to tell the inhabitants of the decadent village of Winchelsea that it reminded her of London! She must have been in high good-humour that day, though she had been constantly on the move through Kent, dining and wining and no doubt " swearing her favourite oaths " with the squires, as was her wont, and eating their paddocks bare in a night with the enormous herd of horses she generally carried with her. But she only spent the inside of a day at Rye, camping at a locally famous spring under Rye hill, where all the big-wigs of the town in full war paint came out to do her homage. The Queen's-Well is one of the historic spots of the neighbourhood. It carries a contemporary inscription, and as a small pool is now the much valued ornament of a private garden.

The Ryers too must have been in a good humour at that moment, for it was the year after the massacre of St. Bartholomew. This sounds worse than cryptic, but as a matter of fact that frightful atrocity of " the Medicis " and the French King possibly saved the town from irreparable decay. At any rate its population badly needed recruiting, when some fifteen hundred Huguenot refugees stepped into the breach. Jeake at least reports that number as being in Rye ten years later, though no doubt the Spanish persecutions in the Netherlands contributed no little to the influx. A century later the Revocation of the Edict of Nantes brought in many more. Numbers no doubt drifted away elsewhere on both occasions, and indeed the town records show that a great many, being penniless, had to be shifted to places better able to support them. In the records of 1573 there is an order by the " Mayor, Jurats and Commons of Rye " forbidding the landing of any more French and Flemish " to dwell among them, being very pore people, both men, women and children to the great crye and greeffe of the inhabitants of Rye and other places about the same, onless they be marchants, gents, poste-messengers or the leike." The difficulty in determining this question is aggravated by the tendency of immigrants to adopt English names. There are names, however, of French or Flemish origin, though often mutilated, still in Rye, and there must be a great deal of French and Flemish blood, but the notion that foreign traits are in any way noticeable, though sometimes suggested, is, I think, quite fanciful.

But of the frequent influx of foreigners from Alva's time to the Revocation of the Edict of Nantes there is no doubt whatever. Sometimes the foreign element was legislated against and forbidden to exercise certain retail trades. There

CORNER OF WATCHBELL STREET, RYE.

seems to have been some justification for such action. To the All-Highest, the Lord Warden in 1573, it was complained that one Cornelys Sohier had, in modern parlance, made a corner in candles, bought up the entire stock, in short, and held it, "as well as causing Frenchmen to make them for him,'' so that eventually the whole town had to go to bed in the dark! Flemings or northern French, however, are sufficiently like us to be quickly assimilated and to cover in two or three generations all traces of their peaceful invasion but their names, even supposing they keep them.

But Elizabeth was not always so enthusiastic about Rye. It was a time-honoured duty and service of the town to supply her daily with fish, as already indicated. It was some twenty years after the Queen's visit that she had cause to send the Mayor a sharp reminder that the Royal table was suffering all sorts of inconveniences through the slackness and delinquency of the Rye fishermen, who were dilatory in the sale and delivery of their catches and, worse still, sold them away secretly to casual London dealers and others before " Mr. William Angell, Yeoman purveyor to Her Majesty " had made his selection. This matter was to be put right *at once* or there would be trouble. Perhaps it was : but in the last year of her life the old Queen had once more to reprimand the town authorities. The fishermen seem to have come to some nefarious understanding with the London fishmongers with a view to " restraining Her Majesty's Prerogative Royal for the provision of sea fish for her own house." This last expression might suggest perchance the modest consignment King George no doubt requires at Windsor or Buckingham Palace. But the number of people who fed directly or indirectly at the Tudor tables was enormous. Probably the Queen refused to give the market price, hence the delinquencies of the Rye fishermen ! But the Stuart Kings in turn brought the same complaints, and despite the secret French subsidies they *did* all cry poverty, though they were not all parsimonious.

From now onward the story of Rye ceases to have any national interest, though its local ones are enlivened by just those incidents, tending often to the humorous, that make the records of so many English country towns of character good reading. Rye, too, and not unnaturally, was always on its dignity and the less likely to forget the trappings of its ancient privileges, because it was shorn of the substance of them. Moreover, it was never under the shadow of a great House,

One might almost call it a democracy of freemen, till under the corruption of the eighteenth century they had reduced themselves to an unblushing single-figured oligarchy. And this reminds me that I have omitted to note that the town sent two members to Parliament from quite early times, till the Reform Bill, at which decadent epoch they were elected of course by the eight or ten freemen for a substantial consideration. Judging by other boroughs of the kind, this last represented no doubt a four figure bonus. A good local authority on such matters puts it at from one to two thousand pounds per vote. The Mayor, it seems, had the right of electing one freeman annually, and one can imagine how charily he used the privilege and what discretion he showed when he did so! What about the hereditary freemen, who must have been pretty numerous; it may be asked? But these people had to "take up their freedom" on coming of age, a formality only possible on the calling of an Assembly by the Mayor. In the glorious days of the Georges the Mayor merely omitted to observe this time-honoured rite, and if there were plenty of people to jog his memory, they soon found that it was not that which was at fault. For no one could coerce His Worship. The Stuart Kings and their Councillors were democrats compared to the Mayors of Rye and their relatives. One family occupied this civic chair forty odd times, and it must have been well worth sitting in! In the earlier and really democratic days of Rye, in its fighting days that is to say, the Mayor used to be elected annually at the Cross in the churchyard by all the freemen, then a goodly assemblage. But apparently the post was not regarded as an unqualified honour and privilege, for there was a legalized proviso which extended also to Hastings and Winchelsea, that if the chosen one refused to serve the crowd should immediately adjourn to his house and "beat it down."

But we must leave for the moment, at any rate, the later and the lighter phases of Rye's domestic record, which of itself if judiciously handled would provide material for quite an entertaining little book. For it is high time to have a look round the old town, a proceeding which will no doubt be frequently arrested by the memories of bygone men and things. I may at once, however, disclaim any attempt at a house-to-house guide-book visitation. It would most assuredly bore the armchair reader, while the pilgrim can easily equip himself locally for such an exhaustive enterprise. As a matter of fact, however, it is not so much in individual buildings, as with Ludlow or Tewkesbury, that Rye makes its chief claim to distinction, but rather in the quaint trend of its streets and in the atmosphere of a bygone day, which breathes all over them.

OLD ROOFS, RYE.

The High Street and chief business thoroughfare running sideways across the sloping face of the town is cheerfully typical of an average old-fashioned Kent or Sussex country borough. There are modern houses in it of the worst kind, but most of the buildings are in quite reasonable harmony with the traditions of the place. They are Georgian-fronted for the most part, but if you can snatch a back view of them, you will get a glimpse of many a quaint old tiled gable, while there are plenty of interiors very much older than their Georgian fronts. That, however, is the way of most of our old English towns. You want to know them to realize what treasures so often lie concealed behind these modern fronts with their plate-glass shop windows, or beneath later roofs that decay or self-respect has made inevitable.

There is probably not much domestic work in Rye of older date than the sixteenth century, which may be said indeed of every old English town. Conflagrations have usually seen to that, even in the absence of foreign foes, and rare surviving specimens are after all curious in themselves rather than any very particular asset to their surroundings. Moreover, the handiwork of the sixteenth and seventeenth centuries gives the full effect of such antiquity and thoroughly satisfies our English standards and desires, for the excellent reason that it is practically the oldest we have got and is no doubt but a more perfected expression of what went before and fed the flames of earlier days. What is more, we can re-people the houses of the Tudor or Jacobean periods more vividly than those which harboured the less intelligible and ruder beings who groped through the darkness of the Middle Ages. But the Georgian period, after all, perhaps is as conspicuous as any in Rye, and that also in its way is almost as alluring and suggestive of days that are quite far enough away to engage the sympathy of the retrospective soul.

The great flat eighteenth-century front of the *George Hotel* in the High Street is assuredly not reckoned one of the architectural gems of Rye, though it contains some fine old rooms, including the banqueting hall with the musicians' gallery still *in situ*. Indeed it is exactly what I would have there myself. It seems to reek of elections, racy and innumerable, and is just the place for a dozen electors, all relations with their cheques in their pockets, to pledge one another and the new members from Northumberland or Cornwall at the latters' expense, while the great disfranchised were getting gloriously drunk outside at the same generous fount. The Lord Warden of the Cinque-Ports had at one time the right of recommending one of the two Members returned by each of the towns : it only remained for the favoured one to square the Corporation. The Duke of Wellington in his youth was M.P. for Rye probably through this channel.

Just opposite the *George* is a sombre but rather remarkable red-brick structure of the time of Charles the First. Conspicuous for its row of lofty pilasters extending from the street pavement to the eaves, a distinguished architect sees in it the handiwork of an ambitious but rather rustic member of his own craft and points out its shortcomings, altogether too

OLD COTTAGES, WEST STREET, RYE.

technical to be of interest here. This is Peacocke's old Grammar School, quite recently abandoned for new buildings outside the town. For some to whom the pageant of history does not appeal, this is the most interesting building in Rye, as Denis Duval, the hero of Thackeray's creation, is put to school here. Personally I would sooner recall the slight figure of the future Victor of Waterloo, at the *George* window thanking the population of Rye, with an effort no doubt, being a blunt man and always scornful of mobs, for allowing their Corporation to elect him without bloodshed (though not put quite this way); for the free citizens of Rye were even then getting restive!

Short thoroughfares run straight and steeply downwards from the High Street, through interludes in the old town wall, to where the town ditch outside is now obscured by a firm well-made highway. From this street you may look right up on a long section of the original Edward the Third wall, if duly warned. For it has been rather carefully concealed from the casual visitor by an ugly modern wall along the roadside; whereas if iron railings had been substituted, the north front of the town, as it once was, would be revealed at a glance to all and sundry. This fine display of Edwardian work is not sensibly marred by carrying necessary garden walls on its summit, but it has been further obscured by recent structures in a manner quite inexcusable. Above the eastern end of this surviving section of wall—the chapel of one of the two monastic foundations of ancient Rye—that of the Augustinian Friars, stands up conspicuous; more so unfortunately as regards its north side, which has been filled with modern windows. As a new roof was necessary, and has not yet toned, its true character, despite its old grey walls, is not realized till it is encountered at closer quarters, or viewed from the south side, when a row of original pointed windows, bricked in and with their tracery rather mutilated, still display themselves above an old flower garden. An east and a west window, a west door on to the street, and an old stone staircase are all still *in situ*. This chapel was erected just before the Dissolution, but the monastery itself is said to have been existing in Edward the Third's time, though little more is known of it. At one time used by the French Refugees both for habitation and in later days as a store house, the chapel has recently been acquired by the church for gatherings of various kinds and remodelled to suit the purpose.

The Landgate, erected simultaneously with the Edwardian walls, is an exceptionally fine example of its period and type. It forms the chief entrance to the town by road and a singularly noble one it makes with its two massive drum towers, machicolated parapet and deep archway. Still more it is most felicitously situated, commanding the upward approach to the town and on the inner side looking up an almost open road mounting to the High Street and thereby displaying itself to equal advantage both from within and without. Indeed this eastern end of the long High Street provides one of those pleasant surprises in which Rye abounds. For it abruptly terminates, while still apparently in the height of its cheerful little bustle, at the edge of a precipice, opening out the whole twenty mile length of Romney Marsh, with the sea on the one hand and the distant downs behind Hythe, Folkestone and Dover on the other.

But it is above these thoroughfares, higher up the slope of the town and round about the great church which crowns all amid its spacious square, that Rye is at its best. No cars or wheeled traps that can avoid it ever come up here into what is more than elsewhere its residential quarter. This last rather grandiloquent phrase smacks maybe of space and trees and tennis grounds and ample villas and of modernity. But not so in Rye, for it is along these silent cobbled streets, where grass really does grow (without any stealthy top-dressing), and round the large square, almost filled by the well-ordered, leafy churchyard, that those discerning folk who have been attracted to Rye by one or other of its many appeals mostly abide. For again I must repeat, Rye is unique. I have not the faintest hope of making the outside reader understand precisely why this rather daring epithet is fully justified. Many nimble pens have attempted it and none have succeeded, and the better qualified they are for the task the more obviously conscious they feel that it is a hopeless one. The artist of course has a more effective weapon, he can at least transfer the physical charm of the place to his canvas.

But there is something more than that, something elusive that even the artist cannot seize, for it is invisible. We all recognize the thing and are content to leave it at that, without attempting to reduce it to terms of words. The effect upon outsiders, such as guests or visitors, is quite curious, as everybody in Rye who is much in the way of encountering them well knows, and I was going to add to their cost, brutal as it sounds. But I should be misunderstood, and in any case it would be more just to say, to the cost of the harried house-agent. In short the familiar symptoms generally show themselves about the end of the first or second day in a consuming desire to acquire a house in or near Rye, a holiday house as a rule, of course, and that too unfurnished and on a seven year lease at the shortest, lest the prospective joy of occupation should be unduly curtailed. The second stage of the complaint takes the form of an inspection of the rather limited number of available tenements that such a popular place, in its essentially quiet way, has to offer. The crisis usually comes after the departure of the infected person, when one is left to imagine that under the cold light of reason and hard fact or the pressure of a predominant partner the scheme is shown to have been from the very first utterly impracticable. Occasionally perhaps the dream merely fades. There is some ground too for believing that there are cases in which the vacant houses in and about Rye, duly forwarded by sanguine agents, are wistfully perused for months, or even years, much on the principle that drives some people, whose opportunities for travel have been cut off, to read Bradshaw as a substitute! The impulse is only worth noting as a proof of that mysterious something about Rye which is not to be set down either with pen or brush, nor of course is it to be confused with the premeditated action of the serious house hunter.

Watchbell Street is a quarter we never allow our visitors to miss. It runs a short, straight westward course from the

IN WATCHBELL STREET, RYE.

church square along the highest ridge of the town, and like the High Street dissolves suddenly into space at the edge of another precipice, unfolding here also a wide and lovely prospect. In this case it is the western levels of the Marsh with a fine background of woody upland country. Winchelsea on its own leafy ridge rises conspicuous in the foreground with the long and lofty hogs-back of Fairlight Down filling in the distance till it dips its noble headland into the sea. We are here looking right over the old harbour, whose waters washed the base of Rye and Winchelsea alike and served them both, while a mile away, brooding in solitude grim and grey upon the wide Marsh is that quite imposing looking fortress known as Camber Castle, which Henry the Eighth erected on what was then a long tongue of shingle washed by the waters of the harbour it was intended to protect. That it was soon left much higher and drier, and that its guns were never, I believe, required to fire a shot in anger, in short, that it was quite useless, in no way detracts from its present value to the landscape. For the shell is fairly perfect, both that of the big central and circular Keep and the outer curtain walls and their curious circular flankers. The science of fortification had travelled a long way when the Italian engineers of the new school fortified Berwick for Henry's famous daughter. Camber was but one of a group of fortresses which Henry erected as a coast defence, Walmer, with Hurst Castle on the Solent and that on Holy Island in Northumberland being others that occur to me.

Watchbell Street derives its singularly felicitous name from the fact that it marks the site where in the days of old the first alarm of approaching danger was sounded in the manner indicated. The houses confronting the cobbled street on either side are practically all residences and, within modest scope, of almost every size and style. If a few would not stand a too searching inspection the general effect is wholly admirable. For there are no palatial mansions in Rye: they would be outside the picture. People who anywhere else would probably insist upon the modest minimum of three sitting and six bedrooms will often be found in Rye in picturesque snuggeries of half that accommodation. Watchbell Street at one time was, in part at least, a picturesque disarray

WATCHBELL STREET, RYE.

of rather tumble-down old houses, and one by one they have fallen into the hands of leisured or artistic persons who have made them habitable within and attractive without. With Sussex materials, a south coast climate, and a judicious training of vines and creepers, a window discreetly thrown out here and there, and a little fresh paint, it is surprising how much can be done on an old background of mellow brick wall and gabled tile roofs.

Watchbell Street looks, and should look, quite pleased with itself. From behind its open windows in the dead silence of a summer afternoon it must be quite uplifting for its occupants to listen to the prattle of wandering tourists discussing which of the houses he or she would most like to annex amid such an embarrassment of riches. No wheeled traffic to speak of rattles here, it is as quiet as a college precinct in the long vacation. A nice layer of verdure too spreads delicately over the cobbles, and a narrow paved footpath on each side of the street seems to say, " Please don't walk on the grass." The street is becomingly flanked upon its western edge by the *Ship and Anchor Inn* which looks down and out upon the world below and can be seen miles away. One of the notable old hostelries of Rye in its smuggling period, it duly looks its part. In the cheerful glow of red tiling on roof and walls and fresh white window frames it easily justifies its presence in such excellent company. Its romantic situation and air of modest but sufficient comfort makes it one of those places which the stranger is apt to take note of for a quiet and secluded week-end. If a gale from the south-west happens to be blowing, a circumstance not unknown in Rye, his or her sensations may peradventure be like those of two lady acquaintances of mine who sat up all night in their sitting-room holding one another's hands. But then they were Londoners ! This uplifted south-west angle of Rye town meets the gales from the Atlantic as the point of a breakwater meets the fury of a storm. But it is used to them, and I do not think its slumbers are seriously interrupted on such accounts.

The other corner of the street in Church Square is formed by the combination of two old seventeenth-century timbered houses into a single private residence, a most effective piece of restoration. Just here too is another of the few mediaeval relics in Rye. This is a small chapel of the Carmelite Friars, who had a branch here, probably a cell of Newenden, ten miles inland, which was their first English settlement. The gable end fronts the churchyard, and though obviously a residence, would attract attention instantly as an early ecclesiastical building in good preservation. With its large pointed and traceried window above, a triple lancet, with a Gothic doorway for a portal, and lofty corner buttress, all unmistakably pre-Reformation work in design, though I believe a good deal restored, the building fails to pass itself off as in any way associated with the row of seventeenth and eighteenth century domestic dwellings of which it forms a unit, while the interior contains a good deal of contemporary work. The three adjoining houses also cover the remains of this little monastic off-shoot, and contain among them small portions of the original building including a sort of crypt with a vaulted roof.

While on the subject of Rye's mediaeval relics, by far the most important stands just below the south-eastern corner of the churchyard. This is the Ypres Tower, or castle, already alluded to. Its situation is commanding and significant. It tells its own story as the Norman fortress of the town: not the ordinary Norman story of Feudalism and Saxon coercion, for such dues as Rye paid to an overlord had gone to foreign monks before the Conquest, and remained unchanged, but as a watch tower and defence of the town against alien foes. This Ypres building itself is comparatively small and of no special interest, save as a complete example of the ruder type of twelfth-century defensive architecture. It forms a square with a single room above and below and a circular tower at each angle, the whole dimly lighted by square-headed and lancet windows. Few watchmen, in days when the scope of vision and the naked eye meant so much, had a better perch than the warder on Ypres tower, who commanded every point that threatened Rye, from Fairlight Head to Hythe and Folkestone. The coast of France is so rarely visible from Rye as to be outside consideration. For myself I have never seen it. But always on clear nights the lighthouses of Cape Gris-

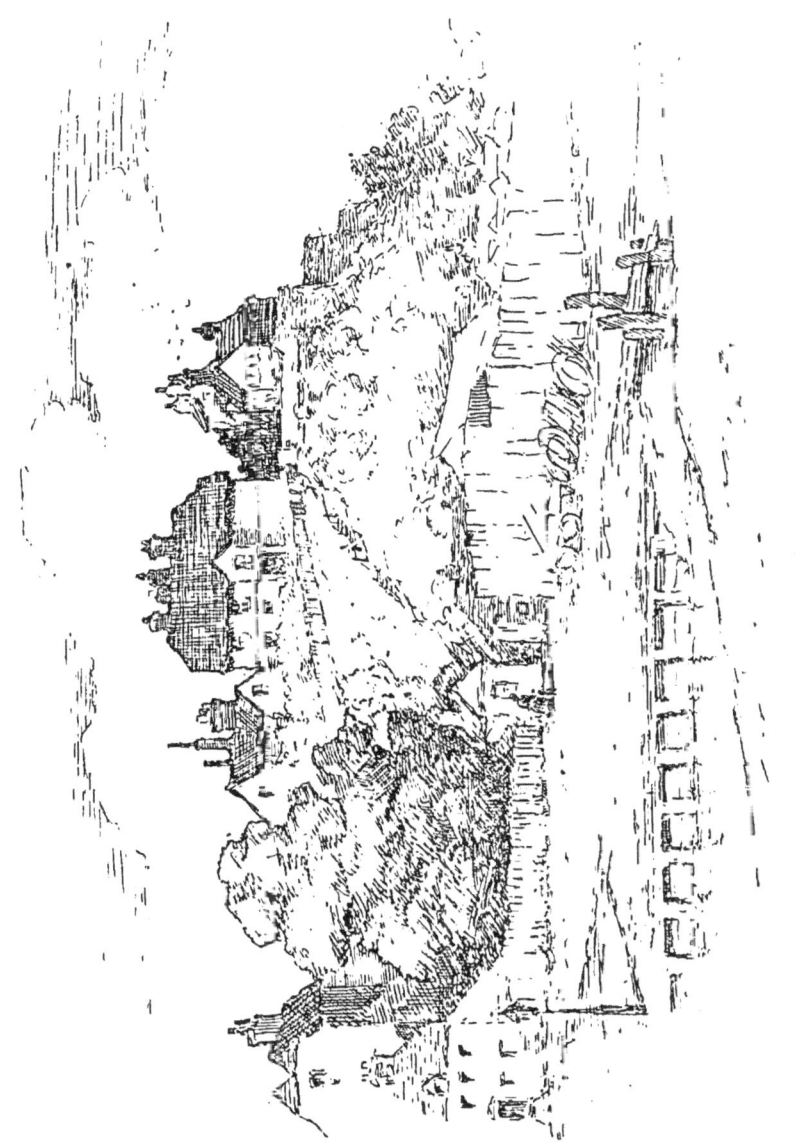

Ship and Anchor, Rye.

Nez and Etaples, which last is always known to Rye fishermen and their equivalents with characteristic contempt for lingual amenities as *Eatapples*, are in shining evidence.

Since Tudor times Ypres Tower has belonged to the Corporation, which held its meetings here till the days of the Commonwealth. After this and till quite recently it served as the town gaol, and an uncommonly dismal one it must have been. Under the demand for less primitive accommodation a small addition was made to the eastward of a well-intentioned wing whose elaborate crenelation is quite a reproach to the long-vanished battlements of the old tower, and on a dark night might almost pass for the handiwork of the semi-mythical William of Ypres. The tower has been always known in the Rye vernacular as " Wypers," and it will be readily imagined how the home letters of Rye soldier-boys in 1915, suddenly confronted with its hitherto unheard of original in Flanders, contained characteristic references to " good old Wypers." Just below the tower is a broad and pleasant terrace much frequented by Rye people and always exhibited to visitors for its noble prospect. This is the Gungarden, so called from certain ancient cannon that till lately pointed their harmless muzzles towards France.

From " Wypers " a stairway leads down the face of the cliff, where once stood a small portal known as Baddings gate, to the flats bordering on the present course of the Rother. Here there is always a picturesque if scant array of the masts and hulls of fishing boats or small traders, with a sprinkling along the bank of those irresponsible little buildings of tarred or painted wood that seem to spring up in the quiet corners of a quiet haven for the special benefit of the artist. The old ferry house is conspicuous among them, a quaint low wooden structure of several rooms which for a couple of centuries, till the modern bridge was built over the river, did a great business, and that too over waters much wider than those of the now bridled channels of the Brede and Rother which meet here.

The pleasant tree-fringed strip of meadow, between the river and the base of the town, reclaimed from the sea not many generations ago and known as *The Salts*, is the arena upon which Rye athletes disport themselves in happier times, fortunate in this ample scope afforded them for cricket and football. Eighty years ago country towns did not trouble themselves much about open spaces for popular recreation. They were quite capable of resisting encroachment in directions along which the burgess took his leisured stroll after his Sunday dinner, but that I think was the limit of public protest. Eighty years ago, however, when it was first embanked there were a few disinterested men in Rye town who protested against a proposed subdivision and leasing out of this now invaluable ground and urged, fortunately with success, that it should be allotted as playing fields to the commons of Rye. Cricket particularly was mentioned as became a community in the very home of that greatest and most truly national of English games, for any foreigner can play football, but cricket beats him.

Rye church enjoys the immense advantage of never having been submitted in any structural sense to the deadly ordeal of modern restoration. If its exterior were even less admirable than it is, its most inspiring situation would alone cover many deficiencies. But the scope and proportions of the building seem precisely to fit the site. The central tower, massive but not too lofty, the long body of the church with its several gabled roofs, forming as we have said the apex of the pyramid which Rye suggests from almost every point of view, harmonizes excellently with the generally rather low pitch of the town buildings. The more usual west tower with nave and chancel extending eastward, would interrupt the symmetry and half spoil the picture. A lofty spire again, though rarely to be seen in this district, would tend to dwarf the elevation of the town, which as it is culminates so felicitously in the pointed cap of the central tower. Two flying fourteenth-century buttresses at the east end are perhaps a trifle disturbing to so dignified a building, though they are admirable examples, one, however, being a modern replica of its fellow. But the only other peculiarity of the exterior is a sixteenth-century clock on the north front of the tower flanked by quarter boys of cherubic proportions and nearly five feet high, fashioned out of oak and gilded. These industrious manikins have been striking the quarter hours on two bells for over 350 years, and had been at work for some time when Rye ships sailed out of the harbour to fight the Spanish

WAREHOUSES, RYE.

Armada. Rye is justly proud of its clock, and a legend is in the air rather than upon the pens of serious chroniclers that it was presented to the town by the Virgin Queen in recognition of its services on the above-named great occasion. As a matter of fact the Corporation purchased it for so round a sum as to suggest an exchequer hardly according with the woebegone pleas of poverty sent up to headquarters from time to time and recorded in the chronicles, together with tales of fire and pestilence, of channels silting up, and the ruinous encroachments of foreign fishermen.

Some one has written, by the way, that it is the wails and

misfortunes of these Ports that stand out in their story. Their long intervals of snug comfort leave no such resounding record. It is quite true, however, that a century later the financial needs of the Rye Corporation were so urgent and its security so deplorable that when a patriotic citizen came to the rescue with a loan of £60, the official gratitude was such that he was excused all civic duties for the rest of his life !

I have never met with any other country town that has inspired a local chronicler to write its history in over six hundred pages of small print ; Rye has achieved this triumph, or rather a patriotic citizen achieved it, nearly seventy years ago. It is quite true that the surprising copiousness of Mr. Holloway's volume is not altogether due to the town's overcrowded past. For since Tudor times, at any rate, its story has been not more remarkable than that of many places which have failed, alas, even to find an abbreviated Holloway to tell us all about them. Its later record is of course wholly domestic, but for that very reason perhaps the more racy, and if the wielder of this industrious and faithful pen had been as afflicted with as strong a scent for humour as for detail, the pages of his monumental work might possibly have run into four figures ! Perhaps he held himself in, as he skips a good deal that he must have yearned to enlarge upon, with a hint that the subject is too delicate to handle freely. For the writer himself was allied to the Purple, or in other words to the crimson of the official robe.

I sometimes wonder how many people, patriotic though Rye people are supposed to be, have read *Holloway* through. Assuredly it is not a bed book ! But that does not matter, it is a notable compendium of most things, great and small, that have ever happened in Rye and of a few things perhaps that never happened, and of all the people that ever lived there, and if the small things are inevitably far more numerous than the big ones, that is not the historian's fault. Probably he is quite right to record them as seriously as he does the

French raids or the disfranchisement of the Borough. At any rate, Mr. Holloway was determined to give his subscribers full value for their money. All honour to him in any case, and it is a pity there was not a Holloway in some other interesting towns we wot of. Some day perhaps a tablet will be affixed to the fine old house he so long occupied upon the High Street. If any are going around he deserves one, in spite of the disarray in which his store of facts and figures are presented to the intimidated general reader and the unforgiveable sin in such a book of shirking an index. The big Georgian fronted house upon the High Street, known by his name, is assuredly of the type to stimulate any such feeling for the past, above all for the past of an old country town, as its occupants may have been endowed with. One could well imagine that any leisured and reflective soul who lived there long enough would sooner or later feel almost obliged to write a History of Rye, even to six hundred pages!

The numerous and quite spacious rooms, the deep cupboards and closets cunningly wrought into every nook and corner, after the good old fashion, the finely carved Tudor fireplaces of Caen stone, ruthlessly chipped by late Georgian chisels to make way for the layers of Georgian plaster from which they have only recently been delivered, oak-panelled chambers and massive beams hewed by Tudor axemen out of the lusty oaks which then covered the heights of Playden: all these things would surely turn such a man towards the story they symbolized. In one room is a French folding bed recess, relic of remote Huguenot occupation. More curious than all perhaps, because slightly mysterious, are the great arched vaults fifteen feet high running under the whole breadth of the house. "For smuggled goods," says Rye with one voice, for the retrospective Ryer, and not unnaturally, has smuggling on the brain, and he has good cause to. It is possible, however, that these subterranean chambers received nothing more nefarious than the big casks of French wine in which the town did a legitimate and thriving trade. From half an acre of old-fashioned garden sloping down to where the old town wall ran, and in part still runs, you get picturesque glimpses of the contrast that the back of an ancient High Street exhibits to the spruce front where it does its business.

There is a tradition that the original church of Rye stood in the Gungarden. If so, this was merely the Saxon church, which like most such buildings was probably of wood. Mr. Holloway takes the trouble to deal at length with the absurd notion that the present church was built up from the ground on a new site after the French burning in 1448, and quite laboriously points out for the benefit of any idiot who could imagine such a vain thing the salient fact that a good deal of Rye church is Norman and Early English work. Mr. Holloway, like every one else, admits that the pre-Norman church may very likely have stood on or near the Gungarden, though as a matter of fact church sites were very seldom shifted. He also rather naïvely defends himself for stating that a Saxon

RYE CHURCH—NORTH DOOR.

church "may have been of wood," whereas it is pretty sure to have been, particularly upon the fringe of forests which flourished abundantly till Tudor times.

Coming to the interior of the church, its ample proportions and clear evidence of the work of successive centuries give it a character altogether in keeping with the fortunes of its historic parish. When one remembers that it was burnt by the French, both in the fourteenth and fifteenth centuries, so far as a stone church can be burnt, the variety of design common enough in English churches that have never felt an invader's torch gives it here on that very account a rather special interest. Which was the most destructive of the two catastrophes seems not quite certain, the evidence being rather conflicting. The variety of styles as well as some curious differences in detail of the same style are so numerous that nothing short of a pilgrimage from point to point could cover them, and such a pilgrimage would be quite out of place here, even if there were space to record it. The church is still cruciform as when it first arose under the hand of its twelfth-century builders with its Norman work probably, indeed one may almost say obviously, drifting into Early English before the whole was completed. It contains a transition Norman nave with clerestory and side aisles of later date, a tower space, north and south transepts and a choir with side aisles or chapels of similar elevation and conterminous.

The earliest Norman work extant is mainly represented by two side arches at the east end of either nave aisle, some arcading on the west wall of the north and south transepts, and in the latter some sedilia with profusely moulded arches, springing from slender pilasters with Norman capitals. The choir with its chapels is in part Early English and otherwise Perpendicular, of which last style the spacious east window is a fine example and of rather unusual pattern. Two of the three north arches of the chancel rest on clustered columns, the third being of a later period owing probably to the French ravage. Looking up the centre of the church from the west end, the arches into the transept and choir will be seen to be conspicuously out of line with the nave arcade. In the north aisle of the chancel, otherwise St. Clare's Chapel, is a beautiful carved mahogany Communion table, vulgarly associated with the Spanish Armada. As a matter of fact it has been pronounced a Chippendale of the early eighteenth century, flamboyant though it may seem, and was presented to the church by one of the Lamb family. The verger, however, relates that three experts in his presence all disagreed upon this point, so we will leave it at that. A rather startling feature to strangers in the congregation is the long pendulum of the famous clock, which swings slowly backwards and forwards in full view, above the choir. It seems to me an arrangement that no church should be without. For anything better calculated to enforce the preacher's warning and to give practical illustration of life's fleeting tenure I cannot imagine. The wide arches of the nave, which contains five bays, are slightly pointed and transition Norman, and are ornamented with dog-tooth moulding. Most of the piers are cylindrical, though two are replacements of recent date. There is much evidence of the reconstructional work that was necessary in the late fifteenth century. The clerestory is of that period and shows the remains of a passage which, descending by way of a small priest's room over the north porch, is continued in the chancel, while as a last word in this brief notice the pulpit of linen pattern is partly fifteenth century.

Forty years ago that afterwards distinguished architect and graceful writer, Mr. Basil Champneys, in a brôchure entitled *A Quiet Corner of England*, stood in Rye Church and thanked Heaven that there, at any rate, was no modern restoration, the rage for which had even by then obliterated all trace of the mediaeval builder's hand in scores of English churches. And still more, Rye church seemed to him to offer a quite exceptional object lesson in the style of successive periods since none of the original examples had been interfered with. At that date, however, the church rejoiced in galleries and high pews, and it is quite refreshing to hear an expert fulminating roundly against the indiscriminate holocaust of pews offered

MONASTERY, RYE.

up to the new idea. As a mere amateur I have often groaned at their disappearance from certain churches, of whose atmosphere and character they seemed part and parcel. Rye church is too spacious and noble a building to feel the loss of early Georgian furniture. But there are some churches, nevertheless, to which it has meant or would mean ruination, an irreparable break with the past for a mere convention. We have an old writer's word for it that Rye church, before the French fell on it, save for the Cathedral, was the most beautiful in Kent or Sussex. It is among the finest to-day. Like nearly all its neighbours, far and near, it has no monuments of any pretension to historic interest and but few surviving brasses. The only Rye worthy who has the honour of an altar-tomb and effigy is John Fagge, and he lies upon one eight miles away in the heart of the Marsh at Brenzett church, where we shall pay our respects to him later. A good deal of restoration was done in 1889, but in no way affecting the fabric of the church. Many memorial stained windows, as well as oak screen work, have been inserted in recent years. But these are matters for the local guide-books and will be found detailed at length therein.

In 1701 Rye church seems to have been in a bad way, for the " minister, churchwardens and inhabitants of the ancient town" petitioned the King to the effect that their church " being a large and stately fabrick hath by the negligence of former times been suffered to fall into ruin in many parts, and that they have already expanded £200 upon it." The humble petitioners go on to affirm that they are " fearful to assemble for public worship lest it come down on top of them." The steeple too is a famous seamark, and in short if Rye church was to continue to be of service to its own people and a beacon to the British mariner, His Majesty must grant them letters of patent to collect moneys throughout the country for that end. No doubt he did, and it was duly collected. So many " piteous cryes " ascended to the throne from Rye throughout the ages that, apart from the French ravaging, one may be bold enough to wonder whether its people were not inclined to be alarmists. They are constantly by their own account upon the brink of ruin, but the supply of warm men in the town, of ships and wine and beef and beer and snug houses and good living seems fairly chronic. They never fail, moreover, to remind the powers that be, that if Rye suffers, whether through its indispensable church spire beacon, or its refractory harbour,

LAMB HOUSE, FROM THE GARDEN.

or its confounded French fish poachers, the nation suffers. Indeed it would be almost unatural if its self-importance had not out-lived the days when the ships of Devon and Norfolk dipped their topsails as they went down the channel past its harbour mouth.

Horsfield, the historian of Sussex, when visiting Rye church about a century ago, quite lost his temper at the regiment of pauper children which twice a day under the ineffective command of an aged parishioner, were turned loose in the north chancel. The distracted historian, who was taking his notes, professes ignorance of whether this turbulent invasion was for the purpose of education or amusement, and inclines to the latter for the uproar that went on. He adds ironically that the sick poor were sometimes brought into this chapel for *quiet!* He must have had some cause for complaint, as he lost his bearings and has mistaken in one case the east for the west !

From the south-western corner of Church Square, a short cobbled lane, conspicuous at its outlet for some gabled half-timbered houses that might well be of the fifteenth century, turns sharply just below them at a right angle. Here, looking backwards up the narrow vista, past these same old cottage fronts, at the church rising out of its encircling foliage, is a spot beloved of artists. The thoroughfare has been known to be entirely blocked by some wandering art class settling down on it out of nowhere like a swarm of bees. At the same corner, its front door and windows commanding the very scene that hangs on so many walls in England and America, or lurks unappreciated no doubt in a hundred folios, stands a dignified-looking Georgian house. And this definition is more than commonly appropriate since it has actually sheltered Georgian Royalties beneath its roof on two separate occasions. It was the property and home of the leading family of Rye in the good old times, and still preserves their name in its own, " Lamb House." For the last twenty years of his life it was owned and occupied by that distinguished author, Mr. Henry James, who till his health declined spent the greater part of almost every year in Rye, and there wrote many of his books. He was fond of jesting in his own inimitable way on the artistic crowd that set up their campstools and easels so thickly along the approach to his front door, with their rows of backs turned towards it. By pure accident since writing the above lines I

LAMB HOUSE.

have run across a humorous confirmation of it in a fugitive chapter on Rye in his *English Hours*. Here it is:

"At favoured seasons there appear within the precinct sundry slouch-hatted gentlemen who study her charms through a small telescope formed by their curved finger and thumb. Leading a train of

English and American lady pupils, they distribute their disciples at selected points, where the master going his rounds from hour to hour, reminds you of nothing so much as a busy *chef* with many saucepans on the stove and periodically lifting their covers for a sniff and a stir. There are ancient doorsteps which are used for their convenience of view and where the fond proprietor going and coming has to pick his way among paraphernalia, or to take flying leaps over industry and genius."

Those who knew the author only through his works or from biographical sketches of him in the newspapers would never, I feel sure, suspect him of those particular qualities that made his familiar and striking figure so much missed from the streets and field paths of Rye which he had trod so perseveringly every possible afternoon of his life there, chatting and cracking jokes in his own delightful and absolutely inimitable way, which like the atmosphere of Rye defies not merely description but even classification. Buttonholing this one who might have some local tale of interest to unfold—for he had the liveliest curiosity in all Rye concerns—or pausing for a word of sympathy with that one who at the moment was in need of it, he pursued his leisurely and genial way towards the open country, which in his later years, when declining physical energies were overmastered by an unimpaired mental activity, he often for his very sociability failed to reach!

Lamb House, both within and without, has all the attractive characteristics of the early Georgian style, even to its ornamented capped doorway and the flight of steps ascending thereto. It is flanked by a large old-fashioned garden which provides the dwellers upon the north side of the already favoured Watchbell Street with a green and bowery outlook from their back windows. It is only worth noting here that the house was built and first occupied by the Grebells, a family of note in the town, because the chief Grebell of the day was stabbed by an irascible butcher (1742) in mistake for his relative Lamb, into whose possession the house had by that time passed. Mr. Lamb it seems had passed a severe sentence on the said butcher for using false weights. The murder made a tremendous sensation and has rung down the ages in Rye town, and if so remote an incident may scarcely seem worth

LAMB HOUSE AND GARDEN ROOM.

the telling, it must not be shirked, as the skull of the butcher, as well as the gibbet in which he hung upon the marsh outside the town, is carefully preserved in the Town Hall, and duly exhibited among its other treasures to visitors.

But it really is remarkable that it should have fallen to a simple gentleman in a country town to entertain Royalty on two different occasions in the same house. For George the First, in the year 1725, on returning from one of his numerous visits to Hanover, was blown ashore while making for Dover on Camber sands. Tradition says that he and his party had to grope their way on foot to Rye through snow-storm and darkness, but Lydd has something to say about that, as we shall

RYE, FROM CAMBER.

see later. At any rate, Mr. James Lamb, both as Mayor and as owner of a well-found house, gave food and shelter to the boorish little German for one or two nights and days, as the weather had destroyed communication with London, where it was seriously feared that the King was lost, as a reference to the history of his reign will show. Great though the honour, it must have been an extremely inconvenient moment, for an addition to the family occurred that very night. The King, however, though he hated England and English ways and could not speak our language, seems to have made himself agreeable on this auspicious occasion With a dry suit, before a good fire and plenty of beer and tobacco, George the First was probably at his best, such as it was. In any case he did the right thing, became Godfather to the boy, blessed him and gave him his own name George and a gold cup into the bargain, which is still preserved in the family.

The second occasion was in 1755, just before the outbreak of the Seven Years War, when the Duke of Cumberland, the so-called " butcher of Culloden " but the best of the whole breed, visited Rye to inspect the defences of the neighbourhood, and was entertained by Mr. Lamb, who was still Mayor.

These particulars have been kindly given m e by almost the only living representative of the Lamb-Grebell families—which have otherwise died out in Rye. In regard to the Grebell murder, which took place from this house, my informant gives some particulars, unknown to the local chroniclers, in part at least, that are physiologically interesting. Mr. Grebell had been supping with his brother-in-law Lamb, and having some business in the town borrowed his scarlet overcoat. On returning late through the churchyard, he felt some one push heavily as he thought against him, and merely remarking " Get away, you drunken hound," passed on to Lamb House, quite unconcerned. He duly reported the incident, but as the family were going to bed, said he felt so tired that, instead of going home, he would have a sleep in the arm-chair by the fire. In the morning he was found dead, with a stab in the back, which had caused internal bleeding.

MERMAID STREET, RYE.

CHAPTER THE THIRD

Rye (continued)

BUT it is Mermaid Street after all that Rye holds in most regard for what may be called exhibition purposes. Our visitors, to be sure, are not so often seized with a burning desire to take up their abode there as is the case with some other quarters, for the street is narrow and under most lights a trifle gloomy of aspect. But beyond a doubt it is more eloquent of the past, and to the eye at any rate seems to contain more ancient houses than any other thoroughfare in the town. Moreover, it is interesting as having been a popular residential quarter among the wealthier burghers in Tudor and Jacobean times, and no doubt at a still later date. The ship-owners, the wool-buyers, the ship-builders, the wine-importers and other snug people, who knew no doubt exactly where to lay their hands on any good little bit of property that was going cheap, to say nothing of those "in the know" who derived handsome incomes from smuggling, to the incidental comforting of neighbouring squires, parsons and yeomen. In the French and American wars too a great deal of money came to Rye by more legitimate means, the town being active in the matter of building and manning privateers.

From the corner by Lamb House, Mermaid Street slopes downwards and westwards till finally with a much steeper pitch it debouches on the Strand, among the timber warehouses and other picturesque accessories to the present extremely modest wharves. And if you pause down here and look up the street with a western sun behind you, throwing its light up the long rows of quaint, diverse and many-coloured houses, and upon the green-clad, roughly cobbled way that parts them, you will withdraw the verdict probably passed on the street till you tread it again on the next dull day. They are small enough houses these for a once substantial quarter, but not ill consorting with the picture of a compact burgess community, that leaned, one might fancy, rather towards good living than to competition in bricks and mortar. There are, however, three out-standing buildings in Mermaid Street : *The Mermaid Inn* for one, near the top of it, and two lower down again connected with the Jeake family, already referred to.

One of these last is rather exceptional in Rye. It stands detached and is of sixteenth or early seventeenth century date. In the latter period it is referred to by its owner as about the best house in the town, which is interesting. The building itself is of half timber with three overhanging front gables and latticed windows, a dignified but now rather decadent looking spectacle ; the sort of Tudor house you may see over and over again in Hereford or Shropshire, except that in the Welsh Marches the tradition of blacking the timbers and keeping the plaster fresh accentuates the character of the style and, as I think, to great advantage. The stranger will probably not be much concerned to hear that Samewell (*sic*) Jeake Junior came to live here on his marriage at the end of the seventeenth century. But Samewell Jeake Senior and Samewell Jeake Junior are both great people upon the rolls of Rye and not undeservedly so. The former laid his country under obligations by his publication of the Cinque-Ports charters, as we have already pointed out, while the latter has deserved equally well of his native town for the personal and other notes he left behind. The elder Jeake was for a time Town-Clerk. Both were authors, sectaries and expounders and were out for trouble all the time, which they easily found when the other side was uppermost. Both too were astrologers, the younger being also a "demonologist," as the phraseology of that day had it. For in spite of his Calvinistic zeal he believed spirits of a rather

OLD HOSPITAL, RYE.

inferior order to be constantly about his bed and about his path, groaning and sighing and among other trifling pranks meddling with his walking sticks. Perhaps the house had something to do with it! To-day, at any rate, it looks as if it ought to be a very nest of spooks. It is known as the Old Hospital from having been put to that use in the Napoleonic wars when Rye as to-day was an armed camp.

A house nearly opposite this one, though of less striking

appearance, proclaims itself by inscription the work of the younger Jeake, and he seems to have built it as a store house in 1689. On its gabled front is a Latin inscription indicating the date of its erection and the position of the heavens when the first stone was laid, while around the inscription is an astronomical plan of them. The mental activities of father and son seem to have been phenomenal, both in a religious and secular direction. For besides his *magnum opus* the elder Jeake wrote many other works and no doubt preached any number of extemporary sermons, in spite of his Town-Clerkship. The list of studies covered by the son, according to himself, before his twentieth year, would make the hair of a modern graduate in first-class double honours stand on end. To this list, however, is added the qualifying statement that he was " something acquainted with all of them." For a rigid Puritan he was on singular terms, not merely with troublesome spirits, but with the magic of the stars, and he cast his horoscope upon every possible occasion. He falls one night through a hole in the floor into a cellar half full of water. Before he had apparently even changed his clothes he cast his horoscope and duly discovered in it the " watery signs " he looked for. Another time on riding home from Robertsbridge in the dark, and crossing a watercourse in a lane, the saddle, wanting a crupper and loosely girthed, slipped forward on his horse's ears. At this critical moment his theocratic side being uppermost he " sought guidance " and " the Lord," he says, " directed him to retire at once," before, that is to say, he was quite over the horse's head, which he did. The beast was fortunately gentle, otherwise he " might have been drowned, trod on or at least soaked through." He immediately consulted the stars, again finding water in the ascendant.

But the marriage of this singular man, as described by himself, is still more interesting as possibly typical of the procedure then in vogue with the golden youth of Rye in the year 1680. The lady was " Mrs. Elizabeth Hartshorn," the daughter of the

Grammar School master, and she had reached the mature age of twelve years and eight months. " Having resolved to seek her in marriage," Mr. Samuel Jeake, Junior, took the preliminary step of calling upon her mother the very same afternoon. But " she had company," and to broach the subject was impossible, the stars no doubt being adverse. So next day he dropped in again, and finding his prospective mother-in-law alone, expressed his intentions immediately, was accepted and " the portion argued." This was in the Old Hospital we have just been looking at. A week later he returned to the house to interview the daughter, and these are the words with which he wooed the twelve-year-old child : " My dear lady, the deep impression your person and your virtues have made upon my mind oblige me to become your servant, and I beseech you, Madam, be pleased to return me the favour of having a place in your heart." · Whereat the infant replied : " Sir, it is so weighty a business that I am not capable of returning you an answer without a long time of consideration."

So Jeake returned home and consulted the stars again, which seemed favourable to his project, and he was right, for a week later he was betrothed, the settlement arranged, and within eight months he was married, the lady being thirteen and he twenty-nine. From this union sprang a third Samuel Jeake, who in due course inherited the old house, as well as the literary tastes and slightly eccentric ingenuity of his forbears. For he purchased the Rye Statute-books for a guinea, the very figure for which his grandfather had acquired the

ANCIENT VICARAGE, RYE.

Charters, though he failed to utilize them. But he invented a flying machine which would not fly, and Mr. Holloway tells us that he knew men who remembered seeing this prehistoric aeroplane reposing in the attic of the Grammar School.

Just here, too, there is an old chapel in which Wesley preached once at least, though he often visited Rye. There was a strong element of Methodism in the town, but it would not give up smuggling, and a smuggler Wesley insisted to his quite unconvinced congregations was just as bad as a highwayman. He robbed his country, and with equal violence if necessary, instead of his neighbours, that was all the difference : " How large a society would be here," he laments, " if we could but spare them in one thing, but then all our labours would be in vain, one sin allowed would intercept the whole blessing." But the men of Rye were incorrigible on this point and remained so long after the great Evangelist had been gathered to his fathers.

The Mermaid Hotel stands near the head of this street and it is quite a famous house, not only because it is a large, picturesque and rambling building of fifteenth-century date, but having been for some twenty-five recent years one of the chief resorts of visitors to the ancient town—golfers, artists, Americans and others—it has acquired quite a cosmopolitan reputation. In ancient days it was the chief hostelry of the town and seems to have done a great coaching and posting business, though its premises have been since curtailed. In the late eighteenth century it ceased to be an inn until its comparatively recent resurrection. Its premises run a long way back into a paved yard, and it is from there only that its curious medley of stone, timber, wattle, and casement window, and its irregular tiled and gabled roof can be rightly appreciated. The street front alone is comparatively modern but so ingeniously unassuming that the scope of the building behind would hardly be suspected. The interior is a regular rabbit-warren of tortuous narrow passages and stairways leading into rooms of mostly varying character, size and shape. The general sitting-room is oak panelled of the folded linen pattern, with a fine sixteenth-century stone chimney piece carrying the Tudor rose. The smoking-room, with its low

MERMAID INN, RYE.

oak-ribbed ceiling, its leaden casements and quaint corner staircase, its carved oak chests and glorious old open chimney space fifteen feet long and supported by a huge beam, is the gem of the house. With a big log fire blazing on the dog irons it is as perfect an unfaked example of an original Tudor interior as could be found, I think, anywhere.

Some twenty odd years ago when Rye was being " discovered " the house was bought up by a small syndicate and restored to its ancient uses as an hotel, but for quite another sort of guest. A clerical acquaintance of mine and a Canon of S——, visiting *The Mermaid* for the first time a few years ago, carried home a story which being possessed of a waggish tongue he used to be fond of relating to his friends in Blankshire. For some technical reason that I cannot precisely recall, probably in connexion with the licence, a visitor using the smoking-room had to enter his name as member of some recognized social or golfing club. This demand by the head waiter, who was himself something of a character, took my reverend friend by surprise and he hum'd and haw'd and demurred a good deal at what he thought was a piece of nonsense. George, the waiter, however, proceeded to smooth him down and assure him it was a mere formality that every guest went through, and intimated that any London club or golf club would serve the purpose. The Canon (he was not in clerical garb) being unjustifiably petulant, as he admitted, at what seemed to him a ridiculous proceeding, after a considerable pause snapped out the fact that he was a member of The Athenaeum. George's face fell; he thought the Canon was pulling his leg. " The what, sir ? Never heard of that, sir. Haven't you *any* other club, sir ? " My friend was restored by this delightful anti-climax to a good humour: " Why, of course I have," he said, " I am a member of the Chalkley Down Golf Club, Blankshire." (Where he was a twenty handicap.) George's face cleared at once and the entry was duly made. The Canon, who had some gift of dry humour, used to tell his friends in Blankshire how as a member of the Athenaeum he came very near being kicked out of his hotel in Rye, but that his ineffectual connexion with the Chalkley Down G.C. had pulled him through and saved the situation. However, he told me the incident as here set down the day of its occurrence with enormous satisfaction.

Where Mermaid Street dips to the flat by the harbour stood the old Strand Gate of the town, demolished in the early nineteenth century. Almost the only group of old buildings outside the line of the Walls is in this quarter and immemorially

PUMP STREET, RYE.

known as "The Wish." Here are the wharves where the few small trading sloops, barques and barges still owned by Rye merchants unload their coals from the Tyne or ship their cargoes of timber to France or elsewhere. For though the forest of Anderida no longer waves unbroken to the brink of Playden cliff, this corner of Sussex still abounds in woodland and its produce is burnt pretty freely even on the hearths of

Rye. In a few of the remaining open Tudor fireplaces piles of big logs roar as merrily up the huge chimneys as they did in the days of our friends the Jeakes and in those of their fathers before them. A little old port like this one, even apart from its peculiar associations, a quiet backwater of a haven, devoid of stir and bustle and almost of life, up whose narrow channel only an occasional sailing ship comes stealing on the top of the tide, has a fascination of its own that needs no telling. There is a tall warehouse or two of black weatherboarding and a little custom house at the foot of Mermaid Street which last is apt to surprise the visitor doing his duty by that notable thoroughfare and probably quite unconscious that Rye has any longer an interest in sea-borne trade. An old inn, *The Ship*, broods under the shadow of the sombre warehouses, displaying a barque in full sail over its low door. It would seem to have nothing in common with the other taverns of Rye, though a few even still wear a slightly amphibious aspect, and nothing to say to anybody but the thirsty mariner just off a voyage and no topics to air in its snug-looking bar than those which smack of salt water, such as the mariner gives utterance to in his own forceful and breezy style. But such an exclusive appeal in a Rye waterside inn would I fancy spell a poor living to-day. However that may be, I have never met any one familiar with this particular spot who does not associate it with his favourite author in salt-water fiction, if he have one.

A picturesque-looking wooden dwelling-house, with a gabled roof and an old stone stairway leading up to a front door twenty feet above the Strand, strikes a cheerful note from above, while adjoining a most noble expanse of mellow tile roof covering a warehouse that used to delight many eyes has been disfigured by a hideous local trade advertisement sprawled in white lettering all over it. A little farther on a handsome ivy-covered old Georgian house looks on to the wharves; as if peradventure some Rye magnate of former days had declined the fashionable quarters of the town, and preferred to see his cargoes dumped out before his front door. This, I believe, is not far from the actual truth. The here uniting waters of the Tillingham and Brede rivers run right round the southern base of the rock to that junction with the

CLIFF GARDENS, RYE.

Rother which we spoke of at the Ferry house below the Ypres tower. Their course is sufficiently clear of the town to give any one who follows it perhaps the most engaging of all the nearer views of Rye. For the entire back of Watchbell Street and Church Square and on to the south-eastern corner marked by the Ypres tower, fringe the cliff edges with their quaintly irregular line of gables and chimneys, while their narrow strips of flower garden and fruit trees cling to the steeps above the sharp face of the rock. There is a wealth of colouring in this southern front of Rye with its varied shades and tones and the sunshine streaming full upon it, that almost persuades me to forswear myself and suggest something of a continental parallel, illusive though it be. All about this waterside trail too, with its stacks of timber and litter of immense tree trunks, hauled down from Sussex woods, lies the flotsam and jetsam of the sea, those far-flung and promiscuous relics of forgotten voyages, and forgotten men, of rotted and abandoned craft.

Why the broken figurehead, or the rusty anchor of a long vanished vessel, the water-logged ribs of a defunct smack, the stem of a ship's boat with its faded name still partly legible, should thus move one is not far to seek. That these inconsequent fragments touch a cord left quite unstirred by the abandoned skeleton of a carrier's cart, or a prehistoric railway carriage transformed into a bathing shed is a question which the mystery of the great deep sufficiently answers. Perhaps upon this particular spot they may also seem emblematical of the vanished maritime glories of Rye, and assume additional pathos thereby. If such be the case, I do not know whether a still surviving shipyard just round the bend, with a half-built vessel probably on the stocks, may serve to modify or to emphasize these sombre reflections, purely academic though they be. For Rye still builds on an average one ship of about fifty tons and sometimes a sailing barge or two of larger tonnage every year. The former is launched in normal times with some ceremony. The Mayoress breaks a bottle over the stern and the assembled youth of Rye raise a cheer as the great ship glides down into the muddy but historic stream. To such a pass have things come where once were built and manned fleets to fight the French and Spaniards, and privateers in the Napoleonic wars, and even pirates in earlier days when a good opportunity occurred. At any rate neither Winchelsea, nor Romney, nor I think Hythe nor Sandwich turns out even one ship per annum, for the best of reasons not of their making.

It is to the glory of Rye, however, as I have always been assured by those who ought to know best, that this solitary contribution to the British mercantile marine, whether smack or coasting trader, is built as is no other vessel in the whole kingdom in these hurried days. There are still ships' craftsmen in Rye, having the pride of other days within them, who would rather hurl their tools into the harbour than hustle over or scamp the smallest fragment of their work. Lowestoft and Yarmouth and Hull are fully conscious of this unique characteristic that has apparently no longer any place among themselves, and if a small vessel of extra stamina is required they send all the way to sleepy old Rye for it. Whether the hustle of war which has of course absorbed in strange and varied occupations all the salt-water element here as elsewhere will break this old tradition is neither here nor there, as regard the record of its survival and the retrospective nature of this book.

THE STRAND, RYE.

Speaking of the near view of Rye from this southern side an outrage was perpetrated upon it some twenty years ago that has leaped to the eye of every soul who has beheld it since. That a row of artisans' houses should be built along the base of the cliff from one end to the other may have been a necessary evil from a practical point of view, but in a land of red tile roofing common decency might have prevented the offender from fetching slates out of North Wales and thereby multiplying tenfold the disfigurement to a prospect that stands alone in the south of England. Neither, alas, is it only in the near view. For when miles away over the Marsh gleams of sunshine out of shifting skies are lighting up the high perched old town with an effect that is unforgettable, this monstrous quarter-mile fringe of sordid slate catches the sun also, and only too effectively.

Ascending to the town again, which from the shipyard can be most readily done by the stairway leading up to the Ypres Tower and the church, I seem to fancy myself incurring the suspicion of that house-to-house visitation which I have so emphatically disclaimed. But in the eyes of any one familiar with all the nooks and corners in Rye worth looking at, even when I have finished, which I have not quite yet, I shall be assuredly acquitted of inconsistency. On the contrary, I am quite certain to be reminded of innumerable omissions. To this as always I can only make answer that this volume is neither a guide book, nor a directory, nor a history of Rye, and furthermore that I have not six hundred of even these comparatively short pages at my disposal like the excellent Holloway for the whole of this little pilgrimage. But the old Vicarage, wholly or partly rebuilt in 1707, standing under the north side of the church, must not be passed over. For here Fletcher, the dramatist and collaborateur with Beaumont, was born in 1579, son of the Vicar, by repute an ex-Fellow of Trinity, Cambridge. This was in the last year of his Rye vicarship, and as he was subsequently Dean of Peterborough, Bishop of Bristol and Worcester and finally of London, the talents of the son were doubtless hereditary. Some, however, including the present writer, believe the original Vicarage to be still standing in the form of a very ancient house, within a few yards of the other now being internally renovated. It is of the fifteenth century, in the half-timbered style and has both the York and Tudor roses on the door lintel. It faces, at a few yards distance, though a later building now intervenes, a closed-up door in the church, strongly suggestive of a vicar's private entry.

The Bishop did not live long enough to witness the staging of his son's plays. As a fierce Protestant he would hardly, I take it, have sat them out! He bullied poor Queen Mary in her last moments at Fotheringay and gave much offence to her friends, calling out in a deep voice when the bloody head was held up by the executioner, " So let Queen Elizabeth's enemies perish ! " But he was a great favourite with the Queen, for his handsome person, courtly manners, and " elegant sermons." She even instructed him how to trim his beard ! He was in truth deplorably subservient to his masterful mistress, alienating the episcopal properties, not to his sons and nephews as did many Bishops of his day, and of much later ones, but to the Queen's favourites in payment for his own preferment. He squirmed under it, to be sure, poor man, when he had to play the same game as Bishop of London. Nay more, he resented it all too openly, and his friends gave him away, whereat the Queen shut him up a prisoner in his own house.

He had hardly made his peace with her when he was fool enough to commit the one unpardonable crime in the eyes of the Great Eliza. For he fell in love with a young and extremely pretty woman, and worse still married her. This of course instantly extinguished him as a royal favourite, and London following suit lampooned the poor Bishop and his apparently foolish young wife with the utmost scurrility of a coarse age. The Queen could not deprive him of his Bishopric merely for marrying a lady of respectable family, but she gave him a most parlous time for the last year of his life. She did eventually consent to pay him one visit at his house in Chelsea. The Bishop died suddenly, just after helping to consecrate his successor at Worcester, while smoking a pipe in his bedroom, for he was much addicted, we are told, to tobacco. He died moreover in debt all round, even to the Queen herself for *first-fruits*, and small wonder, poor man, considering the way she had encroached upon his episcopal income in every See he held. His eight children were left totally unprovided for, and a petition on their behalf was presented to the throne. He himself was buried in St. Paul's in an unrecorded grave. Such in brief was the rather meteoric career and the sad end of, so far as I know, the most distinguished of the Vicars of Rye. Perhaps he would have done better to have spent those sixteen years in the quiet haven of Church Square and reserved his " elegant sermons " for the congregations of St. Mary's and his courtly manners for the ladies of Rye. His brilliant son, who only just managed to be born here in the very year of his father's promotion, died of the plague at forty-six, which, according to Aubry, who knew everything, he caught by going up to London to see his tailor ! as we should now put it. One other Vicar of Rye rose to the Bench, namely Lewis Bagot, who was appointed to St. Asaph in 1780.

In a small book of notes on Rye, written by Holloway and rather scarce, he relates that a very old lady of ninety, one of the Lamb family, told him that she remembered the trees now bordering the churchyard, mostly elms, being brought over from Holland by a Captain Gosley. The same old lady too explained to Holloway the meaning of a cryptic illustration carved upon a tombstone in the churchyard, now worn wholly away, which depicted a woman sitting up in a coffin, the inscription being even then illegible. It appears that this is in memory of a Mrs. Gibbon, who in the middle of the eighteenth century lived in the house at the corner adjoining the present *Fresco House* upon the south side of Market Street. She was subject to fits, and one of them lasted so long that she was laid out for dead, prepared for burial and placed in her coffin. On the morning of the funeral the woman who was baking the cakes, then usual on such occasions, was horrified at the sudden appearance beside her of the corpse holding out its hands and complaining of the cold. It was a case of catalepsy, a risky complaint in those days ! The woman lived many years after this and was remembered by old Mrs. Lamb whose relations employed her.

Just under the north side of the church is the Town Hall, and on its flank, at the corner of Church Square and Market Street, is another notable building, *The Fresco House* just alluded to, but in olden days *The Flushing Inn*. It has quite recently, after more than a century of private occupation, resumed its former calling, in much the same fashion as *The Mermaid* and for the same class of guest. Some few years ago, while still a private residence, quite a flutter was caused in Rye by the discovery, on the wall of a front room beneath some panelling, of a remarkable mural painting of the sixteenth century. It is now exposed and practically covers one side of the smoking-room. The colours are well preserved, though the subject is rather confusing and an idle hour might be pleasantly spent before the wide Tudor fireplace picking out the birds from the beasts and both from the flowers and foliage among which they are so quaintly distributed. Bands of old lettering of a devotional character cross the scene. There is a good deal of panelling and oak in the house, while a Tudor doorway with an ogee arch opens into Church Street. It is now one of the chief resorts of visitors to Rye. The original sign, *The Flushing Inn*, has been discovered and hangs over the door.

An Interior, Church Square

The Town Hall, which stands in the very heart, as well as almost on the crest of the town, now demands a word. As a structure from the Georgian civic building point of view it is admirably typical, dating from 1742 and is of red brick now tolerably weather-toned. Its open-pillared front and round arches upon the ground floor, under which the market was once held, its stone facings, tiled roof and the aspiring cupola beloved by the generations just before and just after the Seven Years War, including the colonial Americans, are absolutely the right thing. Lists of the Mayors from about 1300 may be read upon the court-room wall upstairs, while all the insignia and curios, which last includes the gibbet and the butcher's skull, a pillory and so forth, may be inspected under proper guidance and regarded, not let us hope as the baubles of an ordinary borough town, but with all the reverence due to the symbols of an ancient Cinque-Port. The maces are held, in Rye, to be the finest in England, and there are also the Elizabethan maces and some other treasures. The town records, such as are left of them, are no longer sold by the half-hundredweight for a guinea, as they appear to have been in the days of the Jeakes, but are carefully preserved. But the most eloquent relic in the Hall is the original of an engagement by the chief inhabitants of Rye to be " true and faithful to the Commonwealth " signed by a hundred and sixty-eight of them : in full by those who could do so, and with their marks by those who were " no scholards." It goes without saying that the Rye records contain a mass of interesting details illustrating not merely the life of the town, but English life generally at its different periods. The Historical MSS. Society have by their transcriptions taken care that the best of this, at any rate, shall be at the disposal of all interested in such matters.

The neighbourhood of the town records naturally inclines one's thoughts toward the queer tales they sometimes tell. There were witches in Rye, of course. Indeed the Ypres tower must have made an ideal starting-point for a trip on a broomstick across the Marsh. But there was much more serious talk than that, between the Mayor and Jurats and the Lord Warden, whose advice as an authority, rather comical though it sounds, was sought for in some of these intricate psychological cases! This surely is one of the most shameful pages in all our history, and a hideous stain on the "unco' guid" who chiefly wallowed in the cowardly business. In December 1645, one finds the Mayor ordering the wife of Stephen Bruff, and a certain widow, Anne Howswell, suspected of being witches, to be thrown into the river as "a tryall," whatever the nature of the test may have been. Possibly they began with the ducking stool. Prior to that some excitement had been caused by Anne Taylor, the wife of a gentleman, being incarcerated for witchcraft together with Susan Swapper who practised the like, and had apparently already suffered for it. Bail was refused, till it was reluctantly accepted in £100 from George Taylor gentleman, her husband, when she was at length let out of the Ypres tower. Joan Bayly, aged fourscore, took it upon her to tell the wife of Thomas Hart, a fisherman, that her child was bewitched, and having undertaken the cure, ordered the mother to fetch her threescore needles, a halfpenny worth of pins and a piece of red cloth. Into this last she stuck all the needles and pins and then put it upon the "emeryes" of the fire. She next thrust a dagger into the middle of this mysterious compound which was confi-

INTERIOR, CHURCH SQUARE.

dently expected to allure the person who had bewitched the child to the house in the shape of the first comer. Fortunately for the gossips no one of them happened to call, and in time the red cloth was consumed and " seemed to be like unto a toad." These cases were seriously investigated by the Mayor and Jurats of Rye and depositions taken in due form, but the town, I am glad to say, has no witch-burning to its account.

In 1608 the Lord Warden notifies the Mayor to intercept the passage of Sir Nicholas Hall and Captain Fortescue, who had arranged a duel over sea. In 1593 when the channels of the harbour of Rye were silting up badly, a certain Italian, named Genebelle came to the town with recommendations from the Lords of the Council, to whom he had proposed a scheme for dealing with this chronic trouble. There was a conference with the said Jenebelly, as the Ryers characteristically spell him, and probably called him. But when it was discovered that the drift of his scheme lay in cutting a new channel to the sea in the direction of Winchelsea, precisely what Rye did a hundred and fifty years later, they denounced him up hill and down dale as proposing to benefit not Rye but " other places " (Winchelsea) and declared by order that he had treacherously abused the town by his false illusions in promising to mend the harbour. So exit " Jenebelly," the well-meaning alien, with a flea in his ear. And inasmuch as their final clause ran that they " would no further intermeddle with the said Jenebelly or any of his devices " the intruding foreigner might have considered himself uncommonly well out of it at that time of day!

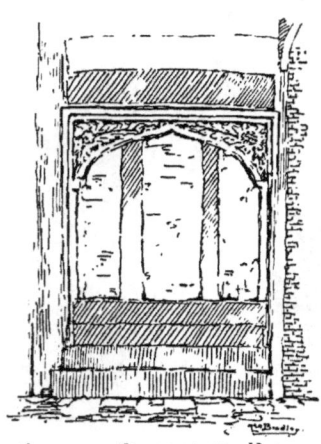

CARVED DOORWAY, RYE

When in the same year the well-known iron foundry at

Brede was first projected, there was a great to-do in the western Ports. Hastings wrote to Rye, and Rye wrote to Hastings to the effect that they would all be utterly undone by the impending destruction of timber. There would be no more firewood, they all protested, no more timber for " building shipps, crayres, botes and other vessels, or for houses, or piles for water works." In short, ruin stared them in the face. A joint Suit to the House of Lords and Council, alone, it was declared, could save them. Lord Buckherst, the potential offender, replies to the three Ports with biting irony, thanking them for their " neighbourly conduct " and telling them that they have enough fuel " within three miles for twenty such towns as theirs "; as to Rye, he wants to know what the deuce its inhabitants have got to do with his woods eight miles distant, and scores rather neatly by reminding them that they had recently exported at least 1000 tons of timber to France, while " as to you at Hastings and Winchelsea " there are better woods, he tells them, than his close to them for their paltry requirements. Rye was always jealous of its wood supply. As late as the Tudor period, when a solitary " agriculturist " came to dwell among them, he was promptly kicked out as a pernicious person with probable designs on the Playden woods. There are constant complaints, too, of pirates, very often of English nationality one is forced to add. In May, 1605, Peter Norry deposed that being in his ship with about ten passengers bound for Dieppe, he was boarded in the night by a ship's crew consisting of about twenty Englishmen. They boarded him, seized his passengers, took all their money, and putting a crew on the captured ship landed the said owner and his passengers at Fairlight and then sailed away with the vessel and all their goods.

So many foreign settlers, it appears, were coming into the town, even in Charles the First's reign, that the natives grew alarmed lest in time they should find themselves outnumbered. So instructions were given to forward all such immigrants to the inland towns, "unless they were men of substance." a method of combing out that Tenterden, Tonbridge or Maidstone may have strongly objected to! George Goodwyn, a carpenter, having been shut up in Bridewell and Newgate for saying that he had a right to the kingdom and was undoubtedly King of England, came to Rye to press his claims. He soon found himself before the Mayor. But when in defence of his pretensions he quoted Ecclesiastes, "that a poor child was better that an old and foolish King," the Bench let the waggish lunatic off as not mad enough, for James I was on the throne!

In 1624 Rye was agitated by a "Mr. Abington," his wife and two children, who were papists, coming to dwell among them and wrote to the Lord Warden for instructions, "For they desired not the company of any of that religion if possible wee may lawfully avoid them." Moreover "Abington had been questioned in the treason of the Gunpowder Plot and not yet cleared." This was possibly one of the Habingtons of Hindlip in Worcestershire, who were indirectly implicated in it. You had to be careful too what you said in Rye in those days! In 1654 Mark Hounsell, bricklayer, was walking down from Playden with Anthony Norton when the latter said, "None but rogues fought against the King and that Cromwell and all who followed him were rogues." His companion, as very often happened in those days, gave him away, but not for three months afterwards, and when the Bench asked deponent to explain his dilatoriness, he replied with unabashed candour that "the prisoner owed him money which he wanted to collect before he had him laid by the heels." All this was soon changed, however, for in 1660 there came an order from Dover Castle to remove the Cromwellian magistrates and restore those whose places they had usurped. Rye must have been rather tired of Cromwellian soldiers, for in 1649 it put forth "a grievous crye" that two companies had been billeted on them free for twelve months, and yet more that their captains had extracted (alleging an Act of Parliament) £100 in cash from the town.

Furthermore they had disarmed all the gentlemen that came to the town so that desirable persons naturally began to fight shy of it. Still more the soldiers had prevented the very fishermen from going up and down the town cliffs to their boats. In short, if the troops were not removed half the town, it was threatened, would migrate and seek a living elsewhere. In 1667 there were more complaints of soldiers at Rye; this time a Scottish regiment, which must have been Coldstreams or the 1st Royal Scots, as they were then the only two Scottish corps embodied. The Ypres Tower was full of deserters from their ranks, and a Rye citizen was paid ten shillings compensation for having been "damnified by Scottish soldiers keeping guard in his house."

Rye nowadays petitions to have troops and is very glad to see them. It was all very well for the soldier-ridden Ryers of 1659 to talk about migration. But the authorities had a blunt method of dealing with that sort of thing. For if the population of a town was visibly shrinking, orders were sent out to those who had settled elsewhere to return immediately, which, unless they had gone to the American colonies, they mostly had to. In Charles the First's time John Withers was placed at Rye as drill sergeant or captain to exercise the citizens in military science. But so many " refused to be drilled or exercised " that the Lord Warden sent for the names of any that should continue refractory and intimated that with the help of His Majesty he would make it pretty hot for them.

The Rye people had a very bad scare in 1689, during the days that followed the Battle of the Boyne and before the result was known. For the French fleet that had escorted James and his army to Ireland came sauntering along the coast of Sussex, with the English fleet for some reason sailing before it to the Downs. A report came that the latter had been beaten, off Beachy Head, and that the French were firing on Hastings, which in a limited sense was true enough. Jeake Junior comes in very useful here with his journal. He had just fetched his mother, wife and children back to Rye from the country on July 5, when to his consternation the French fleet anchored in the bay and began sounding the harbour entrance with the intention as was supposed of burning and plundering the town. " Upon this an intolerable hurry all day ; the trainbands up in arms with the soldiers and sailors of *The Anne*, who were then in town, sending out into the country for more men and planting guns on the beach with a breastwork of deal ; sending of goods out of town in waggons and on horses, and the like confusions usual at such times. I sent my mother-in-law and daughter out of the town again about two in the afternoon and with them my writings and gold. The rest of my money I sent afterwards and my wife's clothes in the evening. But she went not out of the town because my little boy was this morning taken sick of a fever." However, Jeake made preparations for moving them as well as his father, who was also ill, should the French actually enter the harbour. " But through mercy " there was no attempt made to do so. The news of the Boyne soon arrived and Protestant England, above all the Nonconformist Jeakes and family, breathed again. And Samuel Jeake at once, having " beheld the face of Heaven," cast a horoscope.

The most thrilling scenes ever witnessed by the present Town Hall will undoubtedly have been the elections. For long before and just after the Great Reform Bill particularly, those contests already alluded to between the illegally disfranchised householders of the town and the little family compact, which held both corporate and Parliamentary honours in the hollow of their hands throughout the eighteenth century and longer, were at their height. It must be said for them, however, that they contrived to get their Town Hall erected without a penny of cost to any one in Rye. It was quite simple. In 1742 £900 was required for the work, and what more natural than that the pockets of the two members of Parliament should be further exploited by the comfortable little syndicate who had no doubt earned and received from them a considerable *quid pro quo* on voting account. So each member advanced £50 at 3 per cent. (current rate then was 5 per cent.) and might fairly be considered to have cornered the Corporation, so it was not all on one side. Rye Town Hall may be regarded therefore with quite peculiar interest as a monument of the civic architecture which was creditable and of the political morality which was deplorable, of the Georgian age. But after all the slimness which saddled the borough members with the cost of its erection had almost a flavour of civic patriotism about it. When ten years later the senior member died, his executors pressed for payment. But the town in such astute hands had neither the intention nor the money to make any such superfluous disbursement. In brief, the next member, Pelham, assumed the bond with the seat, and finally his brother, the fussy, spluttering Duke of Newcastle—prince, nay, emperor of jobbers—bought them both up, presented them to the borough and so secured for life, as he imagined, its Parliamentary good-will. But Rye got its Town Hall for nothing!

In later years, when the corruption of Walpole's régime had been amplified by sixty years of his more than disciple George the Third, Official Rye was anti-patriotic, or rather anti-civic to a deplorable degree. Holloway may be generally dull, but when he comes to the stirring period that he could not only remember but had taken a sanely active part in, he breaks out of his sober gait into almost a canter. " It was on May the 4th," he tells us, warming into fervour with the recollection, " that the tocsin sounded which roused the men of Rye from their deep slumber of ages, when they flew to arms and sat down before the fortress of the Corporation." In plain words fifty or sixty inhabitants, householders, paying " scot and lot," entered the fortress, otherwise the Town Hall, where the Mayor was sitting in Court, and demanded to have the oath of allegiance administered to them and their names enrolled in order that they might be admitted to the rights and privileges belonging of old to the townsmen. The Court, taken, so it professed, by surprise, was not prepared to reply off-hand. So the company retired to a house near by and drew up a petition to the House of Commons, which was presented by one of the County members, Mr. Curteis, a neighbouring landowner, who sympathized with their wrongs. The petition explained the ancient rights of the town and how unjustly they had been usurped. On the next Court-day the petitioners applied again to the little family syndicate whose predecessors had captured Rye body and soul. The Court declared themselves willing to administer the oath of allegiance to all and sundry, anybody in fact over twenty-one who liked to come along and take it: the more the merrier. But as to their rights they were unaware that any were withheld from them! A fortnight later the petitioners again went to the Court-House, took the oath of allegiance, had their names enrolled and demanded to be admitted to all future meetings of the Corporation. The demand was of course refused.

According to the old custom of Rye, never abrogated, the Mayor was chosen on the Sunday following the Feast of St. Bartholomew at the cross in the churchyard. So early on that day, August 28, the householders of the town proceeded to the spot where the Cross had once stood, and there elected as Mayor Mr. Meryon, the historian's father-in-law, of an old Rye Huguenot family and the sole member of the Corporation at that moment in sympathy with reform. The next morning the Revolutionists proceeded to the Court-House, where the old gang were occupied in choosing their Mayor, and demanded, though of course in vain, that the retiring Mayor should at once swear Mr. Meryon into office. The choice of the Family Compact seemed almost to shout for trouble and touched the limit of municipal paradox, being actually a beneficed parson in Lincolnshire, who happened to be a relative of some of the Corporation. One can imagine only a single reason why the

Reverend Dodson should have aspired to the civic chair of Rye. He was not even a freeman, as the lists show, nor in any way connected with the place except that a relation had formerly been for a short time one of its representatives in Parliament.

Anyway the reverend gentleman came all the way down from Lincolnshire, and took his seat in Court, supported by his cousins and his wife's cousins of various removes, further comforted no doubt by the fact that a general election was imminent and two new candidates for the favours of their little family party there assembled were coming forward. It was in vain that the Rye householders respectfully prayed the Bishop of Lincoln to restrain this wandering sheep of his fold from meddling in the concerns of a distant town, with which he had nothing whatever to do, and to order him back to his parish with which he had everything to do. The Rye householders had obviously a quite pathetic confidence in the Episcopal authority. The revolutionists in the meantime took the matter into their own hands, turned out the family party, put their own Mayor into the chair and held possession of the Town Hall for six weeks, administering justice to such as sought it, and even sat officially upon the body of a man who had hanged himself, whether a patriot "despairing of the Republic" history does not say.

> "No Policemen had we
> No trials nor cares,
> Oh! that was the time
> When we had our two Mayors."

Thus sings a contemporary Rye poet, a Radical printer in the town, who in a quaint and now scarce little book (lent to me by his grandson) has left a whimsical picture of these stormy times, in which his pen at any rate took an active part. But the others had not been idle; they had gone to the Court of King's Bench and returned with an order for the expulsion of the popularists and the re-seating of the Lincolnshire parson, who must have had an astonishing thick hide. The Rye householders then applied to the Court of King's Bench to compel the Mayor to admit certain native-born inhabitants to the freedom of the town which was their hereditary right. But technically such admission, in former days a mere form, lay with the Mayor and Jurats, who for seventy years had manœuvred for the monopoly they now held. In 1758 a private document had been drawn up, to which the Corporation, already settled down into a comfortable understanding, had set the several hands, agreeing to admit no one into the body who would not be subservient to its interests ; a truly amazing production, which furthermore pledged the signatories to secrecy, and arranged for the division of profits arising out of custom-house pickings and Corporation contracts. This precious document was discovered among the Records during the occupation of the Town Hall by the opposite party and placarded all over the town, causing an immense sensation. It may be perused at length in *Horsfield's History of Sussex*. A copy was embodied in a new petition to Parliament by the householders which complained that the Court of King's Bench had set up " the usurpations of seventy years as their authority for a decision." Lord John Russell presented it, and explained how the charter confirmed from Edward the Confessor to Charles the Second had been flagrantly broken.

But the House cared nothing at that moment for the woes of Rye, with its list reduced to thirteen votes, if such they can be called. The disfranchised burgesses, however, were not to be quashed, gloomy though their prospects might seem. The next excitement was a general election in the following year, when Rye having already achieved notoriety in the possession of two Mayors proceeded to elect two pairs of representatives to Parliament. The Reforming burgesses, on a franchise previously agreed upon, amounting to sixty-two votes, including those of two sympathetic Corporation men, elected their candidates, the Corporation with its eleven votes did the same. The Mayor of course rejected all these votes but those of the two above-named councillors. So the defeated party in their turn carried their case to the King's Bench, but to no purpose. The repeated demands of the disfranchised burgesses on the Mayor to call an assembly according to the customal and charter, for the election of freemen, always elicited the laconic answer that the Corporation " were unanimously of the opinion that an Assembly should *not* be called." Their nerve was undoubted and their unanimity always touching, as it would be with any twelve men who were politely requested to hang themselves!

All this was of course in that period of unparalleled excitement and grave anxiety which forced on the Great Reform Bill and extinguished the rotten boroughs, of which Rye had come to be such a shining example. In 1830 the death of one of the members for Rye gave the Reformers the chance of electing a voluntary candidate, one Colonel Evans, who offered to test the matter against the Corporation candidate, Mr. Pusey. The first result was of course as before, but the Colonel was enabled to petition against the other's return and so get the Speaker's warrant to inspect all the town documents, which he did with the aid of outside experts. The results were carried before a special committee of the House of Commons, who after several meetings decided that all the Rye householders who paid " scot and lot," native born or otherwise, were freemen and entitled to vote, in which case Colonel Evans was duly elected. So exit Mr. Pusey and enter the Colonel to the House of Commons in May 1830. Upon this triumph there were tremendous rejoicings and much open-air feasting in Rye. The Reformer's printer tells us that " Rye's unheard of boldness and bravery was heralded throughout the Kingdom, and in every journal occupied a considerable space."

But the triumph was short-lived. For George the Fourth died in the summer, when both the Corporation, clinging to its doomed fortress, and the townsfolk put up their rival pairs again, with the result of twelve to two hundred and six, all but eight votes of the latter being duly rejected by the Mayor. The usual petition to Parliament followed, which this time was rejected. The election of 1831, that stormy one before the Reform Bill, rapidly followed. The Reform leaders, regarding their old plan of recording disfranchised votes as hopeless, now determined *to act upon* the twelve or so unfriendly and three or four friendly registered voters. This proved the most sensational struggle of all. Colonel Evans had abandoned Rye in despair, and was wooing Preston, but some enthusiastic Ryers travelled the whole way into Lancashire and virtually dragged the Colonel south, just in time to be nominated. The twelve Corporation voters seem to have been so effectually " canvassed " that they sent for a company of armed coast-guards, whose appearance infuriated the mob. And while the former remained outside the rough element took the town in hand, tore up the pavement, wrenched off the iron railings under the Town Hall and raised for a day and night such a turmoil that several voters on the unpopular side durst not show their faces, much less approach the polling place. The magistrates were powerless before the pandemonium. So the poll had to be postponed till the next day, when the intimidated voters crept out of their lairs. But in the end a compromise was come to allotting a seat to each party, and here is the poll, which to moderns unfamiliar with or forgetful of political history will read strangely for a town of over three thousand souls.

> For Colonel Evans, 7.
> ,, Mr. Pemberton, 5.
> ,, Mr. Pusey, 3.
> ,, Mr. Smith, 2.

At the passing of the Reform Bill Rye ceased to be a rotten borough, but was deprived of a member, and had to share its remaining one with several neighbouring parishes aggregating a total vote under the new franchise of 379. Local candidates now succeeded the distinguished aliens or open-pocketed seat hunters that had paid liberally for the favours of Rye's little oligarchy, who after all had only followed the prevailing fashion, with a little more success perhaps than some of their neighbours.

The passions generated by this long struggle of the town against injustice found almost a fresh field in the open voting of a comparatively large register, the free and easy methods and the uproarious accessories that attended most elections prior to the 'seventies. It took three hundred special constables to keep Rye town within even such liberal bounds as were then tolerated. Free beer ran for days in most of the publichouses. The fishermen, who were sort of specialists at the rowdy side of elections, abandoned their nets and boats, filled their insides with heady ale and their pockets with rotten eggs. Each side abused one another through their respective printing-presses with a wealth of language both in prose and verse such as reads to-day almost like a lost art. There lies in the Hastings Reference Library a large folio packed with Rye election posters and addresses and amenities generally, of the period following the Reform Bill. It makes an hour's instructive reading. Here is a single specimen worth noting for its significant ending : " Proceed on your dirty task if you choose, you are the fittest person to transact the filthy business of a despicable faction, who for the present may applaud your labours. We shall meet again!! *Remember, we shall meet again!! and when we do, you depart not unscathed.*" The Rye fishermen had not wholly abandoned their rotten egg privileges even as late as 1905. The police sergeant, I remember, showed me his cape the morning after the polling day and its surface was entirely obscured under a thick congealed layer of—Well, let us say, scrambled eggs ! When history as we have known it closed in August, 1914, to reopen in a manner few can guess, Rye, it might be interested to note, like the rest of south-east England, was a stronghold of Conservatism, which surely best became a little town of such venerable complexion. It has had too the quite fortuitous distinction of supplying a seat in Parliament to many famous men. Wellington has been mentioned. Robert Dundas, afterwards Lord Melville, sat for Rye, the bosom friend and confidante of the younger Pitt, but far more famous as having held the entire patronage and practically the government of Scotland in the hollow of his hand for five and twenty years, to say nothing of his impeachment and trial in the House of Lords. Jenkinson, afterwards Prime Minister as Lord Liverpool, also represented the ancient town, and so did Charles Cornwall, who died Speaker of the House of Commons.

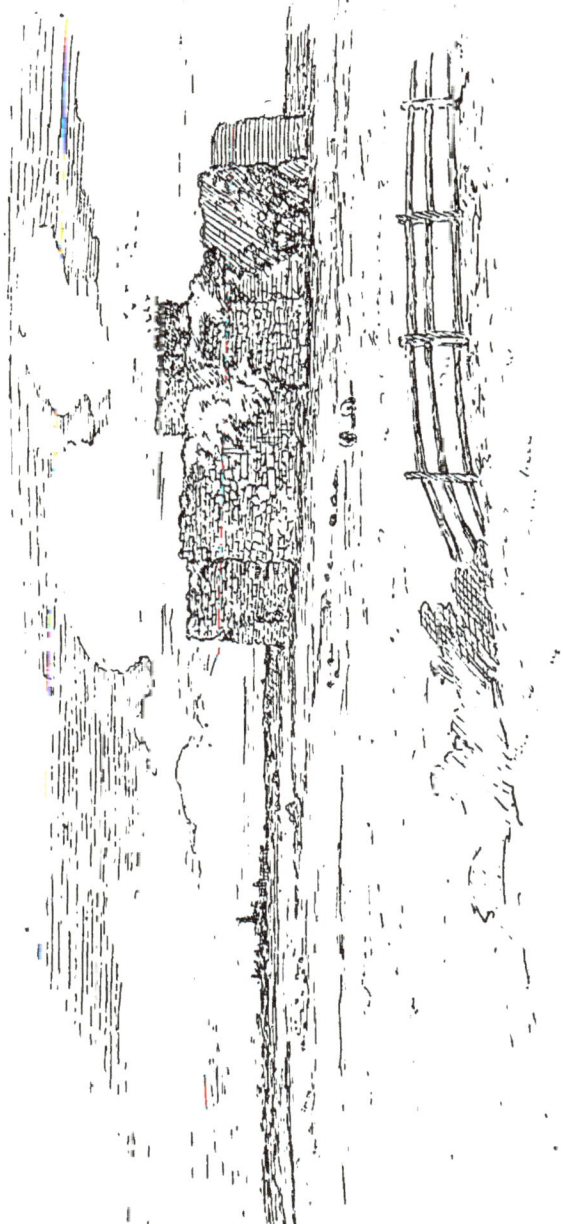

CAMBER CASTLE.

CHAPTER THE FOURTH

Rye to Winchelsea

AS you leave the town for Rye harbour and Camber sands by the Landgate there stands conspicuous behind high gates of wrought iron and within its own grounds, a fair-sized Georgian house. It had been the residence in former times of various well known citizens, but has now for long done duty as a social club, not merely for Rye and neighbourhood but with a much larger membership drawn from London and the Home Counties. This wide appeal is mainly due to the famous golf links at Camber, of which a word later. This establishment bears the significant but not very felicitous name of "The Dormy House." Greatly enlarged at the back it has sleeping accommodation for nearly twenty members and their friends, while the club rooms have all the quality and, for their moderate size, the dignity of their period. In one room is a very finely carved marble mantel-piece; in the present billiard room is part of a much older house, which still retains its great hearth, very similar to that of *The Mermaid*, where small bonfires of logs burn on winter nights, while even in the luxurious age just passed away, the ménage of the House defied the criticism of the most exacting guest. There are Dormy Houses, I believe, elsewhere, partially answering a similar purpose, but this one is no commonplace modern club-house. Indeed we like to think that it has an atmosphere of its own in more ways than one. It has even a ghost, or had, for no ghost would face a club! The cobbled path beneath it, however, bearing the mysterious designation of Turkey-Cock Lane, has an officially recognized one—or two rather. For a monk from the monastery over the way and a young woman having compromised themselves were buried alive standing upright in a neighbouring field. It is they who still haunt the old scene of their meetings.

The London Road, after crossing the railway just below the Landgate, runs in a deep cut straight up Playden Hill, the track followed in olden time by the " Rippiers " and their pack-horses, carrying the daily consignment of fish for the Royal table among other demands. Here, too, within well-timbered grounds is the only house of consequence in the old Rye circle that lay without the gates. It belonged to the Lamb family till their reign in Rye closed. It was here, indeed, at the famous election of 1831, as already described, that the last of the old Corporations waited with their armed body-guard while the Reformers and the fishermen held the town.

Turning from Landgate seaward, one is soon on the iron bridge which spans the Rother, where it rolls its turgid waters between shining mud banks, or in high tides—always interesting at Rye, as you never quite know where they are coming to next—brimming over the green banks. On a fresh sunny morning there is quite a sheen of water here, all alight with the reflection of chasing cloud, and whirling sea birds, and the filling sails of fishing smack, or coaster starting for the mouth of the river and the harbour bar. Just here, too, all about the Rother bridge on either side of it, is the view of Rye that of all others the artist most affects, and partly no doubt on account of the river foreground. But at one particular moment, that of departing day, when the sun is sinking, or has just sunk behind the uplifted town, it is so dramatically effective as to be altogether outside this or that capacity for appreciation. It would give pause to a brake-load of bean-feasters, or provoke even a costermonger to some sort of fervid utterance. For myself, I do not remember to have seen anywhere so striking a silhouette in landscape, as under certain and withal not infrequent conditions, a sunset behind Rye displays from this quarter and the meadows beyond. It is, I think, agreed that the atmosphere of Romney Marsh accounts in a measure for this unique effect; when all detail has faded from the face of the town, into a monotone of blue-grey, and its clear-cut gabled outlines climb gradually up to the dominant church tower, in sharp contrast against a flaming sky. But I will forbear any further attempt at description and merely repeat that the Marsh beyond a doubt owes something of the charm which it has in so many eyes to this subtle atmosphere.

The main path to Camber runs more or less parallel to the Rother, over continuous sheep pastures of crisp and verdant turf, edged with great sweeps of sea gravel in wave-like ridges, that some day will be green like the rest; for less than a couple of centuries ago the wide waters of the steadily shrinking harbour were still rolling backwards and forwards above it with the tide. There is a speedier way of reaching Camber than on foot or cycle by the Marsh path. For Rye has naturally enough connected itself more effectively than this with its sea-board, its golf links, its noble sands and the considerable fishing village that clusters upon the western bank of the river mouth. For a steam-tram plies backwards and forwards pretty frequently, accomplishing the two miles or so in about ten minutes with a further short extension in summer-time to the very edge of the sands. This miniature railway seems to vastly amuse some of our visitors, laying them thereby under a double obligation for a single fare! But it is quite invaluable: for among other things, it gives Rye almost the advantages of a town upon the sea front without those drawbacks, structural and social, inevitable to a watering-place, and altogether disturbing to the romance of a seashore.

The village known as Rye Harbour is modern, to be sure, but the general effect of this river mouth, with its quite respectable fleet of smacks, trawlers, ketches, coasting traders and smaller miscellaneous craft, is notably picturesque, and worthy of the mother town, which far away above the long gleam of the river and the green of the Marsh, shines conspicuous upon its rock. Long stone embankments running seaward on the Camber side and the steep edges of the great shingle waste upon which the village stands upon the other, lead the river out to the harbour bar, along that treacherous channel which for generations has caused such constant anxiety, such alternations of hope and despair to the good town of Rye. In brief, the keeping open of a harbour exposed to the full drift of the ever moving shingle from the south-west, has been a chronic problem to a place where large expenditure is out of the question. East of the river mouth, for a couple of miles or so, a long line of sand dunes front the sea which rises and falls upon as broad and firm a stretch of sand as there is in the south-east of England ; the paradise of Rye infants, their mothers and their nurses through all the hours of summer, though even in their full strength hardly more than specks upon the waste. More numerous companies are to be seen in August in normal times, when many Rye folk let their houses, and all the places of entertainment, not a very great number, are full of visitors, artists, golfers, and their attendant families. Occasionally there are excursions, from whence or where I do not know, but they are not welcome in the rather exclusive atmosphere of Rye, as may be imagined ; nor have they always·behaved themselves.

All along and behind the sand dunes stretches Rye's famous golf course. And I use the epithet advisedly, for every fine golfer in the country, and no doubt a due proportion of what may be called the rank and file, who are less critical but at the same time familiar with national golfing standards, class Rye in the small group that with Sandwich, Deal, Westward Ho. and Hoylake, stands a bit out above all the next best in England. In short, the course affords what the scratch and plus player designate as the finest test of golf, and that should be good enough, if it is not too good, for the less gifted of all degrees. Founded about twenty-five years ago as little more than a local club, it has for a long time now drawn its members from all parts of the south of England and elsewhere. With a limited membership of five hundred, there was in 1914 a waiting list which reached three years ahead. One of its undoubted attractions, however, is that from its comparatively out-of-the-way situation, crowding, except of that normal kind inevitable at the big meetings, is virtually unknown at Rye. On no other of the first-class sand courses is there so little of that delay in starting, or again of waiting on the tee, which upon the great Scottish courses so tries the Southern visitor. Neither has the club lavished its substance upon a palatial and exotic-looking club-house. A quite sufficient frame building of the bungalow order serves every purpose and crowns a ridge near the middle of the course, affording a most inspiring outlook on every side. It stands in the centre, as it were, of an eight, so that a half-round may be played out and back from the premises, or again any slight pressure may be avoided by starting some pairs from the tenth tee which, like the first, together with the ninth and eighteenth greens are all close to the club-house.

From the Rye links much is to be seen. In truth the view in all directions from the club-house on the top of the sand dunes, or indeed from anywhere hereabouts is both far-reaching and inspiring. There is nothing at all like it in Kent or Sussex, and the two counties share the picture about evenly between them. With this its loneliest end in the foreground, the Marsh spreads its illimitable green levels to the east and to the north, with Lydd church tower seven miles away, springing conspicuous above its oasis of woodland. Early summer when the rich grass is at its greenest and the newly sheared sheep in their thousands are at their whitest, is the best season for this and all other outlooks over the Marsh. From here too the whole of the ancient sea-coast from Lympne heights above Hythe, twenty miles away, displays its indented ridge around the back of the Marsh with here an upstanding church, and there a windmill, to the very gates of Rye. And on again from Rye past the woody hill of Winchelsea to Pett and Fairlight Head, which makes upon the western verge of sight such an astonishing spring above the level shore. Rye too from here, as indeed from almost any neighbouring point, is the centre, the pivot and one might say the jewel of the whole spacious and wide-open prospect of land, sea and sky. The fine effect of light and shadow, gleam or gloom is for ever drawing the eye back from east or west to that spire-crowned cluster of red roofs upon the rock that seems, though filling so small a space in it, to dominate the whole.

Upon Camber links too the migrant wheatears find a congenial landing place and feeding ground, when they arrive in springtime from the South, flitting or running over the smooth sheep-nibbled turf, while the innumerable skylarks that breed in the bents fill the balmy south coast air with song. The delicate yellow of the sea poppies then glows upon the ruddy brown sweeps of shingle. Potentilla, bedstraw and trefoil fleck the turf with their faint gold and saffron spray; while the vivid blue of the bugloss, and the pink of the mallow in their season spread gay patches upon untrampled portions of the course that the more erratic golfer knows as no one else does. The sea does not break upon the Sussex coast in those green translucent waves which the Atlantic flings upon the rockbound coasts of Pembrokeshire or Cornwall, nor again with the clarity of those of the North Sea that boil so menacingly upon the gridironed floors of the Northumbrian and Lothian coast. The yellow tinge of the sand is generally upon it even on calm days, stirred up no doubt by the rage with which it expands itself in stormy weather on lines of sand dunes, or on endless barriers of beach that heap themselves high against it and year by year win slow but sure victories in their age-long contest with its fury. For the land is making here at a great rate,

Winchelsea, from the Marsh.

both on dune and shingle. High ridges of the latter that five years ago had no existence have thrust themselves for half a mile or more along the formerly smooth sands of the west end of Camber Bay, entirely altered the in-running of the tide and disconcerted at this point the unimpeded onslaughts of the sea. Recently cast-up sandhills, already in the grip of tufts of bent grass, cover spots that eight or ten years ago were overrun at the height of every tide.

West of the river mouth where all is a flat shingle waste with a sharp front to the water, firm land has been made within the easy memory of elderly men to a depth in places of nearly a quarter of a mile. I sometimes wonder whether the foundations of old Winchelsea which lay off the mouth of Rye harbour and was submerged in the thirteenth century, will re-appear! A bank of shingle has quite lately begun to pop up occasionally at very low tide in that direction, and some day perhaps the vexed question of the precise situation of the old Cinque-Port town may be settled by some unmistakable sign or token that has withstood the ocean turmoil of five hundred years: who knows? The great inundations of the thirteenth century on various parts of the southern and western coasts are among the most difficult things to realize, and furthermore to account for, in later and authentic history. For nothing like them has ever since occurred. The first really serious inbreak seems to have been in 1250, when the important town of Winchelsea lost, according to the chronicles, three hundred houses. Two years afterwards it was again attacked by the sea, and of this second misfortune Mathew of Paris writes: " At Winchelsea, a place extremely important to the English and especially to Londoners, there was a great inundation, the sea submerging mills and houses and drowning a large number of the inhabitants." Being built on a low-lying island, it was probably protected by embankments which gave way under this perhaps unprecedented storm.

It has to be remembered too that the Rother did not then as

now run to Rye and out at Camber, but crossed the middle of the Marsh, part lagoon as this nearer half of it then doubtless was, from Appledore, finding its outlet between New Romney and Lydd to the sea. It was these same storms that blocked the mouth and turned the course of the river along the foot of the hills where it now flows to Rye and thence to Camber. All hereabouts was then a shallow bay, spreading back to Rye and the present Winchelsea, to the cliff line behind and up into the valleys beyond, as already described. This old Winchelsea, most important at that moment of all the Cinque-Ports, and one of the first naval, mercantile and shipbuilding ports of England, lay on this island, as it probably was, with evidently a fine harbour upon its landward side. It possessed about seven hundred householders, representing some three to four thousand inhabitants, a populous place for the period. Battered and ravaged by the storms of 1250 and 1252, the town recovered sufficiently to maintain a precarious existence, though emigration seems to have even then set in, till another raging tempest in 1287 wiped it for good and all out of existence.

Just east of the golf links along the sand dunes is the old parish but modern church and trifling settlement of Broomhill. This in the days of old Winchelsea was a flourishing little port, with almost certainly a large amount of reclaimed land behind it. " A pretty little town much frequented," Camden, who lived nearer its time than ours, calls it. An ancient tradition with the exuberant arithmetic characteristic of the Middle Ages, credits it with fifty public-houses, which may account for its popularity. A few centuries later it would no doubt have accounted for its destruction and been a priceless triumph to the teetotal enthusiasts. The storm of 1287 wiped out this place also, and quite as effectively. But the contests between sea and land have been here so strange that Broomhill, or Promhill (some think it was Broom-isle) arose again in due course from the waves and in a much chastened frame of mind, no doubt, while its greater neighbour of Winchelsea has remained irretrievably sunk beneath them. A strange enough story all this, but one upon which as regards broad facts no sort of doubt rests. It would be altogether another matter to draw a precise plan of the great harbour of that day with its deeps and shallows, its sandbanks and its shingle-spits already risen and to rise gradually through the coming centuries till at last crops and sheep took the place of mud and ooze, sand and slime. Whether it can be said of the Rye fishermen like those of Tom Moore on Loch Neagh, that in drifting homewards to the harbour bar,

> "In the cold dark eve's declining,
> He sees the round towers of other days
> In the waves beneath him shining,"

I do not know. But he has not, I fear, the imagination of Moore's Irish friends, though a much sounder and more serviceable person—particularly at the present moment. But at any rate, one of the greatest and busiest seaports of thirteenth-century England lies at the bottom of the sea, just off the Rye golf links, and even St. Andrews has nothing so dramatic as that to tell of to its innumerable pilgrims. It is interesting too to note, since local antiquaries and historians treat Romney Marsh inundations purely from a local standpoint, that very similar havoc was wrought by the same tempests upon the levels of the Glamorgan coast. It took the form of sand storms or sand deposits as well as inundations, leaving behind it immense tracts of dunes surpassing in extent any others in Britain, and resembling rather those on the coast of France around Etaples. The corporate town of Kenfig was buried by one or more of these tempests. The tip of a tower emerging from the sand, if I remember rightly, still marks the site of its vanished glories.

The more or less contemporary accounts of these Romney Marsh inundations are most concise. "The tide flowed twice without ebbing, and to many was heard for miles inland." An uncanny red light was seen by all men to burn along the advancing course of the waves. "The moon upon her change, appearing exceeding red and swelled, began to show tokens of the great tempest of wind that followed, which was so huge and mighty both by land and sea that the like had not been known and never heard of by men alive." Another writer tells us: "The sea forced contrary to its natural courses, flowed twice without ebbing, and appeared in the dark of the night as it had been on fire and the waves to strive and fight together after a marvellous sort so that the mariners could not devise how to save their ships when they lay at anchor, by any cunning or shift." Beyond the actual lands already "inned" that it destroyed, the salt of the sea in the earlier tempest of 1252 was flung so far inland that the next year's crops declined to grow, nor would the leaves of the trees and hedges put forth their full foliage.

The whole shore of Romney Marsh has been from the earliest times, though not so much, perhaps, under present conditions, one of the most likely points for the landing of a foreign foe. A Martello tower near the harbour village and another just outside Rye are but reminders among some sixty other "inverted flowerpots" planted along the coast of the great Napoleon scare of a century ago. A mile away across the Marsh, in the direction of Winchelsea, is the new rifle and machine-gun range, and beyond it stands the grey fortress of Henry the Eighth, Camber Castle, which we noticed from the summit of Rye in the last chapter. It was built upon what was then a broad spit of shingle running from the direction of Winchelsea and upon the very edge of the water. Landlocked by more than a mile as it is now, the slight elevation of its site above the surrounding pastures beneath the level of the sea is quite noticeable.

A good deal of the castle remains. It is one of the largest of Henry the Eighth's coast fortresses, and a most striking feature in the landscape though of no very special interest.

save as an example of the transition period of fortification with its inferiority to the later work of Elizabethan engineers. This and its many fellows were, like the Martello towers, built under an invasion scare. For Henry the Eighth with all his physical strength, and, when young, athletic achievements, was in truth not over stout-hearted and so possibly an alarmist. But the chronicler Hall puts Henry's precautions on very different grounds. " Since the King was laterly enfourmed by his trusty and faithful friends that the cankerd and cruel serpent, the Bishop of Rome, by the arch traitor Reginald Poole enemie of Godes word and his natural country, had moved and stirred diverse great primates and Potentates to invade the realme of England and utterly destroy the whole nation. So His Magesty in his owne person, without delay took laborious and painful journeys towards the sea wastes. Also he sent diverse of his nobles and counsaylors to view and searche all the ports where any metes and convenient landing place might be supposed."

One of the results of all these surveys was Camber Castle. It was placed under the command of the Lord Warden of the Cinque-Ports. Its Captains were appointed for life and seem literally to have carried out the terms, for there were only two in the first sixty years! These gentlemen were very well paid; with only twenty-six soldiers and gunners under them and apparently without any occupation but that of annoying their neighbours, they must have had a very soft job. Indeed, the two of them together very nearly outlived the castle, for in less than a century the sea had hopelessly receded and Charles the First gave orders for the dismantling of so useless and expensive an establishment. The order was not carried out, however, till the beginning of the Civil War, when the Parliament wanted its ordnance and munitions, after the removal of which the castle was effectively sleighted. To the northward, and confined between high banks, the Brede now flows across the Marsh from Winchelsea to Rye. In the

Napoleonic wars it formed a link in the military canal that was cut from Pett to Hythe, using the Rother in like manner for two miles beyond Rye. And just beyond it, following the same course with still more precision, is the military road that was made at the same stirring period when troops, as at this time, were quartered in all the Kent and Sussex coast towns.

Here and there the solitude of the wide stretch of marsh land that lies between the river and the yellow glint of shingle that marks the sea-line, is broken by some small homestead with its screen of trees and girdle of hedges. But as the road approaches the foot of the Winchelsea hill it crosses the Brede, and passing out of the open into the momentary shadow of some noble elms breasts the sharp ascent to the high promontory upon which the great Edward renewed the life of his recently vanished Cinque-Port. Like Rye, Winchelsea is entered by an embattled gateway. Unlike Rye, however, in its lack of destructive modern needs Winchelsea still retains three of its gates; two of them coeval with the town, and a third built in that fateful year when Henry the Fourth had to defend his crown against the Percys on the bloody field of Shrewsbury. This Strand gate at the high corner by which the road from Rye climbs to the town is one of the former. Though much smaller than the stately Landgate of Rye it has the usual drum towers, with string course and deep port-cullised archway of the period.

The village—for Winchelsea has been nothing more for centuries—straggles picturesquely about the still wide-open spaces of the plateau upon which Edward originally planted it. Much as a village stands around some ample green, so Winchelsea fringes the spacious breadth of churchyard, in the centre of which rises that beautiful remnant of the original fabric which serves it now as always for a parish church. Out of this great square, wide streets, but essentially village streets, run direct to the cliff edge of the plateau to the north

and east, while others to the south and west drop down through
the old gates into the country behind. Even apart from the
great distinction of the church itself, the whole effect of the
place is vastly pleasing, and perhaps also a little puzzling to
an observant visitor unfamiliar with its strange story. For

STRAND GATE, WINCHELSEA.

though in some respects like any other of the many charming
villages that sprinkle the country around it, to the stranger
who did not know that it was the skeleton of a once considerable mediaeval town, there would seem something rather

unaccountable about the place. Its rectangular lines would strike any one wandering about it as something unnatural and quite at variance with the tortuous ways of the ordinary English village.

But any suggestion of utilitarianism quickly vanishes before the leisurely flavour that pervades Winchelsea. The very shops are inconspicuous. Most of the houses of all degrees suggest a snug and peaceful life and, unlike the rather concentrated humanity of Rye, with plenty of elbow-room in which to lead it. High perched though it be Winchelsea offers no such striking silhouette from a distance as its neighbour, the foliage of its many spaces being more conspicuous from below than the gabled roofs which show among or above them. So Winchelsea folk looking across the Marsh to Rye, which from here poses as effectively as from most other points, have this advantage over their neighbours. It is strange that two such places, the dead and the living, should be confronting one another across a mile or two of pasture land. That they should be coupled together in the minds and on the lips of such part of the public as knows anything at all about them is of course inevitable.

Some ten years before old Winchelsea was finally washed away, existence there had evidently become precarious and uncomfortable, and King Edward himself came down to look into the matter. He had been there before on a less genial errand. For in the preceding Civil Wars, Winchelsea and Rye (then of less importance) had taken advantage of the lawless condition of the realm and devoted themselves to a course of unmitigated piracy. It was in this fashion that they professed to show their partiality for Simon de Montfort, who had visited and fêted them, and for the liberal views he represented. Young Simon, it is said, after his father's death upon the field of Evesham, repaired to Winchelsea and took a leading hand with the Cinque-Ports men in their marauding enterprises, which spared neither Englishmen nor foreigners.

Less than a hundred years ago, when their boats entered some of the west-country ports hatchets would be held up towards them as vague traditional symbols of wrongs long forgotten by either party. It was Henry the Third, it will be remembered, who took over Rye and Winchelsea from the Abbey of Fécamp into his own hands, so their action seemed the more flagrant. So on the crushing of the de Montforts, Prince Edward came down to Winchelsea and made an example of it. For the town was rash enough to offer resistance, and he had to

COURT HALL, WINCHELSEA.

storm it, a proceeding for which the leading pirates paid dearly.

But Edward set great store by Winchelsea and, as we have said, came down at a later day as King to see what could be done. The conclusion arrived at was that a wholesale removal was the only cure. So Edward set about it at once and secured a site for a new town. The sandstone rock, then a rabbit warren, where Winchelsea now blooms so luxuriantly, was the spot chosen. With the help of the Bishop of Ely, his agent in the matter, the practical King set about the purchase of it from the owners. It was in the parish of Icklesham (then

Igham of Iham) that the new site, comprising about 150 acres, lay. Eighty-seven of these were laid out in town plots ; the rest included the adjoining meadow land and precepitous sides of the hill. The coast line of the western side of Rye Bay runs nearly north and south, so when facing directly seaward from Winchelsea one is looking east instead of south as a visitor might naturally assume. On this side it was even then apparently more or less dry land and the actual sea nearly as distant as to-day, though this point is very obscure. The harbour must have been cut off from the sea by sand, shingle or marsh from below Winchelsea hill to somewhere about the present site of Camber Castle, leaving inside it the great sheet of water that spread from Rye along the Cadborough cliffs and up the Brede valley to Udimore. At any rate, the Winchelsea ships lay facing Rye where the recently built houses now stand and from which the Rye road, now as then, springs from the flat to sidle up the cliff to the Strand gate. There seems also to have been an inner harbour round the point beneath the Ferry gate, which now admits the present road from the station into the village. In brief the fleets from the new town had no short cut of their own to the sea, pebble and sand ridges having already intervened, but sailed out by the same channel, or wide opening rather, as the ships of Rye.

The transfer of the old to the new Winchelsea was as complete as such an operation could well be. Charters, privileges, church endowments, and virtually all of the population which had not migrated elsewhere, were shifted *en bloc* to the high promontory now cut off from the parish of Icklesham. Many persons from elsewhere no doubt were tempted there, as in all ages the building of a new town would tempt outsiders, to say nothing of the advantages offered by a Cinque-Port residence. The distribution of surveyed lots and lands began and the completed town was handed over to the Corporation in 1288, the ceremony being attended by a large concourse of people, including many of national as well as all those of local distinction. The actual work had been done by the Lord Warden and Jurats, supervised by Bishop de Kirkeby of Ely and King Edward in his spare moments. Never before, or since, was a town in England laid out under such conditions. The King had in his mind certain new towns in France, and the design was precisely that which has governed the construction of all modern American cities : a series of parallelograms or blocks

TRANSEPT RUINS, WINCHELSEA CHURCH.

with main thoroughfares bearing no doubt distinguishing names, such as the Chestnut and Walnut Streets of Philadelphia or the Broadway of New York, crossed at right angles by numbered streets.

As in these modern rectangular cities, so in this Edwardian Winchelsea, a man's address indicated to a stranger with a most cursory knowledge of the town precisely in what part of it he lived, and like the stranger in New York he would presumably have had no occasion to grope his inquiring way to his friend's quarters. The system is as old apparently as Pompeii, which Mr. Inderwick in his delightful brôchure on Winchelsea tells us occupied precisely the space which the vaulting ambition of the re-founders of this old Cinque-Port expected to cover, namely 150 acres. For the details we have no space here, but a good slice of the acreage was laid out in thirty-nine blocks of roughly two acres apiece. A few of them were reserved for specific purposes, as in the case of the church; the rest were allotted to the refugees from old Winchelsea and other intending residents. The town had taken five years to build. With the exception of the present Court House, which as the original Manor Court of Icklesham may possibly be older than the town, and the many vaulted cellars which still arouse interest and curiosity, the houses were of timber and wattle.

To give further confidence in their title to the founders and occupiers of New Winchelsea, Edward sent them from the castle of Acton Burnell in Shropshire (still partly standing) where he was holding a parliament on the affairs of Wales, a Deed of Confirmation, committing the lands and tenements there to " the Barons of the Port and town of Winchelsea " and declaring that the said Barons from the commencement of building should be as free in the new town as in the old and should enjoy the same liberties and privileges as under their old charter. This was renewed in a further charter by Henry the Fourth in 1404, given *in extenso* by Jeake and equivalent to about four of these pages in length. The King was in Wales for the first three years of Winchelsea's building period on weightier matters, but very soon after his return came down there, apparently several times, and as Mr. Inderwick suggests, it is most likely that he resided in the present Court House, as it was already in existence, and as before stated was the official headquarters of the Manor of Icklesham, which continued to hold rights in the new town.

Walls were built around all but the precipitous sides of the new town, and in relation to its fortifications, Thomas of Walsingham tells the story of a miraculous escape vouchsafed to the King. But this was ten years later, after the completion of Winchelsea, when Edward was regarding it, like its predecessor, as one of his chief points of attack and defence against

WINCHELSEA.

foreign foes. He was staying this time with de Etchingham at Udimore, across the north arm of the harbour, waiting for the collection of a force he was to embark for France in the fleet then lying at Winchelsea. Riding into the town one day, either by the Strand or Ferry gates, in both of which the ground favours such an adventure, the King's horse shied at a revolving windmill, and at the further instigation of his whip and spur, leaped clean over the bulwarks. The slope being then as now extremely steep, the surrounding crowd on seeing him disappear gave him up for lost. But by good luck, which was attributed to magic, his horse dropped, all four feet at once, on to a track soft from recent rains, whence having slid several yards, the King, who had kept his seat, managed to turn him.

The new town was early called on for sea-service. For during the next and four following years the Winchelsea fleet was utilized both in Flanders and in Scotland, and the Winchelsea officials were kept quite busy proclaiming wars, truces and treaties of peace with other nations. But the great Statesman and Warrior King, founder of New Winchelsea, died as we know in the act of what he hoped would prove the final conquest of Scotland and Union of the Crowns. But destiny struck him down at the crucial moment and left not only his well-intentioned plans shattered, but a legacy of hatred that brought three hundred years of strife and suffering to both countries. His futile son called on Winchelsea and the other Ports to assist him against Robert Bruce, assembling at Dublin for the purpose. But after the catastrophe of Bannockburn, the Ports mostly rejected Edward the Second's summons, while Winchelsea and Rye, suiting themselves to the laxity of his reign went plundering and freebooting again with slight respect for nationalities.

By the beginning of the fourteenth century the new town had become well established. Its old trade in wine and timber and its fisheries flourished as on the former site. Upon the thirty-nine quarters intersected by seven highways about seven hundred and thirty households were already settled, representing a population of from three to four thousand souls. The name of every householder and his place of abode is transcribed from ministers' accounts in the Carlton House Ride by Mr. Durrant Cooper in his history of Winchelsea. In this remarkable roll of 1292, there are forty odd female householders, both widows and spinsters, among the 730 recorded names, which last are of themselves an interesting object-lesson in the gradual development of English nomenclature. Many of these are familiar to-day in Sussex: Campion, Faber, Lamb, Godard, Russel, Godfrey, Dawes, Fletcher and others. About a fourth of the women have Petronilla as a Christian name, after a Norman saint, I believe, and nearly all have Norman names which would seem to suggest social position. For Winchelsea was far more aristocratic than Rye. Several outstanding families of rank lived and led there. It was not an almost purely burghers' town like the other. There never was a resident family at Rye of the type of the Alards, for instance, whose splendid canopied tombs are the glory of Winchelsea church, or corresponding in rank to the Paulins, the Gervases or the Finches.

In 1297 Winchelsea was the scene of a momentous interview between Edward the First and his Barons. One is apt to recall that great King as an unchallenged if sagacious autocrat. But the protracted Barons' wars of his father's time had encouraged the nobles to expect a little more rather than a little less of their rights as formulated in John's Magna Carta. Edward's war-needs seem to have driven him into some infringement of the latter, and as he was awaiting a fair wind for Flanders at Winchelsea, according to Thomas of Walsingham, a deputation of Barons from Westminster turned up, to his great annoyance, and told him in effect that if he did not give them an undertaking to confine himself in future to his legitimate powers they would cut off the supplies. The King was in an awkward place and had nothing for it but to give way. So a confirmation and something more of Magna Carta was forwarded from Ghent a few days later.

Edward the Third was more frequently at Winchelsea than even his grandfather during those constant wars of his with France, which eventually brought upon it the not unnatural and quite disastrous vengeance of the French. He too occasionally made his headquarters at Udimore, of which a de Etchingham was still lord. It was in his reign too that the persistent draining or "inning" of the Marsh lands had sufficiently dried the north arm of the harbour to make road communication possible by means of a bridge and causeway between Udimore and Winchelsea. The King's family seem to have been here several times. When the great sea-fight with the Spaniards, already spoken of, took place in Rye Bay, the Queen and her ladies were awaiting the result at Udimore. She had spent an anxious day, Froissart tells us, for many of her attendants had been with the crowd who watched the fight from Winchelsea or the Cadborough cliffs, and had fed her fears by frequent reports of the size and number of the Spanish ships.

The King had no sooner landed upon the night of the battle, with the Black Prince, and other Barons, than he took horse in Winchelsea and rode at best pace to Udimore, to report the victory to the Queen and relieve her suspense. The old Court House of the Etchinghams, where she lodged, was only removed a few years ago, and by good fortune the illustrator of this book had preserved the appended sketch, taken just before its disappearance. The Spaniards, says Froissart, had laden their fleet with Flemish merchandise at Sluys and fully expected to meet the English, an event they regarded with indifference as "they had marvellously provided themselves with all sorts of warlike ammunition and the wind was favourable to them. There were forty large vessels of such a size and so beautiful, it was a fine sight to see them under sail. Near the top of their masts were small castles, full of flints and stones, and from their flagstaffs their streamers fluttered in the wind, so that it was pleasant to look at them." If England had a great desire to meet them, it seemed as if the Spaniards were still more eager for the fray, and they had full ten thousand men.

The King commanded the English in person, being with all his household on a ship called *Le Salle-du-Roi*, and he was at great pains to explain to all his knights the order of battle. " He was in the fore part of his own ship, dressed in a black velvet jacket and wore on his head a small hat of beaver, which became him much. He was as joyous as his friends had ever seen him and ordered his minstrels to strike up a dance tune. Then the watch on top cried out : ' Ho ! I see a ship and it appears to be a Spaniard.' The band was silenced. ' Yes,' cried out the same man in the turret, ' I see two, three, four, and so many that, God help me, I cannot count them.' " To the sound of trumpets, the line of battle was then formed, while the King ordered wine for the whole party and they put on their helmets. The Spaniards could have avoided the fight, says Froissart, with their big well-ballasted ships, and could have slipped off easily down channel before the favouring wind. Instead of which, however, they bore right down on the English fleet. As they met, the King ordered his sailing master to lay him alongside a big Spaniard approaching him, or as he phrased it, " to have a tilt at him." The master durst not disobey the Royal command, and so they tilted, and with such effect, " like the crash of a tempest," that the rebound brought the masts together, knocking the turret of the Spaniard with all its men into the sea. The English vessel leaked violently from the impact, but the knights fell energetically to baling and stopped the leak. " Grapple me with that ship," cried the King, " for I will have her." But the Knights said, " Let her go, you shall have better than her."

So the vessel went on, and another large Spaniard bore down and hooked on to the King's ship. And now the archers and cross-bowmen on both sides got to work " and either fought furious not in one place but in ten or twelve at a time and grand deeds of arms were performed." The Spaniards' ships were much larger and higher than those of the English, which gave them superiority in shooting and in casting stones and iron bars on the latter. The King's ship was now in danger of sinking from the leak, and this lent extra fury to its brave crew. At last they boarded the Spaniard whose men retreated fighting hard, till they were all either killed or flung overboard, the usual fate of the survivors in a mediaeval sea-fight. The Black Prince, then aged twenty, was similarly engaged in an equally leaky ship with a big Spaniard, but with less success, till the Duke of Lancaster, seeing his plight, came up on the other side and grappled, shouting, "Derby to the rescue." This settled the matter and all the Spanish crew were thrown overboard just as the Prince's battered ship sank beneath the waves. These contests were repeated all along the now broken line, the English greatly exerting themselves, "and need there was of it, for they found those who feared them not." Late in the evening, an English ship having been grappled by a large opponent was being borne out of the fight by the powerful sailing of the Spaniard. Their cries for rescue were unheard in the tumult and in the growing dusk they would have been lost but for the gallant act of a common soldier, who with sword on wrist leaped on board the enemy, rushed to the mast and cut the cable holding the mainsail and then, with great agility, cut the other ropes, till all the sheets fell and stayed the ship's course. This dashing exploit so heartened the English that they boarded the Spanish ship, vanquished the crew and flung them also to the fishes.

"At last," says Froissart in his spirited narrative, "victory declared for the English." Fourteen Spanish ships (other accounts say twenty-six) were sunk or captured and the rest saved themselves by flight. The King, his son and his knights, as we have before told, rode off at once to Udimore, "where they passed the night in revelling with the ladies, conversing of arms and amours." On the morrow the King publicly thanked his Knights and Barons, who then returned to their respective homes, though not before, as if to repair in some measure his own loss in warriors, he had knighted "four score of the young gentlemen who had performed best in the fight."

So ended a great naval action, fought it must be admitted for plunder, as well as glory, and a memorable August day for Winchelsea and Rye.

The next warlike incident at Winchelsea, years later, was a woeful contrast. For, smarting under King Edward's ravages in France, three thousand Normans surprised the town during Mass, and encountering but slight resistance half burnt it, slew all the townsmen they could catch, ravished women of all

A Street, Winchelsea.

degrees and carried away many of the more attractive. One high-born lady, after being much ill-treated, was killed within the precincts of St. Thomas's Church. The dead were afterwards buried in St. Giles' Church, and Deadmans Lane near by to this day commemorates the catastrophe. On the very same day, March 15 of the next year, while Edward, obsessed by his continental ambitions, and his nobles stimulated by the plunder which for years had enriched them, were besieging Paris, Winchelsea was again attacked and ravaged. No doubt the recent devastations of the Black Death had infinitely weakened the defensive powers of the town and neighbourhood. Nor can one much wonder at the rage of the French, for the occasional plunder of Rye, Winchelsea, or Hastings was a small reprisal for hundreds of square miles of French soil rendered desolate, its people homeless and reduced to literal starvation. This time, however, an English fleet got swiftly on the raider's trail, drove all French shipping into its ports, seized and burned the town of Luce and the next year captured the Isle of Caux, " In revengeing of the Frenchmen's displeasure doone to Winchelsey," as old Leland puts it. I always feel tempted to quote the old fellow, even when as in this case he is of not much consequence, merely for his spelling and phraseology. For in days when both were quite arbitrary, and to us moderns quaint enough, Leland stands alone among notable writers for his whimsicality and is almost an unconscious humourist.

In 1370 a large army went into France and sailed in a great fleet from Rye and Winchelsea, conveying, it is said, the incredible number for those times of 8,464 horses. Richard the Second's reign, and for good reason, was marked by much cross-channel raiding, and Winchelsea suffered again. When Rye rather disgraced itself in 1377, " turning its back in the hour of battaile " and was so ravaged and burnt, Winchelsea with the aid of the valorous Abbot of Battle scared off the French. But they returned later after doing wild work in the Isle of Wight and sent word to the Abbot to redeem the town. The Abbot replied in caustic terms that it was unnecessary to redeem an uncaptured town and advised them to leave it alone as their safest course. The French, exasperated by such a taunt, sent word to the Abbot to come along and fight them. But the Abbot meekly replied that he was a religious man and did not like fighting except in defence against aggression. So the French, making light of such a pacifist, went gaily for Winchelsea with siege engines and other contrivances. But the stalwart cleric gave them such a reception that they were glad enough to depart. Immediately after this Rye and Winchelsea combined and gave the opposite coast some severe lessons, bringing back much plunder including, it is said, many of their own lost possessions, church bells and so forth. Some of these indeed would seem to have chimed alternately on both sides of the channel, being always marked objects of plunder to either nation, possibly because their iron throats could sound such eloquent taunts over the sea.

Two years later the French descended once more on the unfortunate Winchelsea, defeated the valiant Abbot and did such damage to the town that the King and Parliament seriously took up the case of the twin towns and their security, " because if these were taken, which God forbid, the whole country would be destroyed." Mr. Cooper quotes a tradition that on this last occasion the New Gate was treacherously opened to the enemy, who approached from the Fairlight direction before daybreak. Again and again in these days it is stated in print by people who ought to know better that the soil of England has never been desecrated by an invader's foot since the Norman Conquest, and so forth. In regard to such preposterous nonsense we are here only concerned with the soil of Sussex, but other counties have a similar, though on the whole less harrowing tale to tell. From this misfortune Winchelsea never recovered, though the steady retirement of the sea, due as much to the " inning " of marshland as to nature, greatly hastened its decay. When in 1415 Henry the Fifth collected the fleet that bore upon the wings of victory his great army to France and to Agincourt, Winchelsea, though no longer so strongly represented as of yore, seems to have provided the Flag-ship (the *Gabrielle de Winchelsea*) which carried the King himself. The town is said by some writers to have been taken and pillaged again in 1418.

However that may be, it was captured and ravaged immediately after that great burning of Rye in 1448 already described, and for both places this was the last catastrophe of the kind. It put a finishing touch to Winchelsea. The water too had by this time entirely receded from the foot of the rock, and Winchelsea ships were being unloaded at Camber or Rye, the latter gathering profit from the decay of her old rival, and at one time more than rival. Henry the Seventh's reign saw the evacuation of the town by its merchants, followed in the next by all the monks and nuns through the Dissolution of the religious houses. Though abandoned by clerics and traders, and deserted by the sea, a certain number of families possessed of lands seem to have hung on to so delectable a place of residence and an effort was made in 1570 by petition to interest the Crown in the restoration of its trade by cutting a navigable channel from the Brede River direct to the open sea— half a mile in length, according to the petitioners, and more than twice that distance to-day. The petition reminded the Council in moving terms of the former fame and prosperity of the town and of the important services it had rendered to the State. It also dwelt on its fine, broad, straight streets and the still large residue of costly vaults " arched and set forth with pillars of Caen stone and mete to have houses over them fit for famous merchants." Nor was there anywhere else so good a place for a haven, midway as this was between Rye and Hastings. In short this proposed half-mile cut to the sea would once more let in England's navies which would ride as of yore beneath the Rock of Winchelsea to their great convenience and the safety of the nation, and above all the town itself would recover its ancient glory.

But it was all of no avail, and there is little more of general interest to tell in the subsequent story of Winchelsea, unless it be the humours of a rotten Parliamentary borough with two members and a farcically corrupt Corporation, such as we saw enough of at Rye in the last chapter. It returned two members to Parliament, always after the Stuart period outsiders, elected by a Patron, himself an outsider. So it was a " pocket " rather than a "rotten" borough, to draw a fine distinction. The Mayor and Jurats, as at Rye, only still more so, contrived to reduce themselves at one epoch to a trio, and two out of them were creatures of the third, the Mayor, in which office the changes were rung year after year by two or three persons. So it was all very snug and cosy right up to its parliamentary extinction by the Reform Bill. At the later Municipalities Act, Winchelsea, alone I believe in England, retained the *status-quo-ante*, though the distinction is of purely academic interest. The population was generally about six hundred, its figure more or less to-day. The town had previously been twice disfranchised, once by Charles the First, apparently because it had rows with his garrison at Camber, and once by Cromwell, who in his blunt common-sense way transferred its two seats to a rising and unrepresented Midland town.

In the Stuart period, when domestic affairs were in some respects better regulated than under the Georgian Whigs, and when the freemen voted and sent local men to Parliament, Mayors had to be careful. One of them was discovered at Winchelsea playing those exclusion tricks towards voters that in Georgian days were practised with impunity, to the great ultimate comfort, as we have shown, of a few people. But he was sent to jail and forced to do penance on his knees, both in the House of Commons and in Winchelsea Court House! As a case in point a town clerk in the eighteenth century in need of money for rigging an election, purloined the original charters, the Customal and other Records which have never since been recovered. There is still a Mayor of Winchelsea, and there are occasions when the old insignia of the town is bravely displayed as of yore. But the office is no longer profitable. On the contrary it is of such an honorary and ornamental nature that residents of sufficient substance and civic patriotism to fill it could almost I fancy be counted upon the fingers of one hand.

But I have said nothing yet of the visit of Queen Elizabeth

to Winchelsea ; I am not aware that any one but Jeake mentions it, but as he lived in the next century he ought to know, while yet more as a Rye man he would be the last person to invent so elaborate a story in a rival's favour. " For Her Majesty, beholding the goodly situation, ancient buildings, grave bearing of the Mayor and twelve Jurats in their scarlet gowns and the city-like deportment of the people (there being then several resident gentry) as well as the projection (configuration) of the place, she gave it, as she thought deservedly, the name of ' Little London '." This was only after the sore petition for a new harbour already told of, while another authority tells us that there were at this time only sixty houses standing. So the great Queen's joke seems rather a dreary one ! Since the French last burnt it and the sea finally abandoned it, Winchelsea has in all likelihood never been so quietly prosperous as of late years, and for much the same reasons that have revivified Rye. For many well-to-do people have either settled or acquired summer residences in the pleasant and more or less old-fashioned houses that stand along or about the Great Edward's spacious squares. The modern builder has not been quite baffled, but he has been kept tolerably well at arm's-length, and with few exceptions to a single quarter in the Marsh below.

Apart from its generally attractive appearance the chief points of interest in the village are its noble church, its mediaeval town-hall, the remains of the Grey Friars' Chapel, the three gateways and the old vaulted cellars still existing below many of the houses. Above all of them, however, in interest and importance is the church of St. Thomas the Apostle, and even this is but the choir of the original building, or one should say rather of the original design. For it is generally held that the nave, of which there is nothing left, was never completed, while of the two transepts only the ivy-clad fragments remain to add some further charm and pathos to the beautiful choir, which for centuries has served as a parish church. There was possibly at one time a central tower, but at present only a small cap-spire, a later addition, appears at the north-western angle of the north aisle. The choir (in this case the church) has a north and south aisle, each carrying its own gabled roof after the manner so general in this part of England, and terminating several feet short of the east end of the main central aisle, while a flying buttress, obviously erected soon after the building for extra support, extends from the north-eastern corner. The founding of the church was virtually coeval with that of the town. How long it was before the chancel was finished must be a matter of conjecture. Mr. Cooper suggests ten years, probably much too short a period, as the money had to be raised by degrees, though the Church had then much more rapid and effective ways of raising it than it has to-day. The rest is silence. The ruined transepts, the nave foundations, or rather their traces, for the stones were removed over a century ago, remain to arouse speculations that can never be confirmed.

Till 1790 a bell tower stood near the south-western angle of the churchyard, and an illustration of it still standing nearly roof high is given in Cooper's History of Winchelsea. The stones were probably used, as were those of the nave foundations removed at the same time, for the building of Rye harbour. The interior of the chancel, the only existing portion of the noble church which local piety seems to have contemplated, achieves a certain completeness of its own, and in size is more than sufficient for the needs of an average country parish. The arcade of three bays, which divides the nave from the side aisles or chapels, is of beautiful proportions and of exquisitely moulded pointed arches springing from clustered columns, in which are alternating shafts of Purbeck marble. Its great width and the lofty elevation of its oak roof, together with the closed-in west end, give the building a rather unusual appearance, but the effect is undoubtedly one of great dignity. All the side windows are fortunately large and terminate in the rich tracery of the decorated period, the east window being a modern replacement. But perhaps the gem of the interior is its sedilia, particularly that of the two aisles which include in their design some canopied monuments over recumbent effigies, two upon the south and three upon the north wall. Those upon the south wall are the Alards : the easterly one at least is pronounced with certainty to be Gervase Alard who was Admiral of the Western Cinque-Ports in Edward the First's time, and presumably a benefactor to the church. The other

WINCHELSEA CHURCH.

is held by Mr. Inderwick, who restored the tombs in 1904, to be the successor in office to the older Alard under Edward the Second. Gervase Alard was also bailiff of Winchelsea and reputed a man of vast proportions, a fact confirmed, I believe, by a recent inspection of his remains which lie below, but which crumbled to dust immediately on exposure. His effigy is in full armour, with crossed legs resting upon a lion. The gables which form the canopy and wings of the tomb, like the sedilia, are profusely ornamented and crocketted, while the central gable springs from carved heads upon either side, said, and no doubt with truth, to be those of King Edward and Queen Eleanor, the latter wearing a most woe-begone expression. The other tomb is similar in character, though differing slightly in detail. The canopy here too is supported by Royal masks, in this case those of Edward the Third and Queen Philippa. The panels of both are highly decorative.

The north aisle was known as the Godfrey or Farncombe chantry, a family associated for several centuries with Lydd and New Romney but which intermarried with the Alards. Three other effigies lie here under plain canopies, a cross-legged knight in chain armour, a lady and a young man. Whom they represent is unknown, though Alards are suggested, but they are apparently of older date than the church, and tradition has it that they were brought up from old Winchelsea, which seems extremely probable. Above them is a window containing fragments of old glass, remnants of the restored east window, and near by, upon a pillar, is a head said to be that of Henry the Third, another surviving relic of old Winchelsea. There is a small crypt under the south-east corner of the church by the flying buttress. The west porch is thought to have been brought from some other building when the west end was sealed up. A sun-dial in front of it in the churchyard marks the western termination of the foundations of the nave.

Of the other two original churches, St. Giles and St. Leonard's, nothing but the name still attaching to the spots they occupied remains. The former stood near the present rectory, the latter on the meadow slopes west of the town, near the windmill. The small parish of St. Leonard's never belonged to Winchelsea proper, but curiously enough to the borough of Hastings. There is now, I think, only one house in it, but every seventh year the Mayor and Corporation of Hastings come over to beat the parish bounds. Till lately this was quite a little function, associated with time-honoured jokes between native followers and the others and was wound up by a proper and convivial feast at the *New Inn*. Now, according to an old inhabitant who was accustomed to make a day of it, and perhaps a night, it is nothing more than a perfunctory dashing over from Hastings and back in a motor car by three or four soulless beings, who hurry over the sacred rite, with indifference and despatch, and are away within the hour.

The ruins of the Grey Friars Chapel still remain to delight the eye both by the delicacy of its workmanship and the leafy charm of its environment. The pointed chancel arch, still complete, is deeply moulded and with a faint horse-shoe curve rests upon triple shafts and delicately moulded capitals. This stands in the garden of the Friars, a modern house erected upon the foundations and from the materials of the old conventual buildings. From the general appearance of the place one would rather look for an interesting personal history, but there is practically none. After the Dissolution it seems to have passed through various and undistinguished hands till about a century ago its then purchaser pulled it down and with the materials erected the present house, which has been recently renovated and altered. The foundation of the Grey Friars was one of those transferred from old Winchelsea. It was rather fortunate that in the years following the move, the Abbot of Westminster, in some trifling matter, had fallen foul of the Friars Minors, the order to which the House belonged. For he (the Abbot) had been condemned by the Pope in costs to the said Order, whose monks applied them to the re-establishment here of their old Winchelsea House. This was further sustained by benefactions from all the magnates of the town.

There still stands visible from the Hastings road as it leaves the village, though with slight evidence of its character, a fragment of that House of St. John, already mentioned as prior to the Dissolution, a Hospital for Monks and Nuns. It is interesting hearing that apart from its ten acre lot it derived an income from houses in Great Yarmouth. Near the site of St. Leonard's church is that of an Order of Black Friars marked

WINCHELSEA, FROM THE SHORE ROAD

by the remains of a crypt, now blocked up, but which the patriarchs of Winchelsea recall with affection as a place of mystery and fearsome frolic in childhood's hour. Another and a smaller hospital, St. Bartholomew's, towards the New Gate, outlived the Dissolution by about half a century. When Rye and Winchelsea were taken over from the Abbey of Fécamp by the King in 1247, the church and parish of St. Leonard's in Winchelsea were excepted from the transfer until the general ousting of the alien Orders in the fifteenth century. This parish and liberty of St. Leonard's was without the walls, and technically, as before-mentioned, never formed a part of the town but belonged to the Port of Hastings, in which borough till recent times such occupants as it possessed had votes. But St. Leonard nevertheless was the saint who engineered the weathercocks for the sailors of Winchelsea and to whom they and their wives presented votive offerings for favouring winds and quiet seas.

And talking of churches, if Rye sent a Vicar to the Episcopal throne of London, an actual native, a poor boy of Winchelsea, though obviously a refugee from the old town, rose to be Archbishop of Canterbury, and by all accounts was an able and pious one. He set his face against the follies of the second Edward, and at his death application was made to the Pope for Canonization. But His Holiness wanted proof of miracles, which were so slow in coming that the matter dropped through. The Canterbury people, however, seem to have taken his saintship into their own hands, and so frequented his tomb that it was destroyed at the Dissolution as promoting idolatry. He was extraordinarily devout, and so diligent in saying " the Salutation of the angel " that when it was repeated over his corpse at his funeral in 1313 his thumb was seen to travel in unison over the fingers of the other hand. He would shut himself up in the Chapter House and scourge himself so often and so violently that his thigh bones were laid bare and the flesh made livid with his blows. Nor did he ever so much as speak to a woman save in confession. So much for Robert of Winchelsea, by far its most distinguished son.

And while on the subject of saints the great pilgrimages to St. James of Compostella in Spain helped no little to keep Winchelsea on its feet during the fifteenth century. Thousands of pilgrims seem to have sailed from these ports and purchased their outfits from the merchants, who no doubt duly fleeced them. The skippers were bound over to see to it that their passengers carried no more gold and silver than was necessary for their expenses, while the pilgrims themselves were sworn not to reveal " the secrets of the Kingdom " while abroad. A contemporary ballad quaintly suggests the hardships which these credulous souls endured.

> " Men may leve all gamys
> That saylen to St. James
> For many a man hit gramys
>   When they begin to sayle.
>
> " For when they take the see
> At Sandwych or at Wynchelsee
> At Bristow or where that it bee
>   Theyr herts began to fayle."

A Roundel tower, whence the harbour-master in ancient times surveyed his charge below, formerly stood above the Ferry gate and was removed less than a century ago. But far the most interesting secular relic of mediaeval Winchelsea is the old Court House, which, as previously stated, may possibly ante-date the town in its character of the original Manor Court House of Igham or I'ham. It has the merit, too, which some old buildings lack, of looking its part, and is moreover conspicuous near the north-west corner of the Church square. It has played all sorts of parts, Court Hall, meat market, store-house, prison, and has been periodically punched about to suit the elementary needs of each. But no serious disfigurement or destructive alteration can be laid to the charge of these ancient utilitarians. It was presented to the town some twenty years ago. and now serves the admirable purpose of a Parish Hall and Reading Room below, and a place of meeting for the Mayor and Corporation above, on those not very frequent occasions when such are necessary. When the building was converted to its present uses, taste had at last something to say. By merely clearing out the various adaptations which encumbered the ancient window spaces, filling in these last with glass and exposing the old oak roof by removing the plaster ceilings, much restoration was done in the better sense of the word. In both upper and lower chambers the original fireplaces are *in situ*. A small window was exposed in the upper room during these alterations bearing the arms of Robert of Winchelsea the Archbishop, who it will be remembered was contemporary with the founding of the town. The house seems to have been surrounded by lean-to buildings in former days, and retains the traces of them. But the main structure, an oblong, with gable roof and panelled chimney is substantially the same as that which probably sheltered Edward the First when he was building the town. The arms of various bailiffs of ancient Winchelsea may be seen in the south windows, among whom the Alards, Finches, Carylls, and Guldefords or Gilfords, were the most prominent. In Henry the Seventh's time the Crown granted away the Manor to the last-named family, for services rendered upon Bosworth Field.

There may also be seen in the upper room of the Court Hall a curious and crude fourteenth-century painting of St. Leonard. It was discovered during the recent renovations on various pieces of boards. These on being joined together revealed the saint in Episcopal garb, with a windmill over his shoulder, symbolical of his management of the winds in the interest of Winchelsea sailors. He is acting for the moment, however, in a different character, and bestowing his attention. and no doubt his benediction on what looks like a gigantic toadstool. Actually, I believe, he is blessing the crops. Among the older houses of the village one known as the Armoury, carefully restored and converted into a private residence some time ago is interesting. For the most part, however, as at Rye there has been a good deal of Georgian fronting done, and indeed that so much of Georgian work remains may be regarded as fortunate, since in its own way it is almost as much in harmony with the leafy atmosphere of an English village as the more directly inspiring half-timber of the earlier periods.

On summer afternoons Winchelsea and its beautiful church seem generally the object of admiring visitors from Hastings or elsewhere. How many of them realize the part that it has played in England's story in the days of old or the stirring scenes and pageants it has witnessed by land and sea, it would be hard to say. I feel tolerably confident that, apart from the church, Denis Duval, Wesley's tree, the vaulted wine cellars, which the less critical visitor is more than half invited to regard as smugglers' caves, comprise most of the Winchelsea tradition absorbed by the average visitor. And indeed there is some excuse, for the story of the town makes a big subject, and one not very accessible to the busy or the indifferent. If the brief sketch of it I have attempted here serves to enlighten a few of them I shall be content. For the benefit of the potential visitor, it may be noted that the chief hostelry, *The New Inn*, standing in the Church Square, is a worthy house of call and something more, and wears withal the cheerful and animated expression of a good old-fashioned, well kept up, Georgian inn. Very near to it is the old tree beneath which Wesley preached his last open-air sermon in the October of 1790. For he rapidly failed through the following winter and died in March. He himself makes note that on this occasion " it seemed as if all that heard were almost persuaded to be Christians." For the present the great difficulty was to persuade them not to be smugglers. The final note of gentle irony which tempered Wesley's optimism translated into terms would undoubtedly have read " till the next cargo of brandy was signalled from the sea." ·Of Victorian notabilities, Millais occasionally painted here, and Thackeray once at least paid a visit to Winchelsea, which provided a background for his last and unfinished novel, *Denis Duval*. It is not *Vanity Fair*, nor yet *Esmond* by a very long way, but it provided among other things a pair of inmates for the old House of the Friars, who help to colour its rather disappointing story. This, however, was actually enlivened by its tenure for a few months in the eighteenth century by two brothers, the originals of Thackeray's villains, whose apparent wealth and undoubted hospitalities deluded the neighbourhood. For the latter woke up one fine morning to find that it had been consorting with a pair of notorious highwaymen, who were urgently wanted for all kinds of misdoings, among others for robbing the Bristol coach. The great novelist is said to have stopped at *The New Inn*.

This Church Square, large as it is, was but one of the thirty-nine that the sanguine founders of Winchelsea hoped in time to cover, and it was near the centre of the survey. To-day, as you leave it by the Hastings Road you also leave the last building in the village behind you. This is Mariteau House, a lofty mid-Georgian mansion standing in pleasant grounds with some past interest attaching to it as the home of the late Mr. Inderwick, the *Vates sacer* of latter-day Winchelsea, who laid it, both in an archaeological and literary sense under no slight obligations. Its Huguenot builder, too, may be recalled without apology, since he and his friends endeavoured to avert the decay of the town by manufacturing cambric, though without success. Just across the road from here are portions of a wall and a doorway, the remains of an edifice known as the Trojans' or Jews' Hall, which is about all that the Winchelsea antiquaries have been able to discover about it. Half a mile further on into the country, five hundred yards past the turn of the Hastings Road and guarding quite pathetically and in rural isolation an insignificant byway to Pett, is the New Gate. Despite its name this is one of the original entrances to the town, which was expected to grow out to it. Though entwined with foliage, it is still in fair preservation, and while displaying no drum towers, it has attached to it a fragment of the old town wall, and overlooks a deep protecting glen, possibly once moated. More than once the French were able to surprise the town at this point, owing to its aloofness, and effect an entrance. In all England there is no mediæval city gateway to all appearances so unaccountably situated. To my mind there is nothing in Winchelsea more eloquent of its strange story than this ruinous embattled archway, standing so inconsequently aloof and to all seeming as if it had lost its way amid fields and lanes.

TOLL HOUSE—MILITARY ROAD, WINCHELSEA.

CHAPTER THE FIFTH

Winchelsea to Hastings

JUST before passing under the Strand Gate in the descent from Winchelsea by the Rye Road to the Marsh, upon the seaward side, there is a small look-out ledge or terrace. This, like the larger Gungarden at Rye, draws both the villager and visitor to its fine and unimpeded view over the Channel, with the restful and warm-tinted strip of Pett level intervening as a foreground. It must be a pleasant perch on which to laze away a summer hour! A mile and more away as the crow flies, and extending along the straight flat line of the shore may be descried the row of painted bathing huts that is a new feature in the scene since I first looked upon it. This is to Winchelsea what Camber sands are to Rye, the daily stamping ground in summer of infants and their attendant female train. But there are also a few bungalows whose owners have nothing to do with the village on the height other than with its butchers and bakers. The shore here is very different from the widespreading sands of Camber. Bathing there is of the kind invaluable to timid mothers, and abhorred by swimmers. A child could hardly drown itself at Camber without a lengthy and deliberate expedition in the direction of the French coast, while its elders abandon all idea of deep-sea enterprises and engage mostly in those touching domestic gambols so conspicuous on the south side of the Channel. But on Winchelsea and Pett Marshes a high bank of shingle slips sharply into the sea, leaving no great margin of sand even at low tide. At

Camber again the ocean is for ever receding. Here it is aggressive, and before a west or south-west gale always struggling fiercely to break the barriers that its own rage has piled up and that man has strengthened and is always strengthening, lest Winchelsea should once again some fine morning become a seaport.

From this platform by the Edwardian Gateway, on a summer day, the seaward spreading strip of pasture land, the ship-flecked Channel beyond, and the long low shingle-spit of Dungeness craning towards France on the eastern horizon, make a *coup-d'œil* both alluring and suggestive. The coast of France as we noted at Rye, though with an open mind upon the subject, is not visible from here. But once, at any rate, in the eighteenth century it burst upon the astonished gaze of the people of both towns, and of the neighbouring upland villages, with such uncanny clearness of outline and detail, as to fill the hearts of the timid with supernatural fears of some dread portent, if not the end of the world itself! The pyramid of Rye town, too, when the sun is westering and shining on it, looks as well from Winchelsea as it does from Camber beneath the radiancy of noon and morning. The group of stately elms springing from the Marsh by the bridge over the Brede at the hill foot, is a finer piece of foreground detail in this wide sweep of sea and treeless landscape than this mere note of it could convey. The road winding shoreward to Winchelsea's little bathing resort looks from up here like a white ribbon laid upon the green marsh. Before quite reaching the sea, however, it bends to the right and runs for four miles over the level, within more or less touch of the beach to Pett, where the cliffs begin to rise towards Fairlight Head. This narrow southwestern horn of Romney Marsh, roughly four miles long by one in width, is known as Pett level. The old military canal, like several still preserved place-names in Winchelsea itself, a relic of the Napoleonic Wars, here completes its most westerly section, trailing its reedy course beneath the hill slopes to Cliff-end. All the way to Winchelsea beach there are charming backward views of the village ; a blend of gable, chimney and foliage, clustering on its ridgepoint around the church, while westward for a mile the rich woods of an ancient rookery clothe the same hillside from the lush level of the Marsh to the skyline.

At Winchelsea beach, in the dry channel of an ancient watercourse, butting significantly into the high shingle rampart that shuts out the sea, may be read the Rye failure of 1758 to reach it this way and replace the then silting-up channel and harbour at Camber. It formed a cut of about a mile, from the elbow of the Brede which you leave on the way here, just turning towards Rye and offering thereto, by the way, a pleasant river-side walk. Poor Mr. " Jenebelly " the Italian, whom Rye so scorned it will be remembered, had this route in his mind a century earlier. It looks as if he was wrong, after all, though it was not, as we know, for his scheme as such that Rye kicked him out, but for its possible advantage to Winchelsea. But the plan as the Ryers carried it out failed most dismally, for the remains show that it must have been quite a large harbour. Yet it was used, I believe, only for about a year, when the sea, or rather the burden of beach it bore with it, not merely blocked the channel but demonstrated the futility of the scheme for all time. At any rate it was abandoned, and happily the tides of Camber still flow over the old bar with sufficient depth for the modest requirements of the present day. A single block of masonry is all that here remains amid the sand and bents, the short sod and scanty flowerets that fill the abandoned basin, to recall with its more vivid suggestion of human labour, this tale of blighted hopes.

It is not quite all though, for just inland, upon a carpet of crisp green turf by the roadside, and sheltered from the windy quarter by a small grove of trees, is the homestead of a sheep farm that I fancy most artists, who pass it would feel an impulse to put on canvas. It is nothing particular in the way of architecture, merely the pleasant old Sussex blend of lichen-tinted tile and creeper and weather boarding, but with a charm of its own nevertheless, standing out as it does into the Marsh. This is the old inn, originally built, I believe, for the refreshment of the hordes of Early Georgian toilers who must have been required for this laborious and futile excavation. Afterwards it became the *Harbour Inn*, and no doubt helped to make the short life of the ill-fated port as merry as could be expected under the circumstances.

From here to Cliff-end the very middling road twists along between shore and marsh, where the far-flung patches of shingle and salted barrens meet the green meadows of Pett

FAIRLIGHT CLIFFS.

level. Behind the pebble ridge and high embankments that keep out the always menacing sea, you can hear it close at hand, chafing on the breakwaters and groins, or rumbling on its stony beach till everything comes to an end. For here the western limit of Romney Marsh butts its narrow point into the first rise of the great Fairlight Headland. All further progress save on foot is now thrust far inland. A few bungalows and wooden cottages are grouped not unpicturesquely around, and a hideous row of new coastguard houses, well inland, are only worth noting for the fact that the rage of the sea washed away their predecessors from a less secure position some years ago. This is the hamlet of Cliff-end with the church and village of Pett conspicuous on the heights behind. All along here the shore front is more or less of a danger point. The attacks of the sea are more violent and the defences more important than anywhere else at this end of the Marsh, while the road at intervals is frequently obliterated by shoals of beach flung over by the fury of the waves. Nervous people six miles away in the lower town at Rye, are given betimes to fanciful calculations as to how far up the side of their house the waters would reach if the wall at Pett gave way, and turn anxiously on their pillows of winter nights when a south-west gale is howling. I know nothing of hydrostatics, but with the care which I am sure the Commissioners take of us I think we are pretty safe, unless indeed the orgies of 1250 and 1287 recur, when the tide, it will be remembered, " flowed twice without ebbing !" As a matter of fact, a breach is often made under Pett itself with no results whatever beyond the immediate locality and the expense of repairs.

Off this Pett shore are the remains of a submarine forest of oak, beech and pine. At certain states of the tide the stumps can be plainly seen. After a south-west gale the sands of Camber are thickly strewn with fragments of its remains, dark slabs of compressed peat-like substance, in which the chips and splinters of wood are more obvious than in ordinary bog peat. The largest tribute from this pre-historic forest washed up within ordinary memory has occurred since these pages were begun, when the smooth sands of Camber foreshore, littered as far as the eye could reach with uncanny black fragments, presented a most curious spectacle. A stranger coming suddenly upon it might well wonder what sort of wreckage had come ashore in such profusion. For one does not expect to find submarine forests flinging up their secrets in such abundance on these familiar Sussex coasts. Some of the old county historians date their overthrow to the thirteenth century inundations, but this is more than doubtful.

Almost the last smugglers to lose their lives " in action "

fell hereabouts, though it was neither by steel nor bullet. For about 1835 four or five of them with avenging justice at their heels, were drowned at night in the Military canal. The popular story has it that they were endeavouring to swim across. A local ancient, however, has given me the true and indeed more logical version, namely that there was a submerged causeway of faggots, made especially for members of the then most popular profession to wade across on emergencies, and that through darkness and panic these particular unfortunates missed the line, and perhaps also a more painful end by the rope. And indeed this will be as good a place as any to say something of smuggling, popularly regarded in the retrospect as a picturesque sort of game in which high and low took a hand. That is true, in a sense, but the former as a rule took pretty good care of themselves and shared only the plunder, while the more active agents in the trade, certainly in the eighteenth century, who took the risks, were quite often reckless desperadoes, and occasionally as vengeful and cruel as any agrarian ruffian in Mayo or Clare. The rank and file of the service were drawn from the country labourers who were ready to risk their necks—an off-chance risk to be sure—for a few shillings a job. But there were two altogether different branches of smuggling, belonging in broad figures to two distinct periods. Firstly, the illegal export of wool, known as " owling," in the fifteenth, sixteenth and seventeenth centuries ; and, secondly, the import of spirits, tea, lace, and silk in later days.

It is this last one has generally in mind when the contraband trade is referred to. For one thing it was nearer our time, more melodramatic, and incidentally more immoral and blackguardly. Moreover, we still tax these articles for revenue, and with universal approval. But though the export of wool, which was rigorously forbidden or very heavily taxed, through the centuries mentioned and a little later was often for the general good of the country, it was sometimes hard on the wool growers to be at the mercy of the Home manufacturers. It is not surprising that they fancied themselves sacrificed to the community, and illegally sought the much higher and more profitable markets of the Continent. But whichever way it went, it was quite a different matter from smuggling brandy for profit into a country which already lacked nothing for alcoholic drinks; though indeed wool-smuggling at some periods so raised the home prices that bitter and justifiable complaints came from the manufacturers of Wilts, Gloucester, Worcester and Essex, the chief centres of the trade from the fourteenth to the eighteenth century. Whether in smuggling wool out, or brandy and tea in, no part of England was so continually active throughout all the centuries as the coast between Hythe and Hastings, not even the other sea fronts of Kent and Sussex, which came in a very close second.

All our coasts are more or less rich in smuggling traditions, but on this one here, being both close to the Continent, thinly populated, handy for landing goods and favourable for escaping pursuit, smuggling was bitten into the very bone of the people. It is hardly too much to say that it was for a long time the chief trade of the country. The number of snug little fortunes acquired, and the prosperous families that flourished within sound of the sea are themselves a contradiction in terms to the steadily silting-up harbours and the prolonged cry of despair at shrinking trade, which wails through the records of every little port for more than three hundred years. The clip and increase of a hundred thousand or so Romney Marsh sheep, at home prices, and the trade of Romney, Lydd, Rye, Winchelsea and Hastings, from the Tudors to Victoria, can hardly be stretched to account for all these pretty little nest eggs. Nor was it only the double and triple price obtained on the Continent for so much of the Marsh clip that made for all this comfort. Wool was consigned from all sorts of places to the edge of the Marsh and there taken in hand for free export by these master craftsmen in the smug-

OLD HARBOUR INN.

gling art, and frequent Acts were passed regulating the local purchase of wool on this account. It was not all done by stealth, however, for brute force was constantly employed; one or two hundred armed men being frequently engaged in openly convoying both exports and imports, and either fighting or intimidating by mere numbers the guardians of the King's revenues. These last were generally less than one hundred and fifty in number on the whole of the Kent and Sussex coast in the early eighteenth century!

They had a hard time these men, and were not over-well paid, and furthermore were liable to private actions at law if they made mistakes, not always avoidable in the sea-going part of the service, which had to overhaul vessels on bare suspicion. The Preventive force was sometimes supplemented by dragoons, and much use they must have been in a country intersected by a network of deep and broad dykes, that even the headiest native horseman following the hounds does not attempt to jump, but steers his knowing way for the bridges as the smuggler of old steered his, in the dark of the night. "Owling" declined in the eighteenth century, owing mainly to the shrinkage in Continental prices and partly no doubt to the frequent wars with France. Brandy and "soft goods" from France, tea and gin from Holland, then took the lead. Great numbers of horses were used in the trade, both those of the parties interested, and those commandeered from the stables of farmers, parsons or squires, a "tub" being usually left in the stable as payment. But whether or no, the liberty was taken as a matter of course, for sympathy with smuggling was pretty general, while those who denounced it got none whatever. In the mid-eighteenth century intimidation reigned supreme. Magistrates hesitated to arrest lest they should be burned out of house and home. Juries failed to convict on the clearest evidence from mixed reasons, till the *Venue*, as in Ireland, had often to be shifted, while informers, or even mere innocent bearers of letters to active magistrates,

WINCHELSEA TO HASTINGS

were ruthlessly murdered, and sometimes with horrible atrocity.

At the period just named, a too sympathetic public awoke to find itself living under a veritable reign of terror, in the shape of gangs of desperadoes who, though smugglers in the first instance, included robbery and murder in their programme. The Hawkhurst gang are the best remembered of these, and a little book printed in 1749 lies before me giving an exhaustive account of a special assize held at Chichester to try them and others, for which the better element in the County of Sussex had petitioned. The constant failure of local justice to put down crime of this kind was the occasion of this extra visitation of the Judges. A hundred pages of small print give the story, as told in court by two of the actors in it, who had turned King's evidence, confirmed by some of the less guilty prisoners and others incidentally connected with the business. It is a horrible tale of barbarous and studied torture on two unoffending men, such as one is not prepared to find an entire group of Englishmen capable of uniting in, and the way it came about was this.

A cargo of tea in which Sussex smugglers were interested had been seized off Poole and consigned to the Custom House there, whereupon the late owners, assisted by friends from various parts, numbering in all some sixty mounted men, rode into the town. Thirty of them guarded the roads of approach as scouts, while the rest broke open the Custom House and carried off the tea. The whole cavalcade then rode to Fording-bridge, where hundreds of people assembled to see them pass. It was four months before a man was discovered in Hampshire who would give evidence against them, one of the gang, Diamond, a Sussex shepherd, having been seen to speak to him as they passed: the said Diamond being then in jail on suspicion at Chichester. This witness was a shoemaker of Fordingbridge named Chater, probably a Sussex man, and the authorities decided to send him, together with a Custom House underling named Galley, as bearers of a note to a magistrate at Chichester who knew Chater, and would take his evidence.

The word got abroad that the couple were bound for Chichester with a note concerning Diamond, Chater, as he himself admitted, unwillingly, and Galley as a mere Crown-servant. On nearing the Sussex border the landlady of an inn they halted at suspected their mission and sent for some smuggling neighbours, who proceeded to make the two men incapably drunk by means there is no need to describe, while they laid their plans. Next day the devilry began. It is difficult to convey in brief the horrors these miserable men were subjected to, and undesirable as well as impossible to go into the protracted and hideous details. It is enough that after being seated upon one horse with their legs fastened under its belly and their hands tied, they were thrashed mercilessly with horsewhips over head, face, and body as they rode along for some three miles, till the poor wretches in their agony fell down with their heads under the horse's belly. The smugglers' female friends had urged at the inn that they should be hung at once, which would have been infinitely kinder, though not meant that way. Propping the poor souls up again on the horse's back they then cut and slashed them for another half-mile, till they fell once more head downwards.

But the brutes were nothing like glutted. Too weak to ride, the victims, now covered with blood, were carried hanging over the saddle bow and submitted to further and nameless torture. Night found them at an inn on the Downs with Galley's now dead body, and the wretched Chater suffering agonies worse than death. The miscreants then buried the former, and chained up the latter still alive in a shed and maltreated him yet more. Later on he was dragged from there with a rope round his neck and suspended down a well. This not finishing the business, they then threw him down head first, and as his groans were still audible they hurled down stones on top of him and departed; the bodies were found a few months afterwards. Informers and King's evidence came forward. The six ruffians, innkeepers, horse-dealers and the like, were sentenced to death at the special assize alluded to. One cheated the gallows by dying in prison, the others were hung, mostly in chains at the various spots associated with their hideous crime, and the Dean of Chichester wound up the business with a sermon on it in the Cathedral, which lies before me, a monument of stilted and commonplace futilities. Later in the same year 1749, others of the gang, one of whom in the interval had whipped and kicked another man to death, were caught and convicted at East Grinstead and hung in chains. Three more on the old charge of breaking the Custom House at Poole were hung at Tyburn.

Large distilleries were erected in France and Holland at this time solely for the English smuggling trade. In 1779 it was estimated that nearly all of the four million gallons of gin annually distilled at Schiedam found an illicit market in England. English smugglers had their regular agents in the foreign ports, while fast sailing luggers designed for the trade were built in great numbers upon the south shore of the Channel. The more respectable classes in Kent and Sussex were perpetually torn between their practical interests in smuggling and the demoralization it wrought on the rougher elements, reacting on society in the shape of murders, arson and robbery. Even the labour market was sometimes denuded for the more profitable and exciting service with the "free-traders." In parts of the country people were even driven to repudiate smuggling by declaration and band themselves together as a sort of informal militia to protect private property. The Jacobite intrigues in the eighteenth century too were greatly assisted through these channels of communication, while well-paid spies in the Napoleonic Wars regularly transmitted English news and English papers to France by the same means. The London Press paid large sums up to £100 for early copies of the French 'papers, and no doubt Parisian editors were not less niggardly.

Militant smuggling was still ripe in the twenties and thirties of the last century, often with considerable casualty lists, for firearms were freely used by both sides. As late as 1828 nine Sussex smugglers were sent up for trial at the Old Bailey and all condemned to death, though sentence was commuted to transportation, which at that time was practically the same thing. Two years earlier a smuggling galley chased by a guard boat ran ashore at Camber. The watch there turned out to seize the crew, but two hundred men dashed out of the sandhills and opened fire on the Guard House. They were compelled, however, to retreat, carrying their wounded with them. The last recorded fight in these parts was at Camber Castle in 1838 when a Rye man was killed. These, however, are but stray examples out of a lengthy list. Mr. Durrant Cooper, in a paper on the subject written sixty years ago says : " I have been present myself at a house in Rye, when silks for sale were mysteriously produced from their hiding-places, and it has been the custom of the farmers to leave their gates unlocked at night and to broach without scruple the half anker of Schiedam considerately left in a rick or outhouse as an acknowledgment. This and the brandy were carried in four-gallon tubs, swung over men's shoulders or over the backs of pack-horses." This must have been almost in' Victorian times ! After all, one cannot wonder at the state of things upon the south coast throughout most of the eighteenth century. We are apt to think complacently of England during such comparatively recent times as a kind of model for its neighbours, whereas it was in some respects far the most lawless of the more civilized nations of Europe. The Whig oligarchy and the German kings between them in their chronic struggle for power, their Party obsessions, their pitiful intrigues and sordid aims, their squandering of the public money on themselves and their friends on the one hand, with the King and his German mistresses and pensioners on the other, left the internal affairs of the country in a most parlous state. While the less we say of foreign and military enterprises in the interval between the genius of Marlborough and the inspiring patriotism of Chatham, the better. Isolated achievements of heroism were in spite of the Government, not the result of its sagacity.

The reputation for turbulence that England enjoyed throughout Western Europe was not the flapping of the wings of freedom, as Whig writers occasionally insinuate. It was simply rank ill-government, and the interludes of Tory administration were of course no better, for all were tarred with the same brush, that of sordid personal motives and a mere struggle for personal and party power. Drunkenness was almost universal, and licentiousness had been stripped even of the refinements which a veneer of polish had given to the loose morals of earlier days. The mob took possession of London practically when it liked; generally, to be sure, but a mere rowdy mob, dangerous only to individuals, Royal or otherwise, who had stirred its rage, sometimes for most trivial or imaginary reasons. There were no police. A standing army was the bugbear of the nation, from the squire who as a militia officer would thereby have his nose put out of joint, to the workman who dreaded its effect on what he imagined to be his liberty, which then amounted to little more than a licence to brawl. Moreover, a standing army was associated in his mind partly with Popery and partly with Cromwellian recollections. If such troops as there were did fire on the mob the officers risked their necks in a Civil Court.

The private coaches of the most illustrious people, from Royalty downwards, were frequently accompanied in London by a crowd shouting through the windows their opinions of the occupants in the most approved Billingsgate of the period. Sometimes, too, they did more than shout, and special guards had to be employed to protect the lives of unpopular men and women. Peers and Ministers were occasionally robbed in the short drive from Westminster to their town houses. Highwaymen haunted each exit from the capital. Every one had to protect themselves as in the Middle Ages or in an American frontier state a generation ago, though there the robbery of individuals was not a common vice of the rowdy, while the ill-lighted or unlighted streets of London were wholly unsafe after dark. This was not a brief interlude ; it lasted for half the century, and with slight modifications for much more. It was no passion for freedom, for in that respect the cycle was steadily retrograde, but licence let loose; Privilege, exclusiveness, corruption, vastly encouraged by a German-minded, as well as a German-born reigning family, increased all the time, reflected as we have seen in the life of these little Cinque-Port towns.

Nothing is more illuminating in regard to the lawless state of England, more especially of London and the home counties, than the many memoirs of distinguished foreigners on first making acquaintance with the country. One and all are amazed that such things could be. To be insulted in obscene language and with impunity in the streets, to drive about armed or with an armed guard, or in visiting friends in the country to have to travel the dangerous roads as in a hostile territory, was a revelation to a French, Dutch or German Ambassador or nobleman and their ladies. Can it be wondered at then that smuggling flourished and that the preventive force was ludicrously undermanned. The elimination of a trifling fraction of these sinecures would have provided funds enough to stamp out smuggling from Dover to Southampton in a month, and save many times the cost of the force needed to the revenue. More money was squandered on unearned pensions, gifts, and jobs among a small circle, than would have been required to suppress smuggling all over England, and furthermore to make the London streets and the country roads as safe as those of Hanover or Holland. It was a poor result indeed of the Constitution of 1688 and spelt a state of things that needs no comment, and fully justifies that of contemporary foreigners, which was trenchant and severe.

Here at Pett where the Marsh, now narrowed to a point, abruptly terminates, the broken sea-washed sandy road turns inland, climbs the steep hill to Pett church and opens out as pretty a confusion of hill and dale as there is in the county of Sussex. This district is roughly covered in whole or part by the parishes of Pett, Guestling, Icklesham and Fairlight which lie up against the great ridge barrier of Fairlight hill. Tortuous and perpendicular lanes labour through it this way and that, by woods of oak and steep hopfields and cuppy meadows nestling in the glens. Nothing but the gleam and the music of tumbling streams is wanting to this almost west-country arcadia, and the south-country man does not miss that. But then there are always those delectable old tiled cottages and homesteads, that in these more sequestered corners of Sussex lurk in all sorts of unexpected and bosky corners. Homes of dead and gone smugglers beyond a doubt many of them, but they lose nothing in charm by that, and maybe even gather a touch of romance!

On the shore front the cliffs here begin to rise, and overhang the sea for some six miles, till they actually dip into the old town of Hastings. From Pett level westward there is a mile of lowish cliff, much of it densely and picturesquely clad with wind-battered woods of oak and ash, thorn and willow. Following this, after a slight dip to an old coastguard station, the sheer and lofty cliffs of the Fairlight ridge offer their brownish-yellow sandstone fronts to the waves, which at high water lash their rock-strewn base and leave but a rugged way around it at the ebb of the tide. A cliff path, however, along their summits affords a most inspiring walk to Hastings, dipping down on the way into the really beautiful and woody glens of Fairlight, Ecclesbourne, and another without name, but no whit inferior. The huge broad back of Fairlight down, nearly six hundred feet above sea level, with its church tower lying somewhat back, but always conspicuous, and its signal station at the edge of the long slope to the cliff, dominates this whole interlude of uplifted and broken coastline, while immense tracts of gorse, interspersed betimes with heather, spread far and wide from the edge of the cliffs. Between the chalk of Beachy Head and that of the Kent cliffs this great block of sandstone is a curious interlude. Its varied tints of brown and red and yellow catch the sunshine under favourable conditions with an almost eastern radiancy, between the blue of the sea and the green of the overhanging down.

I have seen these sharp contrasts of colouring to great perfection on a clear, frosty winter day, not the less effective for the solitude that at this season reigns profound upon cliff edge and bosky glen the whole way from Pett to Hastings. Looking eastward from Fairlight down, a trifle higher than Beachy Head, the whole of Rye bay with its fringe of yellow sand or shingle, glimmering along between the sea and the green flats of the Marsh, spreads to the long point of Dungeness, reaching out towards France. Winchelsea and Rye are plain enough upon their respective hill-tops, while Romney Marsh, broadening out beyond them spreads like a map towards the distant downs of Kent and the heights of Dover. With a westering sun this glorious prospect is naturally at its best. Nor less alluring is that other part of it which carries the eye over the fine confusion of hill and dale that spreads north-eastward from the foot of Fairlight and over the belt of villages through which we hope later on to work our backward way.

Few churches in England stand out so prominently and make so conspicuous a mark over land and sea as that of Fairlight. A Gothic building with a high tower and comparatively modern, its romantic situation has made it a favourite place of burial among the many invalids who came to Hastings in its palmy days, in the hope of prolonging their precarious lives,

So the tombstones in the wind-swept graveyard mean often something more than a brief page in local history. The manner in which these sandstone cliffs have been eaten away by the sea and have toppled over periodically during past ages is not a little curious. Wide clefts occur at intervals in the otherwise perpendicular walls of rock, where the landslip, whether gradual or instantaneous, has been on such a scale as to leave a ravine, now covered with vegetation and of so moderate an incline that you might readily scramble down it to the sea level. On a much bigger scale than this, however, the cliffs would seem in some places to have retired quite a distance inland, leaving far above high-water mark a fine and broken confusion of rock and turf, of fern, gorse and leafy brush, representing the débris of ages that has fallen from their summits. There are acres and acres of it, facing the sun and the south. One may well fancy the migrant birds from over-sea hailing the sight of such a welcoming harbourage and closing their tired wings with relief in its snug retreats. The broad glen under the western flank of the signal-station hill, where it expands at the sea front, and that of Fairlight just beyond are striking examples of this curious action of time, weather and the restless waves. And when you have climbed out of the former over the intervening ridge you descend into the middle and most famous of the three valleys which drop down to the sea, in a fashion savouring of the west rather than the east of England.

There is a good cliff path, as I have said, all the way from Hastings to Pett rising and falling through the three main valleys. But the average visitor to Fairlight glen from Hastings goes up to Ore, a mile from the head of it, by tram or otherwise and descends it by woodland or hillside paths to the sea. And let me here and at once urge the reader, if the opportunity should arise, not to spurn it for the " trippery " reputation that attaches to its name in the holiday months. Out of the season he will have the whole of this imposing stretch of coast practically to himself. But whether or no, Fairlight, and indeed the other valleys, are on a quite generous scale. They are not of the restricted type of glen, or its equivalent, to which some watering-places I could mention introduce the visitor by way of a twopenny turnstile ! Save Beachy Head and Dover, which with their sharp white chalk belong to altogether another type of scenery, there is nothing on the whole main coast of England between Dorset and Yorkshire at all comparable, either in scale or intrinsic beauty, to this Fairlight district. As for the chalk formation, it is of itself inimical to woody vales and such profusion of verdure as here clothes the long slopes and their lofty broken sea-fronts.

At a high point on the eastern front of Fairlight glen, and overlooking the sea, is the famous " Lovers' Seat." And here again let no one dismiss this lightly as a mere haunt of trippers and of hackneyed name contrived for their edification. For the spot is truly beautiful and the tale *mirabile dictu* is literally true, and this is it. In the year 1786 a young sailor, Captain Lamb, of the well-known Rye family, was commanding *The Stag* revenue cutter and busily engaged in hunting smugglers and privateers off this bit of coast. He loved and was in turn beloved by a certain fair maid, the only child and heiress of a Mr. Boys, of Elford, near Hawkhurst. This gentleman, possibly for financial reasons, resolutely opposed the match, and in those days there was of course nothing more to be said ; action was the only alternative. There seems, however, to have been no thought of this till the girl's parents inadvertently laid the train for it. Now at the very head of the glen there is a charming old Early Georgian house, known as Fairlight Place, with beech groves on either flank and gardens between them which open out a glorious view over the Channel. Either for her health's sake or to get her out of the young man's way, the maiden was dispatched, under the care of a trusty servant, for a period of retirement to this sequestered retreat, then a farmhouse.

But the gallant Captain on his cutter, by some means or other, discovered the whereabouts of his lady-love and meetings were easily contrived. The girl used to repair, unbeknown to her unsuspecting guardian, if such she were, to this conspicuous ledge near the top of the woody cliff, and thence by signals to her hero's vessel on the sea below, arrange their stolen interviews. The upshot of it all was that the couple ran away and got married, quite regularly and prosaically, at St. Clement Danes in the Strand. Of course the lady ought to have flung herself over the cliff and the Captain to have died fighting upon the deck of a privateer immediately after. Some old guide books, despairing of any allurement in the true story, or perhaps not knowing it, have provided various tragedies of this nature for the tourist. The father never, I think, forgave the girl, which does give a further touch of romance to the incident. But the young man, if not rich enough to be a worthy suitor in the parental eyes, had enough to build a house at Salehurst and live there happily and comfortably with his wife for twenty-eight years, when he was washed off a yacht in Southampton Water and drowned. The lady survived him some years, while their only child, a daughter, married a Mr. Ferris and many of their descendants are living. The story, though only moderately dramatic, is worth noting if only for the fact that the preliminaries to the elopement had so romantic and picturesque a setting, and further that the unconvincing name, " Lovers' Seat," has a really genuine origin, and that five generations in their thousands have visited it, with the tale generally distorted as the impelling cause. Lover or no lover, it should on no account be missed. But I am assured that the spot is still thus regarded by sentimental couples in the same amorous condition as the gallant skipper and the squire's daughter. Nay, I need no such assurance. For on visiting the spot one mid-winter day quite recently, when not a soul was abroad between Pett and Hastings but an odd ploughman or coastguard, we actually surprised such a pair, seated on the classic spot, and holding one another's hands too! It is a perfect sun-trap on a bright winter day, so we had intended to lunch there, and I regret to say were unfeeling enough to carry out our programme. If I had been alone I should not have had the nerve to shift' (for it amounted to that) a couple at once so affectionate and so obviously respectable. I won't apologise for relating this really rather picturesque and significant coincidence.

BETWEEN FAIRLIGHT AND PETT.

The Ecclesbourne Glen intervenes between that of Fairlight and the East Hill above Hastings. It is of much the same character as the other, nearly as beautiful and outside the season quite as solitary, and like its neighbour watered by a little tumbling stream. The foot of it is rather marred by a deserted coastguard station. But the cliff from here to Hastings harbour is for the most part precipitous. There are two views from the East Hill at Hastings, and to my thinking the greater is included in the less. In brief there is the imposing

WINCHELSEA TO HASTINGS

coup d'œil of New Hastings and St. Leonards, almost merging into Bexhill, with the faint blur of Eastbourne hanging far beyond on the skirts of Beachy Head. But all the trailing misty wilderness of bricks and mortar, and parades and piers, sprang up within living memory. It is well calculated to swell the bosom of a town councillor, but not what I would chiefly go up on to the East Hill for to see, which would be rather the little old town of Hastings, the ancient Cinque-Port, lying compact and hardly altered in the narrow trough at your feet with the castle ruins rising on the seaward point of the steep, beyond and above it.

You may easily ignore the rest in the complete and perfect picture of an ancient town, squeezed up the narrow valley from the shore front, where to this day its fishing fleet perches on the high shingle ridge, as aloof from the great watering-place beyond as if the latter had never been. The furzy heights we have just come over drop sheer down on to its old red roofs. Green fields and even hedgerows still hold the further slope which with the ruined castle on its point hems it in upon the west. The horrors upon the ridge top do not affect this foreground picture of the little town, with the old church towers of All Saints' and St. Clement's looking diagonally at one another from its upper and lower extremities. Where this tightly packed wedge of fishermen's houses, and such as minister to them, draws to a point up the narrow valley, a pleasant interlude of fine old timber shelters some equally fine old Georgian mansions which harboured its magnates in the days of old, and cuts it off most effectively from the modern disfigurements of Ore and Halton at the head of the vale. It is pre-eminently from these heights that one realizes the true aloofness of Old Hastings, with its three thousand souls, from the huge and famous watering-place which has inherited its name spreading three miles along the coast and sprawling far inland over hill and dale.

The first serious growth of the town, early in the nineteenth century was along the sea front westward, for the high precipitous promontory of the castle rock forced it by this narrow way and so virtually out of sight and eventually, one might almost think, out of mind of the old borough. This last consists in effect of a couple of long, narrow streets, intersected with wynds and courts, running up the Bourne valley for some half-mile, though the stream itself which within living memory splashed down by its houses and gardens has long been rele-

TORFIELD HOUSE, OLD HASTINGS.

gated to subterranean courses. Quaint as Old Hastings is when you get down to it, there is little here of the charm of Old Rye. Much of it is indeed undeniably slummy: the most pervid aesthete has never probably felt the faintest impulse to take a house here and fill it with old furniture, even if one visitor in a hundred to Hastings-St.-Leonards (they have long been united) as understood by the polite world ever saw the old town or realized its existence. Its two churches, All Saints' and St. Clement's, though spacious and dignified examples of the Perpendicular period, much restored, have hardly sufficient character of themselves to allure the visitor interested in such things from the distant purlieus of Warrior Square or Eversfield Place. The thorough-going Cockney, who now haunts in holiday seasons those shabbier eastern portions of the new Hastings once dedicated to Early Victorian aristocrats, probably knows much more of the old town than his betters, though no doubt he would refer to it in uncomplimentary terms as a God-forsaken hole.

It certainly looks to the eye as if the Town Council at least had forgotten it, or did not think it worthy of an occasional wash and brush up. It is not a recognized asset to the great business of entertainment by which Hastings lives, and none too prosperously I fear this last twenty years. Moreover, it contains at a mere guess no more than perhaps three thousand rather humble folk out of the nearly seventy thousand that comprise the whole community to-day. This severance, however, between the past and the present, makes it easier to consider Old Hastings as a Cinque-Port than if it were indefinably merged into its gigantic offspring. So much has been told of early Rye and Winchelsea as to reduce the space necessary for any story of Hastings. For in broad outline it is much the same. The details differ, but even they have a strong family likeness. Perhaps we ought to put it the other way, as Hastings was the premier port of the five original towns, whose common charter was afterwards extended to Rye and Winchelsea. But all of them shared the same privileges, the same responsibilities and the same dangers. They gave and received the same hard knocks with Frenchman, Spaniard and Fleming. They followed the same sea-borne trade and pursued the same shoals of herrings and mackerel in the North Sea and the Channel. All alike wrestled for centuries with the sea, its overwhelming onslaughts, its even worse recessions, and all in the end were beaten by it and left either high and dry or as seaports utterly insignificant. Lastly as privateers, as smugglers, and at times as pirates they were in complete and perfect harmony, while as rotten or pocket boroughs in the glorious days of the Georges, it was not the others' fault that Rye easily takes the lead in racy incident. Though often jealous of one another, they did not often, I think, come to blows, reserving these for outsiders, and when threatened in privilege or dignity they closed their ranks with commendable unanimity.

Hastings, however, has far earlier claims to recognition than the others can make any pretension to. Roman relics have been found in the town; an earthwork on the East hill is supposed to be Roman, while there are people, mostly natives, who declare that Julius Caesar landed here! Pevensey, otherwise Anderida, according to many people, is after all not far off, and brings Hastings within its imperial orbit. But these are shadowy glimpses. It is in Offa's reign, the great eighth-century Mercian King, who with one foot on North Wales and the other on Kent, made so many things happen, and gave such material to the literary monks that Hastings comes into recorded history. For having chastised the "gens Hestingorum," Offa made a present of them to a French Abbot, confirming the grant of the harbours of Pevensey and Hastings to the Abbey of St. Denis. What to our eyes read like spasms of suicidal generosity had probably much method in those of the Saxon and Early Norman Kings. They made beyond doubt for intercourse, trade, church building and prosperity. Certainly Hastings prospered by its foreign connexion, for King Athelstane established a mint there and coins from it are in existence. Like its neighbours, Hastings was given by the Confessor to the Norman Abbey of Fécamp, a much more dangerous proceeding now that the vigorous and predatory Northmen had superseded the old French upon the opposite coast. But as the Normans were fated so soon to conquer England it did not much matter, while as regards this little town the Conquest itself contributed to its still greater importance. Hastings is identified as the *New burgh* of Domesday, for a former town seems already to have been almost wiped out by the sea. It is credited with eighty-four burgesses, besides a few in the remains of the old town, and before the Conquest the Hastings sailors had distinguished themselves against Earl Godwin's intractable son Sweyn, who was playing the pirate in the Channel.

Most people know, I fancy, that the immortal contest to which Hastings has given its name was not fought here but six miles inland, where now stands the little town of Battle. I am thankful it was, as placing it just outside our circuit here, for I should not like to be confronted with the Battle of Senlac, as the purist following Freeman styles it, in this short narrative, which is by way of following a trail not generally familiar either historically or physically to the general reader.

SHOVEL HOUSE, HASTINGS.

The Battle of Hastings as the opening scene in one stage of our national existence, another of which has so recently closed, is altogether too big a business for passing notice. Moreover, the space given to it by specialists, is in inverse ratio to what is actually known of the details. These have in great measure to be supplied by the imagination to which it offers an irresistible field. William, as we know, landed at Pevensey, about twelve miles from Old Hastings, and one or two patriotic Hastings writers accepting the monkish figures (generally divisible by three at least) of the Conqueror's miscellaneous army, have calculated that the extreme right of his fleet would have touched ground near St. Leonards. However that may be, the Conqueror, as we know, marched to the ancient Port and spent a fortnight in the district, much to its discomfort, while awaiting the arrival of Harold, who unfortunately had the Cinque-Ports fleet with him on the east coast.

The ruthless harrying of the Rape of Hastings was for the purpose of bringing Harold and his army down from Yorkshire, so that William could fight near his fleet and escape in case of defeat. Harold, it may be remembered, had just won the hard fought battle of Stamford Bridge over the Norwegian invaders under Harold Hardrada and Tostig. Freeman describes William as uncertain for a few days with which of these two armies he would have ultimately to contest the crown of England. But he was soon assured on that point owing to the incredible speed with which the victorious Saxon King marched his comparatively small force to London. It was there, while awaiting vital reinforcements from the west, the midlands and the east, that the delay of a week occurred, which monkish writers, whose prototypes are still with us, have been prompt to criticize. As it was, Harold manœuvred successfully for his own position at Senlac, and as we know very nearly won the battle. William, in the meantime, had taken note of the castle rock, and when he had completed his own work, commissioned the Count d'Eu and the Abbot of Fécamp the secular and ecclesiastical lords of this strip of coast, to build upon it the great fortress whose fragments are still sufficient to crown this noble height with a lasting monument to its old significance.

Of the present remains, the most considerable are those of the Collegiate church, a part of the original foundation. But the entire fortress was repaired again and again, during the three centuries it served both in a military and ecclesiastical sense any serious purpose, portions having apparently toppled into the sea from time to time. Like all these obvious points of defence, the rock seems to have carried some sort of a wooden fortress in Saxon and possibly in British times. But through the Norman period it was an ideal stronghold, the point of a promontory, unassailable on three sides, and on the fourth connected with the land by a high ridge, sufficiently narrow to be easily defended. In after days when cannon came into use the position lost its value, being commanded by loftier

HASTINGS HOUSE.

heights on both sides. But that was of small consequence, for it had done its work. As a connecting link between England and Normandy, till they fell apart, it proved invaluable, while in the later days of perpetual hostility between the two shores, being often left to a weak and purely local defence, it was gutted, together with the town, more than once by the French. In these earlier days, however, Hastings was a place of note and import, of which its rank as senior member of the Cinque-Ports was an abiding indication, though indeed this last was never challenged, even when in the time of Stephen it had fallen behind Rye and Winchelsea in actual contribution of men and ships.

In these days, though controversy upon the subject has never been quieted, Hastings had almost certainly a natural harbour, running in upon the western side of the castle rock, where the old Saxon town is supposed to have stood and where the newer Hastings of the eighteenth century began its first growth. But the sea in all these centuries has wrought so much destruction, as evidenced by the submerged remains of trees and fences and the traces of buildings, that the work of unravelling the chequered story of this bit of sea front has practically baffled the ingenuity of the most industrious antiquaries. Its present condition, however, can be stated without any ambiguity and in a single sentence—for there is now nothing more hospitable than a steep bank of beach, which the flattish-bottomed fishing smacks have to charge on the top of the tide, and forthwith be hauled up on to the flat above by main force. As beaches go it is I believe just the right incline, neither too steep for vessels to climb, nor gentle enough to make the hauling up process too lengthy or arduous. Still at the best it is a mighty inconvenient operation to be repeated every twenty-four hours by biggish fishing craft, particularly as this is only possible for an hour or so at high tide.

The subject of harbours, piers and breakwaters is in truth a sore one at Old Hastings, for the record is one of disaster ever since the first recorded wooden pier and harbourage was washed away in Elizabeth's time. Twenty years afterwards sufficient money was raised all over England, after the fashion of that day, for restoration, and masons were brought from Lyme in Dorsetshire to build a stone breakwater and pier. The skill and strength of the new work so delighted the Hastings men, that they protested it would defy time itself, but the very next big storm washed the whole concern away. Undaunted by this further catastrophe, the persevering Hastingers rebuilt the work with such skill, care and labour that the mere sight of it when completed gladdened their eyes and with thankful hearts they felt that now at least their ships had an everlasting shelter from the south-west gales. Alack, and alas! before the year was out this too vanished in a single storm. Many schemes were now suggested and some vain attempts were made to break the sea's rage. But in the end the Hastings traders and fishermen had to beach their ships just as they do to-day and have been doing ever since. A shattered stone pier and breakwater of probably far greater bulk and strength than any of those ancient ones, and erected not long ago, bears melancholy witness at this moment to the futility of fighting the onslaughts of the sea at this exposed spot. It says much for the Hastings men that they kept going as well as they did throughout the centuries. Though a port without any harbour to speak of, they turned out four times as many ships as Rye to fight the Armada and became the chief ship-builders of all the Ports.

EAST CLIFF, HASTINGS.

Before Rye and old Winchelsea had achieved full honours of Cinque-Portship, they had been in a sense "limbs" of Hastings. When they became independent and when Hastings in the thirteenth and fourteenth centuries experienced bad times, Seaford and Pevensey became its supporters. They no doubt helped the mother town to maintain its premier rank among the Cinque-Ports, even against Dover, the official headquarters, and the object of ever-increasing care and expenditure on the part of the Crown. There is plenty of life to-day on the beach when the little fleet has come in with its herring catch, but it is such a picture as may have been seen at any time within the last hundred years. The black hulls of the fishing boats resting upright on their rollers, line the crest of the steep pebble ridge, while men and boys, with baskets on their shoulders, hurry back and forth over the deep shingle between the shining piles of herrings and the fish market or the place of packing for the London train. So far as the foreground is concerned, strings of pack-horses might even now be waiting at the foot of the High Street to jangle off with the first instalments for the Royal, noble or civic tables of the Metropolis, instead of commonplace vans bound for Hastings station. And what may be said of the herring season in late autumn applies equally to the visit of the mackerel in May and June, the other great fishing festival and period of weal or woe upon this coast.

To this broad expanse of shingle plateau, on which odd craft of all sorts connected with the fishing trade, but quite unconcerned with modern Hastings, are lying around in temporary idleness, the oldest part, in appearance, at least of the old town makes a fitting setting ; while the quaint tower-shaped black sheds for storing tackle stand midway in serried rows, just as they stand in the oldest prints of this interesting quarter. The precipitous front of the East Hill, punctuated on its face with uncanny looking caves apparently barricaded against potential " home seekers," rises behind, while if one walks eastward for a few hundred yards, Hastings comes suddenly, and in wild weather rather awesomely, to an end. The broad and busy beach, alive with men and boys and girls who drag a livelihood from the deep, the ships, the sheds, the warehouses, the narrow town front beneath the cliff, all terminate abruptly in a high stone embankment which doubtless has its uses. It is probably the easterly horn of the shattered breakwater which presents such a melancholy spectacle at the further end of the beach.

But however that may be, the sea surges in, deep and strong beyond it, flinging its surf against lofty and precipitous cliffs and puts a limit to Hastings in a fashion more abrupt and dramatic than one looks for in a south-country watering-place. Not many of the watering-place folk, however, reach this Ultima Thule of the unvisited end of the town. I think they would be surprised if they did. In winter, under dark skies, when even a moderate sea is flowing and the sheer cliffs rise high and menacing in the misty gloom, it is really quite a gruesome corner.

To say that the fisher-folk form now, as always, a community to themselves, intermarrying little with outsiders, is merely

FISHING SHEDS, OLD HASTINGS.

to record an instinct that is common to their breed on every coast known to me in England, Scotland and Wales. The Sussex man is in any case supposed to be reticent and non-committal above most south-countrymen, though any one from Northumberland or the Lothians might think him almost garrulous. The fisherman, as elsewhere, is the least communicative of his breed, except at election times, when his attentions to the outer world have been often felt to be embarrassing. There is a world of difference between the eloquence of the pleasure boatmen beyond the White Rock and the profound indifference to strangers expressed upon the countenance of the man with rings in his ears upon the foreshore of Old Hastings. But, after all, these things are relative ; the

Sussex native, whether ploughman or fisherman, particularly the former, is discoursed upon by a great many modern writers and sometimes out of their own imagination. Now assuming, which would not always be safe since these things depend so much upon individual powers of observation, balance and intuition, that even the Sussex writer knows his own people, it is more than probable that he does not know any other intimately. The consequence is we have certain traits, habits, phrases, customs, legends and even ballads recorded in the best of faith as if they were peculiar to Sussex, whereas many of them are quite familiar to many other counties and other parts of England.

HOME OF TITUS OATES.

Very few people know much of England from this point of view, and very few indeed who are likely to be interested in or articulate upon the subject. On the other hand, those who best know their own district and are alive to these things would, for obvious reasons, be the most unlikely of all to be intimate with others and so to recognize that many peculiarities believed to be local are common (within geographical limits) to all. This is not of course peculiar to Sussex writers, but to most intimate exponents of their own districts it is inevitable. To any one who does happen to know ten or fifteen counties between the Forth and the Tamar and their literature pretty well, this community in so many presumed local possessions and peculiarities is curiously illuminating. The position of Sussex again, between London and the coast, has made it the stamping ground of a whole army of scribes, male and female, who in fugitive papers endow the Sussex native with all kinds of qualities, good a d bad, but generally meaningless. It is easily accounted for. He is the first more or less unadulterated rustic, though in some parts of the county he has ceased to be such, that they encounter on emerging from the urbanized or be-villad regions round London, and of that far-spread Cockney accent which seems of itself to promote loquacity. He finds the Sussex countrymen irresponsive, as almost any other rustic would be, compared with a job gardener in Epsom, a greengrocer's man in Surbiton, or even the cowman of an agriculturally minded Surrey plutocrat. He finds, or thinks he finds, at any rate he sets down many other things about him that are naturally not characteristic of what may be called the rural Cockney, who inhabits the artificial country which spreads so far round London and has penetrated Sussex, accent and all, at more than one point. And not less artificial because there are pine woods and commons where you may dodge the villas for many miles if you know your way. I think this accounts for a good deal of the taciturnity encountered upon Sussex byways by writers from within the London orbit. It is only the natural reserve of country folk, when questions are fired at them by a stranger in a pitch of voice and an intonation to which they are unaccustomed and so fail perhaps to catch his meaning. If the Sussex rustic is labelled dour, and very often in a wholesale way "silly" like his prototype of Suffolk for the mere sake of alliteration, I wonder what our London rambler would think of the roadside amenities he would encounter on a pilgrimage, say, from Darlington to Edinburgh! As to the Sussex fishermen, a blunter man than the Sussex labourer, I have frequently known him hold a gate open for quite a few seconds. His equivalent upon the north-east coast, Scotch or English, would see you d——d first, worthy person though he be, and a great gulf lies between these two apparently trifling acts of commission and omission.

The open space at the bottom of the High Street, facing the beach, was once known as the Hundred Place, and according to the *Customal*, all the commonalty assembled there on the "Sunday after Hockday" to choose a bailiff, as the Mayor was formerly called in all these towns. Here too, as at Rye, if the favoured one refused to serve, the crowd were instructed to repair to his house and pull it down about his ears. In later periods the commonalty had mighty little to do with the selection of the Mayor, which as at Rye became almost hereditary in a family or connexion. In a map of Hastings *temp.* 1748 there are no buildings at all west of this spot. A haven too with vessels on it is here depicted, partly behind the castle hill and on or about the site of the present Wellington Square. It is connected with the sea by a narrow channel, over which a bridge carries the road leading westward along a then virgin shore-front.

OLD HASTINGS.

It was a dozen years after the date of this comparatively recent map that the Hastings mariners turned pirates again for a time, and for many years a gang known as the Ruxley crew reverted to the practices of the Middle Ages. In August, 1758, two armed Hastings cutters held up a Danish ship carrying no less a personage than the Ambassador Extraordinary from the Court of Spain to that of Denmark. They assaulted the captain and plundered part of the cargo. Six of the offenders were subsequently arrested and two of them hung in London. This example, however, in no wise intimidated these audacious Hastings corsairs, who during the next seven years boarded and robbed many vessels coming up the Channel.

Their outrages culminated in the looting of a homeward-bound Dutch ship off Beachy Head, whose skipper they clove down the back with an axe. This raised a great outcry, and two hundred Inniskilling dragoons were sent to Hastings to seize the culprits. The purchasers of these ill-gotten gains were seized with panic, and one of them, worth £10,000, fled the town. A dozen men were arrested on this occasion and three of them were hung. As wreckers, too, the natives of the premier Port proved incorrigible.

In 1747 a big Spanish ship of nearly 1,000 tons carrying a most valuable cargo, insured for £120,000, the prize of a British privateer, was wrecked near Beachy Head. Desperate encounters took place between the Custom House officers and the wreckers, sixty of whom are reported to have perished from various causes: many, no doubt, from excessive sampling of the ardent liquors found on board. A most curious contemporary print of the scene, now in possession of Mr. Cousins, and reproduced by him in his *Bygone Hastings*, shows the shattered hulk of the big ship lying on the sand and crowds of people on the shore, making off with the cargo. Underneath the picture is inscribed, with other descriptive details, " Ye most extraordinary wreck that ever happened on any part of ye coast of this Kingdom." Two months after this a Dutch East Indiaman of 700 tons, and carrying in cash and cargo £200,000, drove ashore at Bulverhythe, just beyond the western extremity of the present St. Leonards. A private letter, of which anon, describes the ship as standing intact upon the sands with no possibility of getting her off. " I believe," says the writer, " they did save everything that is worth saving to the Great Disappointment of the wreckers who came from all parts of the country for plunder. There was yesterday more than a thousand of these wretches with long poles and hooks at the end. But all the soldiers on the coast are here and Behave well at present. They keep the country people off and their officers keep the soldiers to rights."

The High Street of the old town, which pursues its straight and narrow course up the valley of the now smothered Bourne, does not bear its years cheerfully like the old streets of Rye, but with a shabby and dejected air not perhaps surprising under the circumstances. Nor among its old houses are there many whose exteriors would give the stranger pause. Its fellow street of All Saints, which in former days confronted it across the stream, is still shabbier and yet more dejected, but contains a half-timbered little house that for sheer quaintness exceeds anything we have even in Rye. A plate attached to the wall informs the passer-by that it was the residence of the mother of the famous admiral Sir Cloudesly Shovel, who was himself, however, born in Norfolk. The long, narrow gable of the higher portion and the sideways cant of the projecting storey beneath it, make it rather unique, even among small Tudor houses.

ALL SAINTS STREET, OLD HASTINGS.

Both streets emerge into the few hundred yards of still leafy and rural interlude that suggest the open country in former days, now blocked higher up by the wilderness of buildings comprising Ore and Halton.

Here, however, standing in their easy space of grounds and trees are two fine old Early Georgian houses, one of which at least held social sway over eighteenth-century Hastings and has personal and even territorial associations over and above that. It was owned and occupied by John Collier, who was town clerk, solicitor and steward of several Manors, early in that century, and it may be noted as rather uncommon in the case of a country town house, that his descendants own it to this day. The said John Collier occupied many posts of distinction both in the county and in the Cinque-Port Brotherhood. But more even than these, he represented the Pelhams, who territorially and politically held this bit of Sussex in the hollow of their hand, while the Collier family seem to have added field to field and house to house till they and theirs came to be the leading family of Hastings beyond dispute. They were all-powerful there: John Collier was Mayor doubtless as often as he felt inclined. His son-in-law, Milward, who succeeded to his position, was Mayor twenty-six times, and his son followed suit. But they were something more than country town burgesses with autocratic tendencies and typical of their century, or I should not perhaps have paused so long before their now mellow and embowered stronghold. For the Collier letters have recently been published (1718–1760), and they include not only those of the head of the family but of other members of it, and present quite an illuminating picture of the local and domestic life of the period, that of the first two Georges. For the writers were educated and well-to-do folk, going to London from time to time and meeting well-known people, though it is the comfortable provincial life here depicted which makes the record more than a little valuable.

General Murray (of the Elibank family), who took over the command at Quebec, after Wolfe's death, and held the city under no slight difficulties against the attacks of the French in the spring of 1760, married into the family after the Peace. He was on the point of taking over Hastings House, or "The Mansion" as it was then called, as a residence for himself, being then Lord of the Manor of Ore. But eventually he built a country house near Battle and called it, as it is called to-day, after the Canadian Seigneury of Beauport, that extended from Quebec to the Montmorency Falls and through which Montcalm drew these impregnable lines of defence that forced Wolfe to his immortal exploit on the cliffs behind. The old stone Manor House of Beauport on the St. Lawrence, where

Montcalm lived during the siege that decided the destinies of North America, was accidentally burned some forty years since, though the long, straggling village of the Seigneury which lined its historic entrenchments still looks down upon the almost obliterated traces of the ruin. The Sussex Beauport flourishes in mellow middle age, and one may wonder how many Sussex people realize the significance of its name. It is a curious coincidence that it should be within easy sight of the field where Saxon England fell before the hosts of France, just as the older Beauport looks out over that upon which the French power in America, seven centuries later, fell as decidedly before the arms of Britain.

When I first remember Hastings "The Mansion" was occupied by the widow of a Milward who had married Lord Waldegrave, and again widowed was a conspicuous personage and benefactor to the modern town. It was afterwards, I find, leased for many years by the late Coventry Patmore. It is not often, I think, that a moderate-sized Georgian, or rather Queen Anne, house on the fringe of a country town, has such an interesting story. Just above it, in this same little countrified interlude, and abutting on the road, stands an older building which some might think more entitled to distinction as it was the house of that incomparable villain Titus Oates. Just in front again, in the wide space where the Ore and the London roads part, is the market cross, a reminder that in former days this entrance to the old town from the country served that purpose. So much for Old Hastings in the literal sense of the word. Enough, I trust, to at least awaken some interest in the visitor to the great watering-place beyond it. As for that minute fraction of residents endowed with a feeling for the past, this brief sketch is neither here nor there. They have ample material at hand on which to satisfy their worthy craving. But to them and to any of us who know the town, there is another side to the appeal it makes, and this is in its beginnings as a watering-place.

There is no romance whatever in the spectacle of modern Hastings. Anything more rectangular and conventional than its far-extended front, or more uninteresting than the wilderness of streets and terraces that cover the hills behind could not be imagined. But then what would you have? A watering-place for sixty thousand people is not built to order by a philanthropic multi-millionaire with a staff of inspired architects! It grows under the hand of three or four generations of miscellaneous persons who have got to see their five

THE BEACH, OLD HASTINGS.

per cent. at least and to keep out wind and weather. The fancy town which the critic or the idealist, I presume, has vaguely in mind when condemning wholesale the sea-front of Hastings and other places would probably pay nothing per cent. and therefore never be built, or if it were might conceivably crumble away under the lashing storms that hit Hastings in the eye. Eastbourne was in this aesthetic sense fortunate, and as the property of a wealthy duke was laid out in rather lavish if handsome style. It is an admirable place of residence for persons who pay super-tax, speaking broadly, or for the proprietors of flourishing schools. But the less affluent have to pay for a cramped little house and a cat-run a rent which at Hastings or Bexhill would house them handsomely with possibly a garden to boot. The tall substantial white houses, of the Late Georgian and Early Victorian period with sensible windows, if kept well painted, are surely the least inharmonious as well as the most cheerful type to face an English sea. The red brick or terra-cotta contraptions, or worse still the pseudo " old-English " villas with their plaster and timber gables, are absurd-looking things where salt water is flying at point blank. Depressing looking specimens of all these latter types have crowded westward from the plain white fronts of Old St. Leonards, which came to an abrupt end in 1870 with The Marina, as I have the best of reasons for remembering. A country road led from there to Bexhill, then a pretty little village clustering round its fine old church, without a thought of summer visitors, and divided from the sea by a mile of pasture land on which indeed the present town of 16,000 souls has since been built.

History repeats itself in strange fashion. In the Napoleonic Wars, upon its then marshy shore, the Hanoverians of the German legion had their main quarters, alongside of the Merioneth Militia whom the German C.O. writes that he found helpful and hospitable when he arrived with his regiment from the Peninsular—a strange blend to read of nowadays! But the Baron Ompteda was a German of the old type, a colonel in that small Hanoverian army, " left in the air " by the poltroonery of the then rulers of Prussia before the assaults of the French Republic, and incorporated wholesale into the British army. His autobiography is of extraordinary interest and leaves no doubt whatever as to his admirable qualities of head and heart.

But it is here at Bexhill, a mere interlude of course in his otherwise stirring experiences, that the Baron finds opportunity for indulging in that particular form of sentiment always associated in times past with his nation. Finding his hut damp and the mess-table boring, he retires to quarters in a farmhouse on the ridge above, and life at once becomes an idyll. The fair-haired, blue-eyed daughter tripping with the milk pail, the only less ornamental but virtuous and industrious mother, the sturdy honest farmer himself, not being cringing peasants like his own German tenantry, puzzle him by their frank and independent demeanour as much as by their kindly solicitude for his welfare. He writes verses at the open window on skylarks, milkmaids and shepherds, oblivious for the nonce to soldiering, politics and the woes of his country, which as head of one of its leading families were an always rankling memory.

St. Leonards, it may be here noted, was not a mere extension of the modern Hastings. It was commenced independently while the other also was in the making, and for a time there was a considerable gap between them. But they ultimately grew together and were long since united corporately. In 1869 the long sea front of Hastings-St. Leonards from the Albert Memorial was virtually what it is to-day, if memory serves me, which I think it does, except that there were no piers, while Bo-peep was of course in embryo. I can say this much out of my own recollection, having spent just half that same year there. An archway, however, spanned the Parade just west of Warrior Square, then recently built, which had marked the limit of St. Leonards. If there is no romance in such comparatively recent brick-and-mortar doings, the first expansion of a little old sea-side fishing town into a fashionable resort is by no means devoid of the flavour, associated as is that of Hastings with Regency waistcoats, coats and hats with the tea drinkings, card parties, assemblies, post chaises and stage coaches of the expiring Georgian period. The company, too, was more or less " select," in inverse ratio to the unostentatious quarters they were content to put up with.

There is surely some pathos in the now shabby and always

modest terraces which crept timorously westward from Old Hastings. They arose in the early years of the century for the accommodation of " the nobility and gentry from London and elsewhere " who were being attracted to what was then a really beautiful little place of less than 4,000 souls. The polite visitor of to-day rarely even sets eyes on these rather sad-looking purlieus, haunts and harbourages about Pelham Place and East Parade, where cravated Georgian exquisites ogled and strutted, and be-feathered, pellissed maidens simpered and sighed, or in more serious moments foregathered in the subscription rooms and circulating library to discuss the news of the day or the last popular novel. But some of these people were more adventurous, exploring the country round on foot or horseback or wheels, and had an infinite advantage in this respect over the modern visitor who is caged in by miles of buildings, and a belt of country beyond them disfigured by their influence. All around the little town was then virgin hill and woody valley. The whole of St. Leonards in 1828, when it was purchased of the Eversfield family by Mr. Burton, the founder of the place, was an untouched Arcadia. The busy heart of modern Hastings, around the Albert Clock Tower, was vacant ground. Robertson Street, now the main business thoroughfare, was a Rope-walk, " White Rock," since living memory covered by quite stately terraces on the adjoining sea-front, took its name from a promontory blasted away at their erection. Round its corner the old-time Hastings visitors from the *Marine Hotel*, or the East Parade, begun in 1812, or Pelham Place of rather later date, used to scramble for a view of the virgin shore beyond, the back-lying cliffs and woody valleys that are now covered by New Hastings and St. Leonards. George Street, which conducts most visitors to the old town and seems now almost to belong to it, was being built about the same time.

Mr. Cousins, already alluded to, has recently published a reprint of practically every view that can be found of Hastings and its surroundings at various periods, from the early eighteenth century down to the photographs of recent times, with copious notes thereon. Those who know the place at all and have any sense of the past within them, will assuredly feel the romance, or at any rate the sentiment, or at the worst the interest in the growth of this famous watering-place, so vividly illuminated as it is in the above work. The story of Brighton, which grew out of an obscure hamlet, is a recognized romance of this kind. The appeal of Hastings, the offshoot of an historic and picturesquely seated Cinque-Port should be much stronger, and after all it has some local flavour still and is not, as Brighton, a mere London-by-the-sea. Its climatic attractions have always been in the first place the high hills that shut out the north and east winds, and in the second its high record of winter sunshine. For the last generation or so, Hastings St. Leonards has not been over prosperous. When I first knew it, and for some time later, it was a favourite winter resort of well-to-do people, who rented or owned good houses there, as well as of invalids of more or less the same social type. The Continental resorts, a quick railway service to others in England, and perhaps the trams, have combined virtually to destroy this connexion. The tripper too has helped to displace the class of summer visitor that formerly affected Hastings. But as the world has changed so much, and is now making for a still greater change, such as no one pretends to guess at, it seems idle to waste words here over these things. It is tolerably certain however that there will be thousands of families in the near future who will be compelled by too obvious reasons to forgo their continental rambles and to take their holiday in their own country, winter or summer. Hastings may then perchance get back something of its own.

Troops were camped or quartered at Old Hastings in the Napoleonic Wars, the barracks being at Halton, and the Duke of Wellington himself was in command here for some time. Reading parties, too, from the Universities came to Hastings over a century ago. In my grandfather's journal, I find that in the Long Vacation of 1811 he was one of a party of Cambridge undergraduates reading with a Tutor for the coming Tripos. The sequel may be worth quoting merely as an apt illustration of the trials of travel in those " good old coaching days." For the said journal relates that its owner had been playing in a cricket match on " the Hill," and on returning round a message calling him home to Suffolk at once, to the deathbed, as it turned out, of a relative, and he just managed to secure an outside seat on the London coach that night. It poured with rain the whole way up and soaked him to the skin, but tired with his day's cricket the diarist slept through it all ! There was no time to change his dripping garments in London, as the Bury coach left immediately, and he spent another wet day on the outside. Brain fever and a consequently disappointing place in the Tripos were the results. He lived, however, sound in mind and body, till his hundredth year, and near the end of the last century could talk about the long period of the Napoleonic Wars and the many scares on the east and south coasts as if it were yesterday. I have passed lightly over the earlier story of Old Hastings, partly because it has been dealt with at great length in easily accessible volumes, which is not the case with the other towns and districts we are here concerned with, and partly because it resembles in so many respects that of its sister Ports of Rye and Winchelsea.

CHAPTER THE SIXTH

Hastings to Brede and Northiam

TILL the introduction of electric or petrol driven locomotion, getting out of Hastings into the country behind was, and by any other method still is, a formidable business. A mile or two of stiffish climb through the traffic of uninteresting streets would be more than enough to damp the ardour

TILLINGHAM VALLEY, FROM RYE.

of even a reasonably enterprising visitor. The road to Winchelsea and Rye, which we abandoned at the former place for the Marsh and the cliffs, labours out as easily as any, perhaps, by way of the old town and Ore. A large and rather residential suburb at the end of a tram line now represents what I can myself remember as a country village with an ancient church, long supplanted, and now a melancholy ruin amid a probably over-built outpost of Hastings. Once free of Ore, however, and so over the great hump of Fairlight down, you are in a country that bears no sign of being within a hundred miles of this or any other great watering-place. In no other direction is every trace of the sprawling west-Sussex metropolis so absolutely wiped out. It is a rough-and-tumble country too, much of it, where one always seems to be going against the grain, which fact together with its abounding woodlands all make for an out-of-the-world charm that has been lost to so much of Sussex by its very popularity as a residential county.

In pre-Macadam days, locomotion over its steep clay roads and lanes must have been laborious to a degree, though surface trouble of such kind as one's forefathers put up with complacently is a thing not merely of the long past but inconceivable to the modern. The pitches on the cross roads are still betimes not far removed from the perpendicular. Guestling, Westfield, Pett, Icklesham, Brede, Udimore and many other delectable villages, with their generally fine old churches, lie in the lap of this hinterland of the Marsh, as one may aptly call it. Indeed, long horns of Romney Marsh run far into it, in the shape of the valleys of the Brede and Tillingham, till the broad flat meadows narrow to a point and the sluggish banked-in stream loses itself in woods or hopfields as a prattling brook.

Guestling is the first point on the Winchelsea Road which there skirts the park of Broomham, a plain but satisfactory-looking stone house of the Early Georgian period, possibly a reconstruction of an older one. For it is the property of a branch of the Ashburnham family, which has owned it since the beginning of the sixteenth century, perhaps longer. For most English families this would be accounted a rather remarkable continuity of ownership, particularly in a part of England where contrary to the accepted shibboleths of a singularly ungenealogical public, Manors have been repeatedly changing hands ever since the Reformation. But the Ashburnhams have been landowners in these parts since pre-Norman times, as more particularly represented by the Earls of Ashburnham at the seat and village of that name to the west of Battle. Even that eminent antiquary, Mr. Horace Round, who has driven a coach and four through the claims of so many so-called Saxon families, has had nothing to say here. Following *Horsfield*, the Broomham branch seem to have broken off from the main stem, *temp.* Henry the Third, and held on here with the same tenacity as their kinsmen have occupied Ashburnham. Good old Fuller alludes to them as "a family of stupendous antiquity."

The Saxon Ashburnham was Constable of Dover when William landed. One account relates that he defended it against the Conqueror and was beheaded with two of his sons for his pains, while another represents him as falling in the Battle of Hastings. William overlooked their nationality and left them in quiet possession of their lands. But for a Saxon this meant, of course, obscurity, which continued for about three hundred years, till they lifted their heads up as sheriffs and knights of the shire. The Ashburnhams (of that ilk, at any rate) had a narrow shave of snuffing out altogether in 1626, for the worthy Knight, Sir John, who then represented them was of " such good nature and frank disposition towards his friends " as his monument in Ashburnham church tactfully phrases it, that he had to sell everything to the last acre, leaving, as the same inscription informs us, his wife and six children totally unprovided for. A stroke of fortune, however, such as rarely occurs in such cases, came to save the situation, when it must have seemed irreparably lost. For the property had already changed hands twice when one of the above-mentioned orphans, having in the meantime grown to man's estate, married an heiress, who sold her own patrimony and re-purchased most of the family estate.

It was this same gentleman, John Ashburnham, who is

probably best known of all to history as Groom of the Chamber and friend of Charles the First, and companion of his flight to the Scots and later from Hampton Court to the Isle of Wight. "No man in England," says Clarendon, "was so trusted by Charles." It was he who with Sir John Berkeley crossed over first to the Island, interviewed Hammond the Governor, and brought him over to the King, then hiding at Titchfield, much to Charles' dismay and his visitor's embarrassment. "Why, Jack, thou hast undone me!" cried the King. Ashburnham in passionate tears offered to go downstairs and shoot Hammond on the spot if his master thought that the crisis demanded it. We all know how the incident ended in Carisbrooke Castle, as regards the foredoomed King. It was a bungled business altogether, and led to much after-recrimination between the King's two friends, to gossip and scandal generally, though it was purely an error of judgment on Ashburnham's part. John Ashburnham was also with Charles on the scaffold, and received his master's watch as a parting gift, and furthermore he preserved the shirt and silk drawers which the King wore at his execution, and the sheet which was thrown over his dead body, all still retained as relics in the family. John Ashburnham was later on shut up in the Tower by Cromwell, and only released at the Protector's death. Clarendon gives the whole story at great length with a touch of bias against Ashburnham.

The Broomham branch became baronets in Charles the Second's time, and in the eighteenth century produced a Bishop of Chichester, who enjoyed that position for nearly half a century, and incidentally denounced smuggling from the pulpit with becoming vigour. This might well be expected of a moralist reared at Guestling, which must have been a perfect hotbed of free-traders. A genuine pre-Conquest family is, like a genuine Saxon church, such an uncommonly rare thing outside the pages of lady novelists, that no excuse, I trust, is needed for these few references, even though Ashburnham itself is out of our beat. The Broomham Ashburnhams have a vault in Guestling Church, which last is architecturally typical of the district though a recent replacement of an older one destroyed by fire. It is most beautifully situated on a ledge beneath the woods of the park, with a view from the well-ordered churchyard over a luxuriant foreground to the spire of Pett Church on the crest of a neighbouring hill, and to the great heights of Fairlight beyond; a view that rivals the famous one from Brede, while the picturesque buildings of an adjoining homestead add no little to the charm of the spot itself. Whence the name of Guestling nobody seems to know, for hereabouts it signifies, of course, The Brotherhood of the Cinque-Ports, and there is no record of such meetings ever having taken place here. It is quite a climb back on a hot day up the long steep lane to the high road from Guestling Church, and whether its worshippers come from above or below, the short-winded among them will have one laborious journey at any rate to their credit. A couple of miles eastward, and in sight of Icklesham, it will become evident enough from the wide views that open to the right and left, that we are on that broad ridge lying between Pett Marsh and the Brede valley, which carries Winchelsea on its western point. Indeed the exquisite view of Rye, some five miles distant, from Icklesham churchyard, framed as it here is between the foliage of neighbouring elms, would give, I imagine, another surprise to many who thought they had seen the old town from every possible angle on marsh or hill.

Icklesham is a fair-sized village scattering itself along the roadside and drawing more closely together as it terminates in its fine old Norman church. Architecturally it is the least engaging of all the villages in these parts, though it might pass well enough in an average country-side. Iham, or Igham, it will be remembered was the parish and Manor from which Winchelsea was more or less sliced off by Edward the First. The qualification is necessary, as it may also be recollected that the said town remained within the Manor, and consequently its Court Hall was the old Manor Court till very late times. Just before the Conquest Icklesham itself was hopefully launched as a "new burgh" of sixty-four burgesses with Hastings tributary to it. Probably the Norman Abbot of Fécamp upset the lop-sided arrangement when the Confessor made him a present of all this country. A curious mix-up still remains as a consequence of so much history having been made in this corner. For example, the few hundred fisher-folk of Rye harbour at the mouth of the Rother find themselves ratepayers, to Icklesham, seven miles away, which most of them have never even seen, while the possibly unsuspecting Ryer who erects a bathing hut on the sand dunes away beyond Camber and the Rother mouth at once comes under the fire of the rate collector of distant Winchelsea. In the eighteenth century the Manor of Icklesham, a very large one, produced about £5 a year in direct revenue, one tenant contributed a pound of cummin seed, another fourpence and three ounces of pepper, another seven herrings and three ounces of pepper, to sprinkle on the herrings, no doubt!

It may seem almost insulting to remind the reader that a Manor is not the freehold estate of its lord, who may own the whole or part of it in his quite other capacity of Squire, or its equivalent. But I am quite sure there are thousands of otherwise intelligent souls in cities who suffer under this delusion, for it crops up in print again and again. Now there lies buried in Icklesham Church a former Lord of the Manor, who in the late eighteenth century took the Government contract for supplying Canada with flour, a proceeding that in these days may well make us rub our eyes! But the period was that of the American Revolutionary War. A British army was quartered in Montreal and Quebec. Starving Loyalist refugees were already crowding into the country from the revolted colonies, and the French Canadian peasant was then quite incapable of raising much more than would suffice for himself.

Hence this apparently strange freak in the export trade. The heir to the Manorial honours and the estate, however, must have had sore reason to regret this dubious enterprise, for when his father died his account with the Government was so much on the wrong side that his 1,200 acres in Icklesham, including New Place, the Manor House just below the church, and his estates elsewhere, when they were brought to the hammer failed to make good the deficit! So *exit* after a nine years' tenure one Lord of the Manor of Icklesham.

New Place had been built by the Finches, for long Lords of the Manor in the seventeenth century, out of the materials of Old Place, their former abode. After its unfortunate connexion with the victualling of the equally unfortunate Burgoyne's army in America, it came into the hands of the Cooper family, which produced the well-known Sussex antiquary and historian of Winchelsea. Icklesham Church, dedicated to the sailors' hope, St. Nicholas, is both an interesting and spacious building and its site is well adapted for the display of its qualities. The situation of its massive, rather squat Norman tower, is unconventional, being near the middle of the north front. Both nave and chancel have three aisles, the nave with its aisles being under one roof, while the chancel and its chapels, according to prevalent local custom, each carry their own, of the usual steep-gabled pattern. The Norman arcade of three bays on either side, which divides the nave from its aisles, is very perfect, while the decoration of the capitals, though not profuse as regards detail, is quite unusual in these parts. The south aisle of the nave is Norman too, but the north aisle belongs to the later period of the chancel. Both open into the latter with Norman arches. But in the case of the north aisle the tower is possibly responsible as the tower-space here intervenes and has round-headed arches on all four sides, that on the outer side consisting of a Norman doorway with zigzag mouldings. The small north chapel of the chancel contains three lancet windows and an arcade along its north wall of pointed arches springing from graceful shafts with decorative and apparently late Norman capitals. A very similar arcade traverses the longer wall of the south chapel which is lighted by early decorated windows. Early English arches divide the chapels from the High Chancel which contains an east window of the more netlike lavish tracery of the later decorated style, known to the profession, I believe, as " reticulated." The tower-space is vaulted, while externally the many roundheaded windows proclaim its period with an emphasis not always so pronounced in Norman towers.

Looking northward from this Icklesham and Winchelsea ridge across the level valley of the Brede, an arm in effect of Romney Marsh and of Winchelsea harbour in Norman times, the village of Udimore some two miles distant can be seen straggling vaguely along the crest of the opposing hill. It can be readily reached by crossing these Brede levels, at Snailham for choice, where there is a regular passage both over the railroad (Hastings to Rye and Ashford) and river. Casual wandering about Romney Marsh and its tributaries, even when the floods are not out, as in wet seasons they more frequently are here than in the great Marsh itself, is apt to be disconcerting, unless time is of no object. The deep sunk ditches which drain the levels are only negotiable at certain points, not always visible at a distance, and unless you know these, your wayward course, if marked afterwards by chart, would be apt to resemble the bewildered trail of a barometer needle in, let us say, the period of the Equinox. This does not matter a bit if you are merely out to enjoy the Marsh, with its human silence, its clamour of birds and sheep, its whispering reeds, but if making for a point a recognized track is generally the best. There is a useful motor train halt at Snailham for walkers from Hastings or Rye, whence the road, after crossing the river trails up the steep green hill to Udimore Church, which stands in the fields a little apart from the village. Before this the pilgrim will no doubt have looked backwards from the brow of the hill over the Brede valley and noted incidentally against the sky-line the two conspicuous windmills of Icklesham and Winchelsea respectively, for windmills even in this country are getting scarce.

He might also recall in fancy the days when the sea rolled over here, and when Edward I. staying at Udimore Court House by the church, with his friend de Etchingham, used to go backwards and forwards by water to see how the building of Winchelsea was going on ; or again that memorable night, fifty years later, when the causeway had been made over the shrinking waters and Edward the Third with his warriors galloped up here to report their great sea victory to the ladies and celebrate it in the fashion related in a former chapter. The old Court House by the church has gone, though some of the outbuildings and the pool with its legend remain. Fortunately our artist has a sketch she made of it before its removal. For it was noised abroad that it was taken wholesale to America to rise again in the suburbs of Chicago, but I cannot vouch for such an astounding transmigration of a Sussex Manor House. A licence to crenelate the Court Lodge was granted by Edward the Fourth to John Etrington, treasurer of his household. The tree-shaded pool near the farmyard and just without the churchyard gate, though of fair size would frankly, I fear, suggest the domestic duck and nothing more to the casual eye. But there is an ancient legend appertaining thereto calculated to strain the credulity of the most sympathetic ear.

The church, it seems, was begun upon the other side of the pond, but the work done during the day was mysteriously transferred every night to the present site. Whereupon the parishioners set watch and in due course became aware of a great rustling of wings and voices calling *Over the mere! Over the mere!* So interpreting the omen as the divine disapproval of their choice of site, they shifted the materials across the pond, after which all supernatural manifestations ceased. A dozen such legends concerning the shifting of church sites in various parts of England come back to my mind, though the active agency is generally that of his Satanic Majesty, who takes a practical hand in it. Why this particular tradition should be so common is hard to say. It seems to lack the *raison d'être* that after all lies at the root of most superstitions of the kind. One or two instances would be unremarkable ; but why all over the country ? Horsfield's derivation of Udimore, pronounced Uddimore by the way, as *cau-de-mer* seems the most

KNELLSTONE: BACK VIEW.

convincing, since the estuary may have terminated for a long time at this point in the valley. Odimer seems to have been the usual spelling in the Middle Ages, though spelling was of course capricious till almost the other day, and has no value except as a clue to old pronunciations. When some ingenuous wight claims the lack of an 'e' or an extra 'l' as the particular and immemorial distinction of his family, one longs to tell him how entertained his great-great-great-grandfather, who probably spelt his name in two or three different ways in the same letter, would be at the hearing!

The last occupying proprietor of the Old Court House died in 1690, to wit Thomas Broomfield. He was also Lord of the Manor, and his tombstone inscribed to that effect may be seen in the aisle of St. Clement's Church, Hastings. It passed from the Etchinghams in the fifteenth century, and John Etrington was owner in 1478, getting a royal licence to fortify the house and to form a park in the same year. For a century at least, previous to its removal, it had been merely tenements for farm labourers. The church is a moderate sized and rugged old early-English building, consisting of tower, nave and chancel, the latter containing both in its south-east and north walls the old lancet windows. Three pointed arches with curious floreated capitals extending along the south wall of the nave tell of a vanished south aisle. The porch within the middle arch apparently included part of the old aisle ; the other two arches contain a trefoil headed window, of two and three lights respectively. There are a good many gravestones with inscribed plates in the chancel and beneath the chancel steps. Burdetts, with their arms engraved, of the early seventeenth century account for two or three of these. Woodhams, also gentry of but recent disappearance after centuries in the parish, are much in evidence both within and without the church. Freebodys too abound. A brass plate near the pulpit registers the death of one born in the fifteenth century, while a tomb in the churchyard records the death of " the last of them (1765) to enjoy the estate of Knellstone," which as appears by authentic records was in the possession of the family for nearly four hundred years. Knellstone is still a farm near the Rye road, and a most interesting old house. The Jordans of Jordan (another old homestead) had given out before that. All of these people seem to have been *armigers* and *generosi*, not yeomen.

So vanish by the dozen along the later pages of social history these small squires of a former day in almost every English county. Where now are their legion of descendants ? Any-

INTERIOR, KNELLSTONE.

where and everywhere beyond a doubt, from day labourers to Archbishops ; nobody cares much, that is quite certain. English folk have slight interest in genealogy unless it is well endowed, and even then they take much of it on trust, including sometimes their own, which perhaps is just as well. For in a country like ours where most old families, except the more conspicuous historic houses, have been more or less mixed up with trade from their Tudor or Jacobean origin, and indeed very often spring from it, and still more where the female side by polite fiction is not reckoned as affecting the quality of a breed or the credit of a pedigree, it is difficult to press things to their logical conclusion.

No wonder foreigners are bewildered by our inconsistencies, and with their rigid laws of caste give it up as a hopeless problem. We can afford to leave them in their quite justifiable fogginess. Our failure to recognize, or perhaps even understand, their ideal has in truth been the country's salvation and saved no doubt much misery and bloodshed, and tended vastly to union and strength. If it does involve a good deal of makebelieve, that is a mere trifle. The hardy fiction, for instance, that trade as a genteel occupation is a comparatively recent innovation is the most amazing of all. Yet it is quite common ! Till about the time of George the Second, nearly all younger sons went into trade or into occupations of like grade, sometimes in their own neighbourhood, sometimes in London, if they were lucky enough to have connexions there. There was neither Army nor Navy nor Civil Service to speak of. The Bar was too expensive for most, the Church then meant anything or nothing. Most pedigrees in most English counties, outside a few great houses, bristle as regards younger sons' occupations and daughters' marriages, with goldsmiths, grocers, vintners, woolstaplers, brewers, maltsters, ship owners, millers, river-freighters, revenue officers, tenant farmers, parsons, chirurgeons and attorneys ; though we must not forget the fairly frequent emigrant and occasional soldier of

Knellstone, from the Front.

HASTINGS TO BREDE AND NORTHIAM

fortune on the Continent, which last career the superfluous Scotsman, who had few openings at home, so much more affected.

These were the ordinary careers of the country gentleman's younger son, whose name was legion. There was no other choice, even had such been present in their minds. With the Georges, speaking broadly, our world-wide wars and the vast increase in the country's wealth, came standing armies and navies, Government offices and a sort of echo of the Continental ideas regarding trade and gentility; absolutely logical, if detrimental in old France, Italy, Holland or Germany, but exotic and absurd in a country always abounding in what, by a Continental standard, were *novi homines* and but two, three or four generations removed from the woolstapler or the acquisitive lawyer. Hitherto there seems to have been no shamefacedness whatever about this or that occupation: far less in

BOX MANGLE KNELLSTONE.

fact than there would be in these so-called democratic days. The new idea so coincided with the Hanoverian dynasty that though the ground was perhaps getting ripe for it, it lies under the suspicion with most people who have interested themselves in such things of being partly "German-made." It was at any rate quite alien to English tradition. It is not surprising then that out of this mix-up there developed in the eighteenth century that particular form of national weakness which Thackeray relished so keenly. Snobbery, however, is much better than bloody revolutions or a military oligarchy, and furthermore has been a priceless boon to literature and to the humorist.

Udimore, like its neighbours, straggles in leisurely fashion along its high ridge between the Brede and Tillingham valleys. Half-timbered, weather-boarded, brick, or stone cottages, with roofs as varied, follow one another at easy distances in pleasant gardens and orchards. An old farmstead blinking at the road through its screen of foliage, above which a row of oast-houses display their quaint tops, here breaks the line, or there, a snug red brick Georgian house in many-acred grounds gives a finish to the picture. But the conspicuous note of Udimore is, or rather was, its windmill. Perched high above the road at the topmost point of the village, when its sails were whirling and groaning in a high wind against a wild sky, one trembled in passing for the people of Udimore who lay upon the leeward side, for with such a precarious grip did the quivering body of the huge mill seem to cling to its exalted perch! The last time I passed this way I found that the sails had gone, and sought information of the village oracle. "Yes, sir, the mill has stopped working." "How is that?" said I. "Well, sir, people had begun to think it was not safe." I should think they had! So another ancient windmill and a far-reaching landmark has vanished. It will not, I fear, be secured and pensioned off in the interest of the picturesque like that of Winchelsea when it went out of business a few years ago.

It is interesting to glance through the names of the landholders, great and small, of such villages as Udimore, Icklesham and Pett in the fourteenth century. About forty are recorded in Udimore alone. Trade names like *Cooper, Carpenter, Fletcher, Hogeman, Ferrier, Herde,* and suchlike are naturally prevalent. But *Thonder*, which occurs in more than one list, is curious; more than curious too is *Agatha Robinhood*, of Pett! A dozen or so female proprietors are all *Agneses, Agathas,* and *Alices.* The site of their dwelling-place distinguished many persons. A two-roomed wattle-and-daub frame house by a hazel copse or under a clay bank gives a surname to future generations, to bishops perhaps, to millionaires or what not : Robert-*atte-wood* and Simon-*atte-clyffe* for example.

The view northward from the long ridge of Udimore is nearly always spacious, ranging over the Tillingham valley, another narrow horn of Romney Marsh, to the parallel ridge or plateau, which carries the villages of Peasemarsh, partly visible among the distant woods to the eastward, and Beckley, from here invisible. A further wave of hills beyond mark the Isle of Oxney, crowned by the village of Wittersham, rising high above the Rother levels and the Kent boundary. Westward towards Brede, four miles from Udimore, is a country of far-spreading oak woods—the despair of fox hunters—of hazel copses, of grass and arable, of hopfields, of homesteads nearly always good to look upon, with their flanking oasthouses. A cosy south-country landscape of the very best south-country type. Like all the rest, it needs sunshine to bring out the colouring, to light the radiant patchwork of field and wood, of ruddy wall and rich tinted roof. Water, to be sure, it sadly lacks, like all south-eastern England. Some landscape gathers the charm of mystery from elemental gloom. Mountains and moorland, even downland, rise to such occasions. Salisbury Plain in former days had great qualities even in pouring rain. Romney Marsh too responds in its own weird way to sombre skies. But this inland country, charming as it is, fails you utterly in dark weather, and succumbs to unrelieved depression of aspect. It holds no mysteries, nor any bold outlines, no wild tracts, no sounding waters, nothing in short of solitude anywhere, though much of it is delightfully secluded, which is quite another thing.

Brede, four miles west of Udimore and about eight miles from Rye, lies on the southern end of the ridge looking over the Brede valley towards Guestling, Westfield and Fairlight. A turn off the main ridge road (which goes eventually to Battle) at Broadoak, a well-known cross-roads with an inn, leads quickly down to it. And Brede is a village of note, partly for old manorial reasons, which most readers will no doubt be satisfied to take on trust, and partly for its fine church and lovely situation. The village too is more concentrated than most of its neighbours, which sets off its old-fashioned character to advantage. It lies more or less contiguous to the leafy precincts of its imposing church, which adds to the general effect of rural peace and seclusion that pervades it. And if there is anything in being off the main road in this quiet corner of Sussex, Brede is all that. A mile away too is Brede Place, a notable instance of a late fifteenth-century manor house of the first rank. Built of stone, it was begun by Sir Thomas Oxenbridge and apparently finished by Sir Goddard, while some brick additions were made in Elizabeth's time.

Its secluded position, low upon the slope of a well-wooded valley, opening out into the broader one of the Brede River, gives the rather grim old house that sense of isolation which so well becomes it. But the site is one of no little beauty and the view from the terrace, both of foreground and distance, is quite charming. A good deal of repair and restoration was done some years ago, as is freely shown in the old prints of the house. The long and rather low body of the main building, with its expanse of hip roof appears unaltered, but the frontal projections have obviously been much changed. A contemporary chapel attached to one extremity is an interesting feature, and its gable end forms one of the projections which set the Elizabethan stamp so strongly on the face of the building. Most of the interior is panelled and the original Tudor fireplaces are *in situ*, as well as some of the old doors.

It was known as Forde Place, for fairly obvious reasons, in the days of the Oxenbridges, who had been important people and considerable landowners before they bought this Brede property, being allied with the Etchinghams and the Alards. They obviously sprang from either Beckley or Iden, as there are old homesteads in both parishes bearing their name about three miles apart. The Iden Oxenbridge above the Rother valley is older than Brede Place, and has a strong tradition of being the original cradle of the family, but we shall meet it later on. Sixty years ago Mr. Durrant Cooper hunted up for the Sussex Archaeological Society all there was to know about the Oxenbridges, even to their collaterals who pioneered in the West Indies, or harangued New England Puritans from Boston pulpits. It will be enough, perhaps, here that they occupied Brede Place through the sixteenth century and that some of them lie in their own chantry in the parish church, the one most in evidence being Sir Goddard, a mail-clad effigy upon an altar tomb.

He held many conspicuous offices, and so far as is known was in real life a quite exemplary person. But in legend he lives as nothing less than an ogre and a cannibal. All accounts agree that he polished off a child every night for his supper. A continuation of the legend has it that the children of the county having held a "guestling," as it were, invented a soporific potion from hops and contrived that it should be administered to the destructive monster. Their plan succeeded and their enemy lay stupefied and at their mercy. A big saw was then brought and laid across the middle of the ogre. The infants of East Sussex took one handle and those of West Sussex the other, and getting straightway to work hewed him in two pieces. Sir Goddard, for some equally mysterious reason, was endowed with the proportions of a giant. Brede Place is still quite commonly known among the villagers as "The Giant's House." It is now the residence of Mr. Moreton Frewen, into whose family it passed early in the eighteenth century. For a long time in this same century it was more or less neglected and unoccupied, when its great storage capacities made it a popular resort of the "free traders." Indeed its complete restoration is a matter of quite recent date.

Brede Church, dedicated to St. George, stands conspicuous at the edge of the village, on the brow of the long green hill running down to the Brede valley, and emphasizes its distinction of site by a massive square embattled tower of the Perpendicular period, that for many a mile in many directions is a familiar landmark. The interior contains a nave with north and south aisle, a chancel and a chantry holding the tombs of Oxenbridges, and named after them. The four bays on either side of the nave are pointed, those on the south resting on circular piers and those of the north side on octagonal columns denoting their different periods of construction. Gothic arches lead into the chancel and the tower space respectively, the latter being lighted by an extremely handsome Perpendicular window. A wide semicircular arch connects the High chancel with its south aisle, terminating in profusely floriated capitals. Here is the Oxenbridge chantry, and here too, as, already noted, lies the giant of the fable upon his altar tomb, his hands clasped, his head upon a helmet and his feet upon a lion. Upon the same side is a canopied and recessed altar tomb bereft of any sign to which Oxenbridge it was dedicated. There is a rather notewothy east window, too, of three headed lights, surmounted by tracery of the "flowing" type rather rare in England, the extremities of the dripstone bearing shields displaying the arms of the Oxenbridges and their connexions. A quaint seventeenth-century alms-box is set up near the south door, and a reputed cradle of Dean Swift is on show—why here I do not know, as there is no connexion whatever. Gooderich-on-Wye holds the Dean's own tributes to his famous grandfather the "fighting parson" of that parish in the Civil War.

The large churchyard at Brede is admirably cared for, and further embellished with well-tended flowers and shrubs. On three sides are screens of foliage opening out charming glimpses of mellow roof and wall, while on the south, framed between the trunks and arching boughs of some larger trees is a most lovely view over the broken wooded country of Guestling, Pett, and Westfield parishes, to the high green ridge of Fairlight. Judging by those who lie commemorated here, the

HASTINGS TO BREDE AND NORTHIAM

parish is rich in surnames one does not meet with every day, though evidently of familiar local hearing. Adds, Apps, Decks, Jee, Honis, and Tuppenny may be cited as examples. This was a strong Puritan district, and I have no doubt that the earlier registers of Brede Church would show a fine assortment of those outlandish polysyllabic Jewish names, that among the godly displaced the good old English Edwards, Alices and Henrys. A Churchman writing to a friend from these parts in the seventeenth century declares that the Puritan laymen are even more troublesome than the preachers.

Furnaces flourished in Brede parish in olden days, before the coal of the north ousted Sussex iron and left its much tormented forests to the mild demand for hop-poles and suchlike. Sackvilles, Brownes, Lennardes and others smelted here till 1766, making cannon among other things, which were shipped from Rye. Leland has a note referring to Brede which I quote, not for its intrinsic interest here, which is nil, but for the unconscious humour of style and spelling and delightful disregard for local dignity that pervades the whole immortal work of the earliest Tudor itinerist. "Lale, a Naunchman, hath married the heire-several of the elder House of the Oxenbridges of Southsex, by whom he shall have £140 lands by Zere, Turwith was in court and is sun and heire to old Turwhites sonne in Lincolnshire." As a last word on Brede, it may be noted that Doleham Halt, on the S.E. railway, between Rye and Hastings, gives ready access to the village and neighbourhood. The winding road from Brede to Northiam (about five miles) climbs up and down through a diversified and sequestered region of wood, copse and hop-garden, of small irregular fields of grass or tillage and twisting hedgerows, that belong to the earlier enclosed parts of England, and to the varied but generally rather moderate acreage of its farms. This makes, at any rate, for charm of foreground, while the few homesteads in evidence upon this secluded road are of the most engaging old West-Sussex type. It crosses too the head waters of the Tillingham River, here reduced to a diminutive trout stream, babbling its brushy course through the hollows of wood and field.

A few years ago there was almost a panic among hop-growers from the severity of foreign, especially Californian, competition. Many gardens, not merely in Kent and Sussex, but · in Worcester and Herefordshire, were grubbed up. Whether our recent Governments were right in the contempt with which they treated agriculture it is not for me to say, though I know what I think and have thought for about thirty years. Nemesis at any rate has overtaken them—and all of us unfortunately! The miserable prices paid through much of the 'eighties and 'nineties by a wealthy and luxurious country for most of its farm produce were almost a scandal. Yet the industrials and the doctrinaires squealed at the bare mention of a tax that might raise wheat to 40s. and give a living profit to grain growing. Land went out of cultivation, English hops temporarily recovered through a world failure, if memory serves me, two or three years before the war. Every one knows that they are more or less of a gamble. The profit and loss is out of all proportion to the figures of ordinary farming. The holder of a three hundred acre farm at 25s. an acre, which by ordinary agriculture and the usual calculation of " thirds " would yield a nett income of three hundred and odd pounds to a tenant, may in a big hop year nett him as many thousands, and occasionally more. The losses in bad years are in proportion. Acreage and rent as a matter of fact are almost unimportant features in regard to hops, which cover a relatively small portion of a farm. It is the amount of capital in fertilizers and labour put into them that constitutes the speculation. It has its prototype, after a fashion, in the big potato crops of the great Lothian farmers, just as West-Sussex agriculture outside hops has its antithesis in the big high-rented, prolific Lothian farms.

We have plenty of fanatics among us, numbers of whom in

HASTINGS TO BREDE AND NORTHIAM

normal times over-eat themselves, and still more over-smoke, who would root up all the hopfields in England, and all the vineyards in France, their own particular stimulant from the plantations of Cuba, Turkey or Virginia being of course sacrosanct. The good wholesome old English drink, beer, has never given way in these parts to the insidious poison retailed in many English and nowadays in Scottish taverns, under the name of whisky. Any country innkeeper hereabouts will tell you that they often do not sell a bottle of whisky, or even of gin, in a week. It is interesting to hear the labourer's pint or two of beer inveighed against by gentlemen who inhale into their lungs the smoke of fifteen or twenty cigarettes a day! A leading divine and perfervid temperance orator, known to me and not long dead, was a burning instance of this preposterous inconsistency.

ON THE WAY TO NORTHIAM.

The village of Northiam has on the whole the highest reputation for charm of any with which these pages are concerned.

> O rare Norgem, thou dost far exceed
> Beckley, Peasemarsh, Udimore and Brede.

It has a village green too, an accessory which generally displays to advantage the best that a place has to offer, though the converse, betimes, must needs hold good. This one moreover is on a slope, and shaded in part by large trees, including the decrepit trunk of a once huge oak, beneath which Queen Elizabeth took her dinner on that memorable tour to Rye. The old tree seems in a manner to have enjoyed official recognition, for the Proclamation of the Peace of Utrecht, 1713, which though it gave us Nova Scotia caused so much after trouble, was affixed to it. A living oak beside it is duly reverenced as its offspring. After all, what tree is there that can approach the oak in its appeal to the imagination.

The village is crowned by the parish church, whose stone spire, one I believe of only four ancient ones in all Sussex, marks the site of Northiam from many distant parishes. Nearby the church stands the fine old mansion depicted by our artist, whose Queen Anne exterior conceals, I believe, much of the old sixteenth-century house. There are several quaint old houses of another degree, bordering the village green ; a quite irresistible-looking though not ancient hostelry faces it on another side, while at the west corner are the house and grounds of Brickwall. Miss A. L. Frewen published not long ago an interesting brôchure on Brickwall and Northiam with a record of the house and its former owners. To this I am indebted for all the personal particulars here recorded. Previous to its purchase by Alderman Frewen, Brickwall belonged to the Whites, who, originating in Rye, held the property for nearly two centuries and built the older and more conspicuous part of the present house. This is the only half-timbered mansion upon the scale of a country house in the whole area covered in this book. It is an admirable example, too, as will be gathered from the illustration.

It carries one's thoughts away to the other side of England, and to the black-and-white manor houses sprinkled so thickly along the Marches of Wales and Worcestershire. Marrington, The Ley, Pitchford, Orleton, Wythall, Mere and a dozen others leap to the mind at once. The slight differences too, not only here but in the many half-timbered farmhouses and

HASTINGS TO BREDE AND NORTHIAM

cottages of this part of England from those of the west Midlands and the Marches, are as interesting as they are natural.

BRICKWALL.

The lavish ornamentation, not only of the deeper barge boards but in the fantastic curving of the wall timbers, so frequent in the west, has no counterpart, so far as my own acquaintance goes, in this south-eastern country, nor again have those quaint inscriptions so popular among the builders on both sides of the Welsh Marches. The barge-boards of Brickwall, as one would expect in a house of its class, are decorated, but with overlaid ornamentation. Indeed I do not remember to have seen any open work in these parts.

This gabled front seems to have been added to the older portion of the house, by the Whites in 1617 and 1633, their initials with the latter date being still in evidence. For a long period prior to 1835 the front of the house had been concealed under plaster. It was "stripped" by the late owner, Mr. Thomas Frewen, M.P. for South Leicestershire, who came to live here on his marriage, in 1832. There had been an interlude of non-residence, owing to interests elsewhere, of some seventy years. Besides opening out the front of the house, a great deal was done to beautify and restore it where needed, including the twisted Elizabethan chimneys which make so conspicuously for the general harmony of the exterior. The iron gates fronting the high road are also of the same date. The road in the eighteenth century ran close to the house, a fact only worth noting here for a strangely tragic incident recorded in the above-mentioned family annals. For in 1752 the wife of the then squire of Brickwall caught fire while alone in her bedroom, and her screams were heard by the passengers on the Rye coach passing at the moment, who at once gave the alarm. But it was too late, and the poor lady, whose portrait hangs now in the house, was burned to death. The interior of the house contains much that is interesting, but having in mind the scope of these pages, to say nothing of the journey still before us, a passing notice must suffice.

Queen Elizabeth's shoes, which are preserved in the entrance hall as a relic of her visit to Northiam, must assuredly not be overlooked. She had, I think, more just cause to be vain of her feet than of her plain but imperious face. There are most beautiful plastered ceilings in the drawing-room and over the old oak staircase of seventeenth-century date. But Miss Frewen remarks that the Sir Edward (M.P. for Rye) who was responsible for them rather discounted the obligation by pulling down the timbers at the side and back of the house and substituting the existing bricks. There are many family portraits, and others of more or less historical personages, some of each being the work of famous painters, Reynolds, Kneller, Van Dyke, Lely and Holbein. Among them is a portrait of the virile Prince Henry, whose early death let in Charles the First, and possibly changed the destinies of England. Charles the Second's Duchess of Portland by Lely, and Clarendon's not over filial daughter, Anne Hyde, painted by the same hand, are here, and so too is Henry the Eighth, ever and always, even on the red seal of a charter, unmistakable. Half grocer, half butler and all bully, our Bluebeard friend is always the same puffy-looking egotist, and it is quite an effort to remember that he could jump almost his own height when he was five-and-twenty, and possessed an acute intellect. A brick terrace at the back of the house, facing the gardens, strikes one as a little uncommon. The gardens themselves, with a fish-pond in the foreground, are in admirable keeping with the atmosphere of the house. Yews trimmed in pyramidical or cone shapes line the walks, while the brick wall on two sides is of date about 1700. In the deer park behind, in addition to its natural occupants, are some kangaroos of the wallaby variety. There is something uncanny in seeing these strange exotics leaping over an English pasture on their hind legs. They seem fairly friendly, however, though when one remembers what execution they are said to do with these same hind legs, when out of humour, I admit without blushing to keeping a fence tolerably handy on a recent interview.

The Rectory is near by, and as a building has no particular interest, unless it be for the beautiful outlook towards Fairlight from the back, and the most charming foreground glimpse of Northiam village and church from the front of the house. The long list of Incumbents that have held such parsonages as these since the Reformation, has always, for me at any rate, no little fascination. The English parson is the one feature in the social make-up of England that has no approach to a parallel in any other country upon earth, and one which the foreigner has yet to be born who can understand. Northiam has rather exceptional interest, as the living has not merely been owned, which is nothing, but occupied, which is rare,

CARRIER'S FARM.

by only two families (with a single exception) since the Rev. J. Frewen came here in 1583 and took up his residence in the picturesque half-timbered little house with thatch roof, still standing a few furlongs down the Hastings Road and now known as Carrier's Farm.

It was here that his two successful sons, the Archbishop and the purchaser of Brickwall, were born. The former, though indicating by his rather unusual name " Accepted " (a brother was named Thankful) the Puritan faith of his father the Rector, as a fellow and dignitary at Oxford, imbibed the Oxford tradition, and as an active Loyalist went through the war and the Puritan interregnum, with the fluctuations of fortune inevitable to the occasion. As Bishop of Lichfield his estates were confiscated, but the Restoration brought him back to the higher honour of York, where he died in 1664. With a single exception Frewens were Rectors till the Lord family in 1749 acquired the advowson and produced the needful supply of parsons of their own name to fill the Northiam pulpit up to a quite recent day, when it reverted in effect to the original stock. Five successive Lords covered a hundred and sixty years. It is not often that a detached patron family, to use a convenient expression, are capable of maintaining so prolonged an occupation. Another such instance is familiar to me—in this case a fat country living in the Midlands, which was held by a detached family, if the paradox be admissible, and with the same continuity of occupation for a hundred and eighty years. The succession and patronage in this case came to an unfortunate end in a clerical racing stable over sixty years ago. Some remains of the loose boxes are there yet, converted to more orthodox uses.

But this will never do. For it is not every one who is interested in those lists of incumbents which are nowadays, and very sensibly, displayed on the walls of church porches and vestries. The exterior of Northiam Church has suffered like the interior, though not so acutely, from the hand of recent restorers. For the nave and chancel have been enclosed under one gable roof, which in so large a building gives a length of body out of proportion to the tower, in spite of its stone spire of but moderate altitude. The Frewen Mausoleum, built as a north wing over the family vault, which contains many stone coffins, in 1845, is a handsome example of Perpendicular work surmounted with crocketted pinnacles. The walls displaying a row of carved armorial shields beneath a continuous inscribed band, have mellowed into harmony with the tone of the main building. The interior contains a number of inscribed memorial tablets. In regard to the church itself the base of the tower is accounted the only portion extant of the original

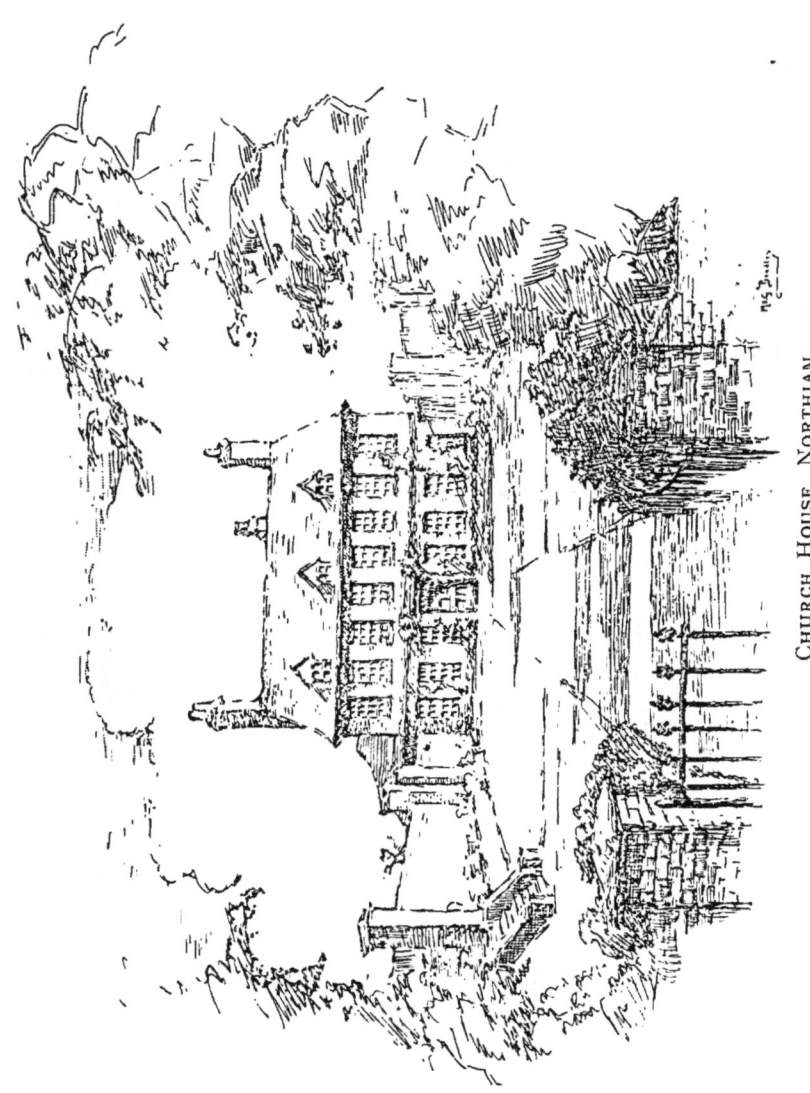

CHURCH HOUSE, NORTHIAM.

Norman building, the remainder with the spire being of various dates up to late Perpendicular. It would have been well if the interior of the church had stopped with the fifteenth century, or at any rate conformed to it. Restorers of the late eighteenth and early nineteenth century have fallen with blighting hand on many parts of the building, which in the main is still Early English and Perpendicular. Some deplorable windows, only too conspicuous in the south chancel, may perhaps be cited as choice examples of the Georgian churchwarden style!

An illustration of the exterior in the eighteenth century, before these and other things were done, gives a good idea of the havoc wrought. Memorial brasses seem to have been freely torn up, but one at least is re-laid, namely that of "Sir Robert Beuford parson 1518." This curious and up-lifting prefix to the clerical office was of course common enough throughout England and Wales. A finely carved seventeenth-century oak table serves as an altar. Among others buried here, are some of the Tufton family, who in the fifteenth and sixteenth centuries owned Tufton (now Northiam Place, in the parish), a notable old house with a chantry in the original church, and land in proportion. They became Earls of Thanet subsequently, and had also connexions with Westminster, one of them being buried in the Abbey. But what will probably touch the reader more nearly, since the back purlieus of Westminster have become residentially fashionable, they gave their name to Tufton Street, one of the best known of its thoroughfares.

It is but a mile from Northiam, northward along the London Road, to the Rother valley, upon the further side of which the little village of Newenden clusters around its rather striking little church, in itself well worth a visit. The river, though navigable for barges for some distance above Newenden is quite small, even at this point, and the flat vale along which it meanders, is but a few hundred yards in width. Here as throughout much of its course it divides Sussex and Kent. Here too as elsewhere the Rother floods its meadows on rather slight provocation. I shall always recall the scene which greeted me on coming down to it from the Northiam ridge one brilliant autumn day after heavy rains. The waters were out all over the little valley below, and were reflecting in the afternoon sunshine with added lustre the azure blue of a wonderful October sky. The surface was everywhere alive with the snow-white forms of hovering or resting seagulls, while patches of radiant sunlit turf exposed here and there above the shallow flood were flecked with the pied wings of restless plovers. The quaint-shaped little church, posed felicitously on its knoll beyond the bridge, with the foliage above, and upon the flanking hills gay in the brief flare of autumn, completed a picture one was fortunate to catch in its all too transient beauty.

Newenden Church lost its chancel, and apparently its tower, two hundred years ago. It consists now of an Early English nave with a narrow north aisle, divided off by three pointed arches. It is not far from square in shape, while a miniature tower stands out from its south-western angle. It contains several Early English windows, a carved and panelled oak pulpit, a very old font, from which that in Rye Church has been copied, and an oak screen, carved with armorial bearings. Now Newenden possesses in its name an unsuspected importance, being no less than Noviadanum " the New town " of the Roman-British period, and this new town replaced an older one a mile away, which disputes with Pevensey the honour of being the site of the famous city of Anderida. It is perhaps only natural for us to take sides with Camden and Selden, and others, followed by Holloway, in his history of Romney Marsh, and rather convincingly supported by Mark Lower, against the more general Pevensey tradition. But about a mile to the eastward of Newenden in the angle formed by the junction of the Exden valley with that of the Rother and on the edge of the first named, stands a conspicuous tumulus, known to the local rustics as " The Mount," and perhaps thirty feet in height. Two or three old trees grow upon it and no road or trail but the single-track railway between Robertsbridge and Tenterden, half a mile away, runs anywhere near it. Very few people but those farming the surrounding land, an occasional sportsman, or a still rarer antiquary, even know of its existence. It is marked in the map as " Castle tolls," the name I believe of the meadow in which it stands.

Near by the mound, which is on the farm of Losenham, is a slightly raised platform and the distinct remains of a vallum about a hundred yards in length. This is the reputed site, upheld by one school of archaeologists, of the fortified Roman British settlement which the Saxons and their chroniclers called Andredceaster, the British Caer Andred, and the Romans Anderida. Furthermore the old name of the parish of Newenden was *Meching*, which Saxon etymologists interpret " The field of the sword." There is no question that in Roman times, and much later, the Rother valley and its tributary channels, like this of Exden, were fiords of the sea. Even to-day though the land has risen, their flats are nine feet below the level of high tide at Rye harbour. Here then were two fiords, of say half a mile in width and probably, judging from the lie of the country, at or near the head of navigation by way of the then half submerged Romney Marsh. A great battle is said to have been fought here, and according to the Saxon chronicler in 490. Hengist had just conquered the Kingdom of Kent, while Cissa and Ella were attacking the British in the great forest of Anderida, in that campaign which resulted in the founding of the South-Saxon kingdom, and " at Andredceaster slew all the inhabitants so that not one Briton was left."

The fugitive Britons from Kent (Newenden stands on the border) seem to have " swarmed like bees " into these works. At this spot within the great forest of Anderida, an attack had been made five years before, but failed. This time it seems to have been delivered by large forces " brought over sea." The ancient accounts of these battles insist on surrounding forests as forming part of the British defence and attack. It seems most improbable that at this date there could have been forests on the wet marsh or water surrounding the Roman works at Pevensey, while the Newenden advocates point out that nothing there favoured a British settlement, nor are there any traces of such, while here the converse is the case. Moreover the Britons had already been driven in from the open coast of Sussex. Gildas, too, is cited by the Pevenseyites, if distinguished archaeologists may be thus irreverently styled, as indicating that Anderida was upon the sea, which is true enough. Newenden was quite sufficiently on the sea for a Breton writer who had probably never even seen the Kentish coast, so we will leave the Newendenites in possession of the field, with the support of the traces of a British town, the mound and the fortifications, which they conjecture to have been raised between the repulse of the invaders in 485, and their overwhelming victory in 490. They further maintain that their Anderida, as evidenced by the *Notitia Imperii* (the Roman Army list) was but a small Roman station and a late one, though a large British settlement, a fact which accounts for that absence of masonry which is one of the assets to the Pevensey theory. At any rate the pilgrim who may peradventure find his way to this sequestered spot on a sunny day and seat himself, as the writer once did, beneath the shade of a gnarled tree on the rabbit-burrowed tumulus, will have every opportunity of reflecting on the matter, with the aid perchance of a pipe, in undisturbed solitude. He can imagine himself, if he feels like it, mounting guard as one of the hundred infantrymen of the second legion who were quartered here (according to the Notitia), just prior to the evacuation, or the much more anxious sentry of an undisciplined British muster, looking out over the broad waters for the pirate prows of the ruthless Saxon.

To-day you may look across over the quiet meadows of the Exden valley, up which these murder-breathing galleys once turned their prows, to the woods upon the summit of the long green slope beyond. These are the woods of Maytham, and just behind them lies the pretty village of Rolvenden and its fine church. At Hole close by lived the Gybbons, or Gibbons, from whom sprang the famous historian; squires there since their ancestor, a clothier, purchased the property in Henry the Eighth's time. About 1700 a young Scotsman, described upon his monument in Rolvenden Church as "of the ancient family of the Monypennys of Pitmillie, in Fife" found his way down here somehow, and married a Gibbon heiress, and purchased Maytham, the male line of Gibbon lapsing some time afterwards. But the Monypennys of Maytham have only recently given way by sale, and oddly enough to another Scotsman, and a late Cabinet Minister, while the plain old house they built there has been removed to make way for a new one. The Monypennys of Pitmillie, however, still hang on to their windswept patrimony near the east coast of Fife. Rolvenden Church is worth a visit, if only for two wonderful family pews, that of Maytham, and another on a scale rarely to be seen in England nowadays. Oddly enough in the kirks of southern Scotland with its quasi-democratic creed, the laird, and sometimes two or three of them, still luxuriate in roomy well-equipped apartments that would make an English High Church rector's hair stand on end.

But returning to our lonely tumulus we at any rate will swear stoutly to its marking the ancient Roman-British town of Anderida and the scene of those sanguinary combats with the murderous Saxons. Pevensey has got William the Conqueror and his invading army all to itself, including a castle and a perpetual stream of tourists, and this should be enough. Here we have a secluded country-side that few even of antiquaries know anything about. The Roman wall-work in Pevensey Castle, instead of a support to its Anderida claims is cited by its opponents as strong evidence against them since the British never fought cooped up behind mortared walls;

nor were there "two waters" at Pevensey, as described by the chroniclers, to say nothing of the lack of forest already touched upon. Thus fortified in our faith, we will go back to Newenden across the fields, noting on our way the old manor house of Losenham on the hill top, not merely for its attractive aspect and position, nor yet for its personal story, as it has changed hands many times, but for the fact that a priory of Carmelite Friars, their first settlement, I believe, in England, stood near the spot for some three hundred years, only to disappear at the Dissolution.

Now Bodiam Castle is right out of our beat, which though of necessity a little wobbly, is designed to move round in a rough semi-circle from Hastings to Rye. But as I have said, there is water transport of sorts from Rye to Newenden, and this continues for four miles westward up the narrowing Rother to Bodiam, and as most persons possessed of any enterprise who come to Rye, or into these parts at all, make a point of seeing Bodiam, it seems only mete and right to say a few words about it. In normal times too a motor boat takes parties up from Rye to Bodiam, some twelve miles, an expedition on a fine summer day that could not fail to please, provided always that the company does also. The hardy oarsman makes the trip betimes, and he can start above the only intervening lock at *The Star* a mile from Rye. Bodiam Castle is a thing of beauty rather than of historic interest. Though it was built in the last years of the fourteenth century it never stood a siege, and I think never saw a shot fired or a lance couched in anger. Like most of the castles in this part of the country it has nothing in common with the war-scarred piles on the Welsh Marches or the Scottish border and some others in less hazardous places that reek of battle, murder, love and legend.

The Wars of the Roses did not touch it, while in those of King and Parliament it was occupied and sleighted without resistance. Like scores of others, Bodiam Castle was built out

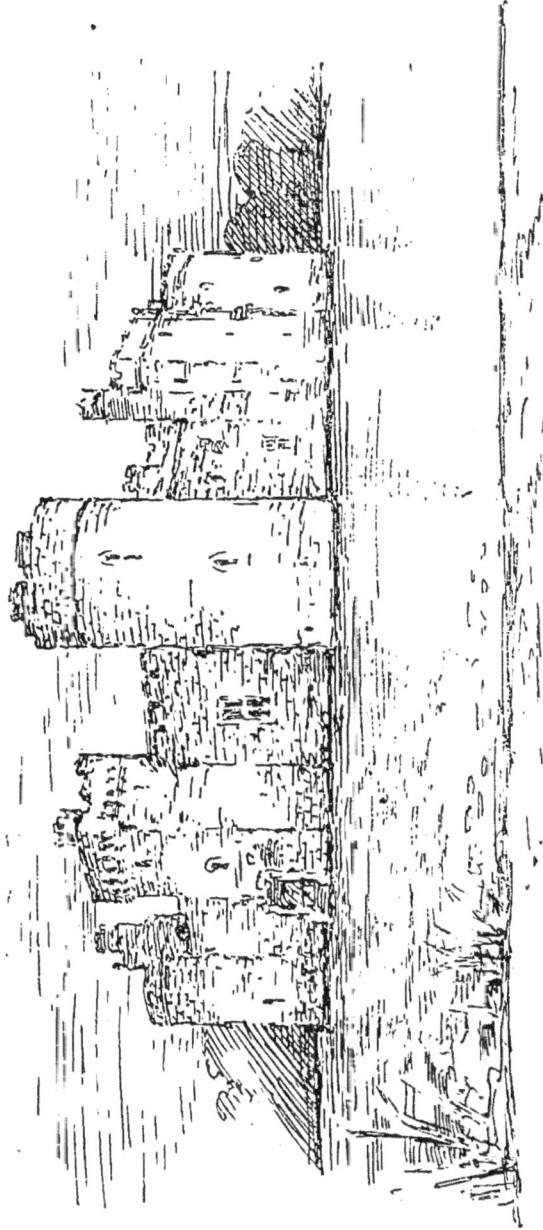

BODIAM CASTLE.

of the plunder and ransom secured from France in the Hundred Years War, not however in this case from the more reputable profits of the Crecy and Poitiers campaign, for Sir Edward Dalyngruge, its builder, was not born till 1346. Twenty years later he crossed to France with Lionel, Duke of Clarence, and fought for a time under the Earl of Arundel. But for some reason, not difficult perhaps to guess at, he abandoned the trade of orthodox war and joined himself to one of the marauding bands under the notorious Edward Knollys, " a man of mean parentage in Cheshire," who by daring deeds had from a common soldier risen to leadership. How these independent companies of banditti bled the wretched and exhausted soil of France, while exacting, among other deeds of rapine, large ransoms from widows or fatherless women of property, is a matter of history. Knollys seems to have had the saving merit of sharing his plunder generously with his followers. So Dalyngruge came back from France sufficiently enriched to build this castle on the Bodiam property which he had acquired by marriage with its heiress. That he built it, not merely as a noble residence, but with a view to protection against the avenging wrath of the French, which in Richard the Second's reign, it will be remembered, was showing itself in ravage and slaughter upon Kent and Sussex towns, there is little doubt, for Bodiam was upon the edge of the danger zone.

Contrived with all the matured skill of that warlike age, and rising from the midst of a small lake rather than an ordinary moat, its lord and his treasures would have been pretty secure from such small forces as, after success at Rye, Winchelsea, or Hastings, sometimes raided the nearer inland villages, even had they reached Bodiam, of which there is no evidence. Nor is there any that the castle proved of that assistance to the helpless burghers or villagers, upon which the petition for licence to build it was based. But Sir Edward was a man of parts as well as a doughty and acquisitive warrior. For he held several offices of note and trust under the Crown. And when the City of London showed its teeth under the irritating actions of the weak young Richard the Second, and his family conclave, the Sussex knight was called up to keep it in check. Stowe says he was soon superseded as too lenient, which may be accounted to his credit, when the circumstances of 1392 are remembered. But he was also employed in treaty making with France, a selection which might seem strange, but that his name in those earlier enterprises of his may have been obscured by that of his ferocious leader Knollys, " Le veritable demon de la guerre."

His fame is not particularly concerned with the fact, though it has some indirect interest, that he was one of the three hundred more or less notable witnesses who appeared in the greatest and most protracted Heraldic law suit of all times, that of Scrope and Grosvenor ; such diverse personages as " Time-honoured Lancaster," Geoffrey Chaucer, Henry of Bolingbroke and his future lifelong foe, Owen Glyndwr, all giving their evidence before the Judges. At his death Bodiam passed to his son John, who apparently fought at Agincourt, after which it came into the hands of the Lewknors, one of the most conspicuous feudal families of Sussex, who held it for many generations. One of these, a Lancastrian, handed it over without resistance to the Yorkists, as in after times its deserted towers were abandoned to the Roundheads. It passed subsequently through many hands, including those of the Tuftons, and is now the property of Lord Ashcombe. Æsthetically beautifully and architecturally distinguished, it seems only to have been occupied for about a century, and even of this there is no certainty, and in truth it must have been an uncommonly damp residence. It has no history but its rather sinister origin, which the arms of that " veritable Demon of war," Sir Edward Knollys, and his appropriate crest, a ram's head, over the southern gateway, serve to commemorate. The building, which is about a hundred and sixty feet square, with circular angle towers nearly seventy feet high and of immense thickness, is in good preservation for a ruin. On all sides, save for the causeway of approach, it rises sheer out of the moat, or rather the large pool, gay in summer with water-lilies, which gives it a rather unique character among feudal castles. One may well forget the empty realization of all this fierce parade of warlike purpose in the charming picture of which its roofless and gutted shell to-day forms so imposing a centrepiece.

CHAPTER THE SEVENTH

Northiam to Rye

LEAVING Northiam by the Rye road, picturesquely shaded for some half-mile by the overhanging foliage of oak and ash, which fringed the Brickwall deer park, and when nothing is to be seen of the village but a tapering spire rising above the wood, Beckley Church, planted conspicuously upon an opposing ridge a mile away, comes into view. Over the meadowy dip between the ridges, distant sweeps of hill

BECKLEY.

and dale, pasture, tillage and woodland fade away beyond Wittersham and Tenterden into the weald of Kent. On nearing Beckley, which tradition says King Alfred left in his will to a favourite relative, its ancient church, a bit back from the main road and supported by a couple of Georgian houses in leafy grounds, makes an auspicious entry to the village.

Encompassed to-day, even as noted by travellers a century ago, by "ancient and goodly trees," the lines of its massive though not ancient tower and well-proportioned nave and chancel are not a little disturbed by some modern dormer windows with pointed wooden gables let into the roof. Its association with the most ancient of Oxford Colleges should have saved it one might well fancy from such a blemish!

Beckley is fairly populous, and like so many other villages in this region holds the high road like a thin line of skirmishers for half a mile or so with every type of rural building, ancient and modern, decorative or simple, but almost always entrenched within its own domain of garden, orchard, or paddock. There are half-timbered cottages to give the artist pause, or again snug leafy retreats with a rather different appeal to provoke perchance the jaded Londoner to a brief passing pang of envy. There are other sorts, too, of quite another complexion, where you may buy picture postcards and tobacco if you need either, and the locals no doubt many other more substantial and useful things. Now in a typical village in Wiltshire, or other Western counties, apart from its aristocratic quarter, if it has one, you will generally pass through rows of cottages, of the local type, whether taverns, shops, or dwellings, over-shadowed perhaps by the larger buildings of a farm or two, and you are at once out in the open again.

But these straggling Sussex villages are quite different. There is not much thatch nowadays, as in the West for instance, though old red tiles with the gay tints that age lays upon them, are assuredly no less picturesque. But the real contrast lies in the obvious presence of so many other social and industrial types besides the agricultural labourer, the farmer, the publican and the parson. Greater variety of occupation and degree accounts no doubt for some of it. And furthermore, while it would seem absurd to credit the Metropolis with any direct influence on this remote corner of Sussex such as it has on so much of the county, the villages somehow lack that appearance of complete isolation from the world, which marks those of many counties but little further removed from it. They probably feel themselves less rustic than these others. Possibly the neighbouring coast towns may impart a touch of in-the-worldness to these back-lying villages. In such a residential county as Sussex, too, even its uttermost corners must catch something of this flavour. Though almost every building in the village may antedate living memory, there is

BECKLEY CHURCH.

little that is shabby or dilapidated; no visible sign, at any rate, of desertion for the towns so obvious in some districts. There seems always some one to step into a vacant house competent to keep it at least in good shape. Roomy cottage residences, with ample appurtenances, at ten or fifteen pounds a year, such as are not infrequent bargains in many counties, are not to be found in these villages, though they may be five miles from a station and two and a half hours from London. With all this, however, the population of Beckley is but two-thirds of that assigned to it ninety years ago, though this will probably be due to the general trend in such matters rather than to local causes.

It requires an effort to imagine the now quiet weald of Sussex, as in Tudor and Jacobean times, the seat of an active and wealth-producing iron industry. Almost every one then who had ore on his land became an iron-master. The forests that had been all too slowly cleared for agriculture by Henry the Eighth's time, were being felled so rapidly for smelting, that legislation became necessary. Again and again fresh laws were passed for the protection of the vanishing woods. Poets, writers and economists denounced the Sussex iron-masters, somewhat after the fashion that the Georgian and Early Victorian Warwickshire Squires inveighed against the spreading blight of the Black Country. Archbishop Parker, voicing the Church, or perhaps merely himself as a great Kent magnate, in a letter to Queen Elizabeth, expresses dismay at a rumour that the iron nuisance is to cross the Kent border, " which plague if it shall come into the county I fear will breed much grudge and desolation." Drayton heads the poets in their attack on the trade in his Polyolbion and utters a wail on behalf of the Sussex woods, which by the way is one of the quainter passages in that portentous and whimsical effusion.

> For seeing their decay each hour so fast come on,
> Under the axe's stroke, fetched many a grievous groan,
> When as the anvil's weight and hammer's dreadful sound,
> Even rent the hollow woods, and shook the queachy ground.
> So that the trembling nymphs, oppressed through ghastly fear,
> Ran madding to the downs with loose dishevelled hair,
> The Sylvans that about the neighbouring woods did dwell,
> Both in the tufty frith and in the mossy fell,
> Forsook their gloomy bowers, and wandered far abroad,
> Expell'd their quiet seats and place of their abode,
> When labouring carts they saw to hold their daily trade,
> Where they in summer wont to sport them in the shade.

Jove's oak, the warlike ash, vein'd elm, and softer beech,
Short hazel, maple plain, light ash, the bending wych,
Tough holly and smooth birch, must altogether burn.
What should the builder serve, supplies the forger's turn.

Cannon, mortars, and arms of all sorts for the use of the nation and indeed for exportation, which last aroused opposition from time to time, were made in Sussex. Still greater was the manufacture for domestic purposes of firebacks and andirons often beautifully ornamented, horseshoes, nails, farm-implements, wheel-tyres, church bells and other of the innumerable articles, even then in demand. Both Germans and Frenchmen with skill in gun-casting were imported and their names may be traced in many a village directory to-day. There would seem to have been about 140 iron forges in the county at one time, each consuming three or four loads of charcoal a day. "Full of iron mines," says Camden, "is Sussex, where for the making and founding thereof, there be furnaces on every side and a huge deal of wood is yearly burnt, to which purpose divers brooks on many places are brought to run in one channel and sundry meadows turned into pools and waters, that they might be of power sufficient to drive hammer mills which, beating upon the iron, resound all over the places adjoining." Nearly a hundred years later, in 1722, another writer tells us: "A great deal of meadow ground is turned into ponds and pools for the driving of mills by the flashes, which beating the hammers upon the iron, fill the neighbourhood round, night and day, with continual noise."

What a contrast to the peace of to-day, which seems to resent even the passing hoot of a motor! Crown surveyors were appointed to uphold the various statutes against excessive cutting and to stamp the iron from the various forges with their respective trade marks. The trade decayed in the latter half of the eighteenth century, though cannon were cast as late as 1770, not so much for the lack of wood, though this too must have been felt, but for the impossibility of competing

with the coal districts. Though the chief producer, Sussex was
not the only one, for North Worcestershire, or to speak broadly
the Black Country of to-day, which was heavily forested, was
forging freely with charcoal long before it used the abounding
coal underlying it. And while Burrells, Ashburnham, Fullers,
Barhams, Bakers, and scores more were waking the echoes,
and lighting the midnight gloom of the Sussex woods, Dudleys,
Foleys and others were forging weapons for the Royalist
armies in the woodland arcady now long buried beneath

OXENBRIDGE (see p. 242).

that wilderness of hideous dump heaps which stretches from
Birmingham to Wolverhampton.

Many a yeoman it was said, and many no doubt that were
not even yeomen, acquired gentility by this roaring trade.
What with iron forging and smuggling superadded to such
normal activities as agriculture and fishing, Sussex must have
been a singularly prosperous county in the good old days.
There is scarcely need to tell that Roman cinders, with coins
and pottery among them, have been frequently unearthed.
For it is not likely that the Romans, who drove elaborate
shafts, some of them almost perfect at this very day, into

remote Welsh mountains for lead and silver and gold, and furthermore extracted them all, would have neglected the iron here under their very noses. Beckley, as before noted, is the limit of the old iron country. There are in this district, however, few or none of those hammer-ponds still existing which are such a familiar feature of the countryside between Cuckfield and Horsham, and all about that region. Holloway says that he knew a man who could himself remember the bellows still working at Beckley forge.

A couple of miles or so from Beckley the village of Peasmarsh begins to straggle along the roadside, and somewhere near its indefinable entry, a milestone proclaims that Rye is only four miles distant. But where the village itself begins or ends would be ill deciding, even if it mattered. It is a mile long at any rate, though much detached and not particularly populous. Moreover, it pitches up and down and straggles sideways here and there, towards the pleasant woody hills and timbered pastures that overhang it on the south, and conceal the parish church which lies away behind them. A pretty place beyond a doubt, both for this reason and for the big cup or basin in which it has the appearance, more or less, of lying, though it actually stands high. But in addition to some attractive cottage architecture pretty freely distributed, there are several private residences either of well-weathered Georgian complexion in themselves, or responsible for the planting of now lusty trees, that may peradventure conceal any shortcomings in age or design, while always an ornament to the landscape. But lands and manors in this parish seem to have changed hands constantly. There is a quite imposing and notable old inn too, *The Cock*, crowning one of the steep pitches on the main highway, capable I should imagine of arresting the steps of the most critical wayfarer at the first glance, if there was half an excuse, and I believe well qualified to entertain the most exacting wight.

Peasmarsh Church, as before indicated, stands alone, upon

the high ridge back of the village, which looks south over the Tillingham valley towards Winchelsea and the Channel. With a tower and shingle spire, a gabled nave and chancel, it is a typical East Sussex church, save for the unforgivable crime in this part of the country of a modern slate roof. I cannot recall another such outrage in these parts. It is, I think and I hope, unique. Nevertheless it covers a most perfect little Norman chancel entered by an unusually fine little Norman arch in all its pristine ruggedness, with a leopard rudely engraved upon the pillar on either side. Three lancets on the north and south side respectively are all in keeping, though

THE *COCK INN*, PEASMARSH.

an east window with the ugly plate tracery of the earliest decorated period, is perhaps a modern replacement.

Now I do not think it is generally known in the neighbourhood, indeed I think it is scarcely known at all, that two hundred years ago Peasmarsh produced a poet who, had he lived, might have reflected upon it no little glory, For though he died in his twenty-first year, William Pattison left enough behind him of sufficient merit to earn a place in *The Dictionary of National Biography*. The son of a Peasmarsh farmer, he was born in 1708, and his budding genius being recognized, he was taken in hand by his father's landlord, the Earl of Thanet (Tufton), and sent to Appleby School and afterwards to Sidney Sussex College, Cambridge. Here his poetic temperament got the better both of his common sense and of his gratitude. For he quarrelled with his tutors, threw up Cambridge to save expulsion, and went to London to mix with the wits, or some of them, for a time and then to starve, sleeping on benches in St James's Park. Ultimately Curll the bookseller took him in and sheltered him, and it was in his house that Pattison died of smallpox. Pope accused Curll of starving the young poet, whereas he actually saved him from that fate, at any rate, and the following year published two volumes of his poems which have placed him, so far as the national record is concerned, among the immortals. One of his poems was a satire on college life. His work was distinguished chiefly for precocity and excellent versification. He was buried where our friends of Lover's Seat fame were married, in St. Clement Danes, Strand.

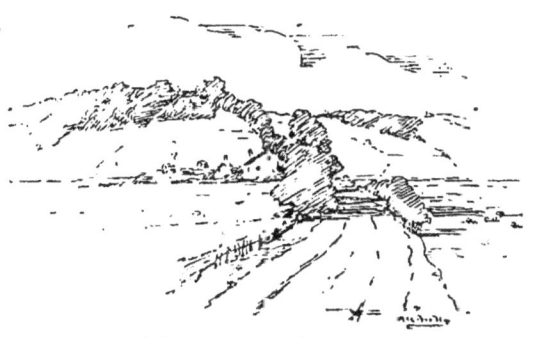

WITTERSHAM LEVELS.

From Peasmarsh a by-road runs due north across the Rother valley to Wittersham, which some three miles away stands conspicuous upon its high ridge near the centre of the Isle of Oxney. The river, here some thirty yards wide, still slightly feels the influence of the tide and in a wet season converts the whole valley into a lake, which from many distant points, miles away, supplies the landscape on such occasions with that glimmer of water which it so generally lacks. There are moments, however, when the inhabitants of the Isle of Oxney have a little too much of it and communication with Rye and the coast suffers an abrupt if brief interruption. The Wittersham people as a matter of fact, even those with the keenest eye for nature, are not likely to clamour for more water. For in normal times the Rother here coils quite a broad and shining course Marshward, through its radiantly green levels, and when the floods are out, or half out, which is fairly often, and when a bright winter sun is dipping towards the distant heights of Fairlight and shooting its parting fires along the

WITTERSHAM, FROM THE ROTHER.

green and silver streaked meadows, the folk upon the north side of the old isle enjoy a rare spectacle. As may be readily understood, too, these Wittersham levels in the rather rare seasons of protracted frost are the resort of skaters from all over the countryside.

"And what is the Isle of Oxney?" the outside reader will most assuredly ask, and indeed I have a strong suspicion that a number of highly intelligent persons living within four or five miles of it might put the same question! The said island, then, includes the three parishes of Wittersham, Stone and Ebony (in part), rising to very high ground in its centre, which is crowned by the village first named. It is still an island, in that channels or "sewers" drain the surrounding low grounds. But in old days and throughout the Middle Ages the Rother and its tributary streams were estuaries filling all these valleys, and not as now well channelled canals liable only to occasional outbreaks of exuberance in stormy weather. The age-long fight with these old tide-swept tentacles of Romney Marsh is in every bit of it so intricate a story that any attempt to labour it in detail is a business in itself, while without detail it becomes incoherent. The interest, too, is

A RESTORATION, WITTERSHAM.

purely technical except in so far as it has altered the face of the country, and the reader will no doubt be disposed to accept a general statement on this account. Indeed I feel sure that he would not stand anything more. One may remark, however, that for centuries all these levels were the care, not only of owners and parishes, but of the Crown. The local Commissions, appointed reign after reign, from the Norman kings onward, give a very good idea of the leading residents of each and every period, who in their turn were liable to render an account of themselves to direct officers of the King. The long tale of quarrels, law-suits and friction generally, always inevitable between land-owners, private and corporate, upon the banks of shifting tidal rivers such as these, would, if collected, no doubt fill many wearisome and lengthy volumes. It may be worth noting, too, that all over Romney Marsh, including of course these its tributaries, local bodies are still appointed to overlook the ever-pressing attacks of the sea upon a wide district which lies below its level, with all the various details thereby involved.

In Wittersham Village.

Wittersham Church stands in a commanding position near the hither end of the village and slightly below the ridge-top along which so much of it straggles after the fashion of its neighbours. Like so much of the country traversed in these pages and a great deal more untouched by them, the Isle of Oxney was both in the secular and Ecclesiastical jurisdiction of Canterbury. In the fourteenth century Wittersham with its Manor seems to have been granted to the Collegiate Church of All Saints, Maidstone, and its Court House bore the name of Wittersham College up to the Dissolution, when its temporalities went the usual way. It is now represented and the old name preserved by College House, a residence just to the east of the church. The latter, recently restored, is a fine building of twelfth-century origin and consists of a tower, nave with side aisles, and a chancel. The tower is Perpendicular work of the early sixteenth century, and in olden days carried on its summit a beacon ready for lighting when the news was flared from Playden or Fairlight of a menace in the Channel. It may be noted by the way that on occasions when these pitch tar and kettle beacons proved ineffective, either from sunshine or fog, it was the duty of certain individuals, known as " hobbelers," to ride around and raise the country. The nave is Early English with a double arcade of pointed arches in five bays. The arches rest, with two cylindrical exceptions, on octagonal piers. Most of them terminate in mask faces, while at the spring of the chancel arch those of a king and an abbot look down from either side respectively. The chancel was rebuilt in recent times. A lofty perpendicular arch opens out the tower space at the west end, which is lighted by a large traceried window of the Decorated style.

In the large parish of Wittersham, which from its more or less dominating village spreads over the slopes and flanks of the Isle of Oxney, there are several private residences of various types, most of them old houses restored, but still in admirable keeping with the atmosphere, and the island generally is well up to the high æsthetic average of this district in its old farmhouses and cottages. Along the high 1 . d from Rye to Tenterden, upon which the upper part of Wittersham stands, the sight can travel far in most directions, and the winter winds from all are free to work their wild will upon the villagers as a kind of off-set, one might suggest, to their inspiring outlook. Just to the south, across the Rother valley, the upland parishes

of Iden with Peasmarsh and Playden only in part cut off the
Rye sea-front. But in the far south-west, all the high country
from Fairlight to Battle looms clearly against the horizon,
while to the south-east down the Rother valley a large extent
of Romney Marsh spreads away to a glint of distant sea beyond
it. To the northward the Isle of Oxney trends gradually
downwards in all directions with the parishes of Stone and part
of Ebony upon its eastward slope to the north channel of the
Rother. On the distant uplands, six miles away, the noble
tower of Tenterden Church rises conspicuously above the

WINDMILL AT WITTERSHAM.

woods. All the country to the westward of it about Cranbrook
and Hawkhurst fades away into a remoter and a dimmer
distance, while to the eastward the long chalk range beyond
Ashford cuts the sky-line.

Among the houses, here sprinkled along the main ridge
road, is a most skilful and charming restoration of a very old
half-timbered house, enclosing in its pretty garden a retired
windmill, rescued from destruction, sails and all for a dignified,
useful and decorative old age, while to the westward another
mill, still on the active list, was whirling wildly the last time I
saw it against a most gorgeous sunset. Near by the former, at

the cross-roads leading to Rye, Appledore, Stone and Tenterden (via Ebony), is the fine old homestead of Stocks. Fronted with age-worn scolloped weather-tiling and capped with a vast expanse of mellow tile roof, culminating in clustered chimneys, it displays itself to great advantage, upon a smooth plateau of paddock and garden flanked with straw-roofed barns and oasthouses. A grove of Scotch firs within the enclosure, if no great defence perhaps against the north on this windswept ridge, must make fine music up here in a south-west gale. Yet this after all is but one among innumerable examples of similar

WHERE THE ROTHER MEETS THE MARSH.

places, so liberally distributed both in hollow and upon hill-top throughout all these parishes.

In truth it is these old buildings and even such as are of but moderate age, with their infinite variety, their homeliness, their unstudied and careless grace of pose, their sunshiny look, that set the seal on this kind of landscape. With the rural architecture, if such it can be called, of some counties I wot of, and those not quite the worst, shifted down here, one would feel perhaps just a touch of monotony in the rather undistinguished prettiness of each fresh scene. But the builders of old days and the good example they set to their successors, quite unconsciously no doubt of any altruistic or artistic intent, have more than redeemed any such negative qualities in nature. Their creations suit the landscape and the landscape suits them and shows them to the best advantage. To say that they put a finishing touch to it would be to say not nearly enough, for they half make it and the result is a very complete blend of its kind. A kind, too, that needs neither lofty hills, nor running waters, nor wild spaces, nor any of those uplifting natural features that have so strong an appeal to most of us. It does very well as it is, representing super-excellently the quiet and peaceful type of English scenery, and has nothing to fear but the Jerry-builder who fortunately has had in this corner, at any rate, small scope as yet for his ill-directed energies.

Away below and to the northward are the two farms of Acton and Owlie, that were both Manors in their day, belonging from the fourteenth century to the time of Edward the Sixth, to the ancient family of Odyarn, or Odiarne, of which I think there are still one or two representatives not far away. From them no doubt the adjoining farm of Odiam was named, and in former days the north chancel of Wittersham Church was known as the Acton Chapel. Further eastward on a long grassy ridge still known as Chapel Bank stood Ebony Church and Priory, the latter being a branch of Canterbury in Saxon times and the first establishment upon the Isle of Oxney. The large original church was destroyed by lightning in the reign of Elizabeth. The graveyard alone remains on a ridge top, and burials still occasionally take place there. A later church erected upon another spot belongs to the parish of Appledore. On the far or western side of Wittersham village is Palstre Court, now a farmhouse. This too is an old Manor and Robert Rudstone its owner, who lived here in the reign of Queen Mary, was deprived of it for his share in the Sir Thomas Wyatt's rebellion, though his son seems to have been forgiven and reinstated. Beyond Palstre on the westward of the two Tenterden roads and lying on the edge of the old north channel is the hamlet of Smallhythe, interesting as having been the port and shipbuilding yard of the above-named town when it was a limb of Rye and attached to the Cinque-Port group. Anything more completely land-locked and less suggestive of sea-going ventures than is Smallhythe to-day, could hardly be conceived. But in the early sixteenth century the tide still

CROSS-ROADS AT STOCKS.

rolled up the north side of the Isle of Oxney, and as late as 1509 a licence from the Archbishop regarding a chapel here includes the right of burial for bodies cast up by shipwreck on its shores.

Turning one's face southward towards Rye, five miles away, the descent from the Wittersham ridge to the valley of the Rother is about the steepest and in summer the hottest to climb of any bit of main roadway in all this border strip of

Kent and Sussex. It traverses a deep cut, picturesquely embowered in copses of hazel and oak which are radiant at the first bursting of their leaves in spring in a spangled carpet of anemones, primroses and bluebells. In no country known to me do primroses riot with greater luxuriance, or with richer colouring than in this network of deep and sheltered lanes that all about here connect the high roads and are as hospitable to spring flowers as the more famous ones of Devon. Being of more generous breadth and often bordered by high copsy slopes, they at any rate display their wares to much greater advantage than the rigid wall-like west country banks, which hem you in for miles, and incidentally shut out any glimpse of the surrounding country, save through an occasional gateway. From the bridge over the broad canal-like Rother, in the centre of its half-mile or more of level vale, one gets a good view down-stream of the quite bold south-eastern promontory of the Isle of Oxney, at Stone, upon which the sea broke in Roman times.

Mounting another steep pitch into the parish of Iden, an old house, on the summit, standing back from the road in a paddock with outbuildings, and tall trees behind it, would bring any wayfarer to a halt. This is Oxenbridge, traditionally and indeed with little doubt the original nest of that famous Brede family, whose august acquaintance we have already made. The accompanying sketch will be far more illuminating than any verbal description. It is indeed a rare old house of its class and as a compact and complete architectural picture not easily to be matched. The bulk of it is fourteenth or fifteenth century; the interior of the older portion has been a good deal pulled about, but the largest sitting-room and some of the upper parts are mostly original work. I might also add that it is in good hands.

One is here on the top of a broad, rolling plateau, pleasantly indented with shallow, twisting valleys, and covered by the parishes of Iden and Playden. The final syllable by the way in

Oxenbridge.

place names of such termination shows upon the tongue of the native a curious fidelity to its origin, which one need hardly say is ' den ', i.e. ' dene.' It is always hereabouts I-*den* and Play-*den*, not Id'n and Playd'n, as would be the case anywhere else. The small village of Iden gathers itself together rather more closely about its four cross-roads than its neighbours and will compare from a picturesque point of view with most of them, its old church and pleasant Rectory with its well-timbered demesne standing apart in the background.

A mile or more to the westward, where the parish slopes down to a tributary level of the Rother valley are two interesting haunts of ancient fame. The lesser, only notable from the reflected glory of the greater, is a farm known as Baron's Grange, approached by a mile and a half of twisting and sometimes watery lane. There is nothing here but a nice old Queen Anne looking house, though I believe some of it is much older than that. Incidentally it might sit for the portrait of an old Virginia country house of the colonial period. But the seat of the Barons, to which the original Grange was obviously related, lies a few furlongs further on, down a branch lane and beside another and smaller homestead, known as the Moat Farm. Though nothing is left of the baronial fortress but the shapeless fragment of a gateway, it is not often that mere foundations tell so plain a tale. For here uplifted and well defined upon a green flat, just below the farm buildings, is a square plateau of smooth turf, each of its sides measuring over a hundred yards in length and surrounded by a clearly marked moat, in part of which the water is still actually standing.

The causeway across is plain for all to see, even if the above-named fragment of gate tower were not there to mark it. One may feel thankful to the locals of olden days, who no doubt carried away and used the materials of this once imposing building in barns, houses, pig-styes, roads and what not, that this eloquent though rough little fragment was spared. For it does make a difference somehow and seems to give Edmond de Passelaye, Lord of Iden, a little more reality and bring him

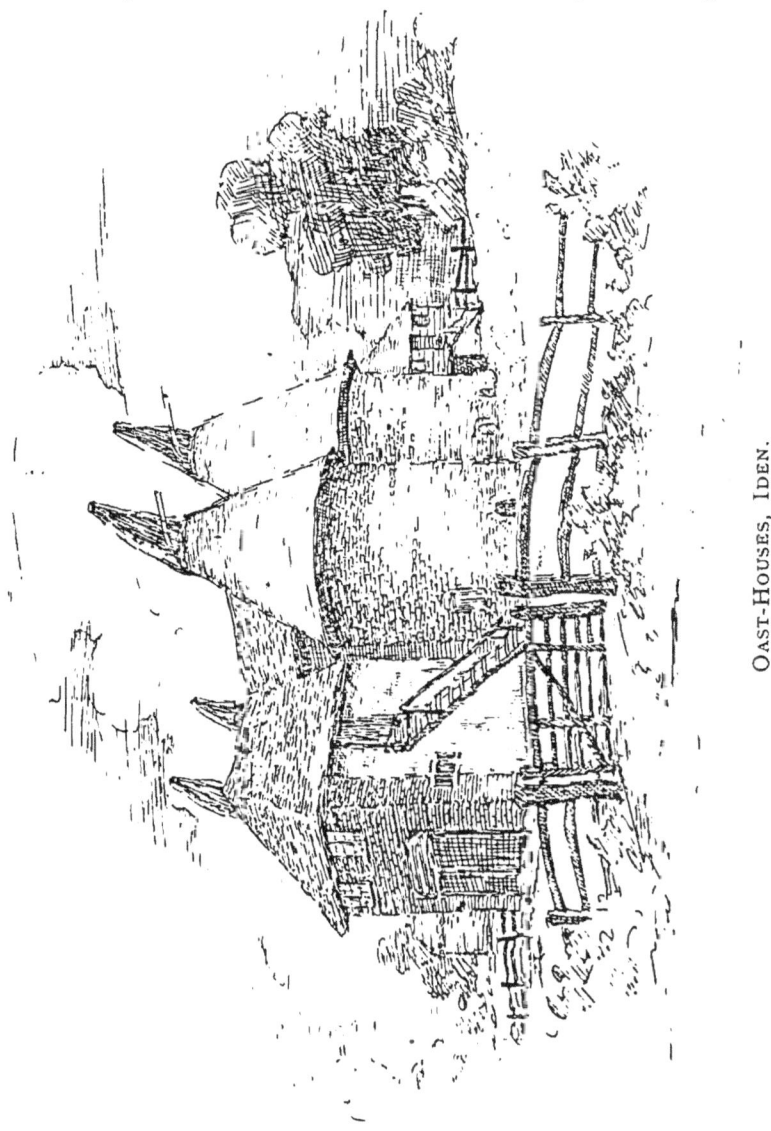

OAST-HOUSES, IDEN.

just a little bit nearer. Edward the First in the tenth year of his reign issued a patent to the above-mentioned gentleman, granting him permission to surround with a wall of stone and mortar and to crenelate his castle at Iden. The document, in the hands of the present owner, is in good preservation. It was reproduced by Holloway in his *Romney Marsh* and is a beautifully executed piece of lettering, with the illustration of a church in the left-hand top corner, showing monks at their devotions. An archer near by pierces to the heart with a well-directed arrow a running deer, while a hare in a sitting position regards the varied scene with apparent complacency. The traces of the walls upon the turf show a building about fifty yards square. In the fifteenth century the place belonged to the family of Iden, one of whom, Alexander, while sheriff of Kent and Sussex in the year 1450, earned the distinction of killing Jack Cade in the parish of Heathfield. He is said to have been buried at Iden Church, and about a century ago a brass, bearing the effigy of an armoured knight, was carried away, as is supposed from his tomb. The church consists of an embattled tower, nave and chancel with a north aisle. The interior is mainly Early English, though there are some Norman arches in the south wall.

Dropping down a bit from Iden and mounting another hill, Playden Church with its tall shingle spire gathers round it what is nowadays in great part an outlying residential quarter of Rye, alluded to in an earlier chapter. There is no collective village and nearly all the surrounding residences are of quite recent date, save Springfield; which is occupied by a branch of the Curteis family (in the female line), the principal land-owners in the district and prominently associated with the country between here and Tenterden for many generations. Speaking generally, as regards this corner of Kent and Sussex, the old county histories which chronicle every transfer of land of the least importance, and of all Manors for three or four hundred years previous to their own publication in the late eighteenth or early nineteenth centuries, reveal a lack of personal continuity throughout the whole period, and more particularly in the latter part of it, that one would hardly expect in a region seemingly so outside the London influence, far-reaching and powerful as that influence has always been. We have already come across more than one exception to the rule and the Curteis family form another, appearing as land-owners in several neighbouring parishes in addition to Parliamentary and other old connexions with the Boroughs of Rye and Tenterden, more especially the latter, since Tudor times. Otherwise, with these few exceptions, it is quite curious what a sharp contrast this part of England affords to the local records of such counties for instance as Shropshire, Herefordshire or Worcester, and indeed of most others. Many yeoman families have proved tenacious, but among *armigers* the personal changes and the land transfers have been surprisingly numerous ever since the feudal nobility fell after the Wars of the Roses and the country gentlemen rose with the Tudors into a recognized existence. Then again the older burgess families, often, nay generally *armigers*, either still extant, or of but recent disappearance from the Cinque-Port towns, nearly always owned lands or Manors in the surrounding country.

Playden Church, formerly held with and served from Iden, is quite a gem of its kind; a very complete specimen of the smaller Sussex church, with pointed nave and chancel, some trace of Norman work and a tall shingle spire. Standing apart in a large and well-cared-for graveyard, it may almost rank as a beacon over land and sea with Fairlight itself. In the old days of buccaneering and invasion scares, a large oak near the church carried, like the tower of Wittersham, an iron basket, filled with coal, pitch, tar and wood, ready to light at a moment's notice. As a last word, on descending the long, steep and deeply trenched hill into Rye, its only exit inland for hundreds of years, Leasam, standing high on the west point of the Playden ridge, should not be omitted. A former seat of the Curteis family, it has changed hands recently more than once and undergone much alteration. Though not, I think, a very old house it is the largest in the neighbourhood and gathers no little distinction from the fine timber encircling it and from its commanding site, overlooking Rye, Winchelsea, and the Tillingham Valley and much besides. Though by devious ways, and without any pretension to guide-book meticulous-

NEAR IDEN.

ness, we have now covered the country to the west of Rye, both seaboard and inland, as originally contemplated, in this little journey. In the space that remains, I propose to strike eastward through Romney Marsh to its extremity and thence return by way of the string of hill-top villages which immediately overlook it.

AT WITTERSHAM.

CHAPTER THE EIGHTH

Rye to Brookland and Lydd

PERHAPS the ancient town may have had some subtly rustic flavour about its name in pre-railroad days. For Theodore Hook declared that at the trial of Lord Melville the presence of " a countrified-looking gentlewoman from Rye," standing next to him among the spectators, stimulated his chronic passion for practical joking beyond control. " Pray, sir," said she touching his arm, and pointing to the peers, " who are those gentlemen in red now coming in ? " To which Hook replied that they were the Peers of the Realm and that the Juniors always walked in front. The lady had two young daughters with her, aged about fourteen and ten respectively, and thus addressed the elder, " Now mind, Louisa, and remember to tell little Jane here that these are the Peers of the Realm, and that the Juniors, that is the youngest, you know, always walk first." " Dear me, ma," said Louisa, " can that gentleman in front be one of the youngest ? He looks very old." " Human nature," says Hook, " with no more mischief in him than a dove, could not withstand such temptation." For soon afterwards the Rye lady touched Hook's arm again, and pointing to the Bishops entering in their full panoply of rochette and lawn sleeves over their robes, said :

" And who, sir, are those gentlemen ? "

" Gentlemen ! madam," cried Hook, " those are not gentlemen, they are ladies, elderly ladies. They are the dowager peeresses in their own right."

The fair inquirer then fixed a long and searching gaze on Hook's face, but the hardened old quizzer did not move a muscle, till at last tolerably satisfied with her scrutiny the lady turned and remarked in a loud whisper.

"Louisa, dear, the gentleman says that these are elderly ladies, the dowager peeresses in their own right. Tell little Jane not to forget that."

RYE, FROM NEAR WINCHELSEA.

A little later the Speaker of the House of Commons attracted her attention by the rich embroidery of his robes.

"Pray, sir," she said, "who is that fine-looking person opposite?"

"That, madam," replied Hook in a grave tone, "is Cardinal Wolsey."

"No, sir," cried the Rye lady, with some heat, and casting an indignant glance at Hook. "We know better than that. Cardinal Wolsey has been dead this many a long year."

RYE TO BROOKLAND AND LYDD 251

"No such thing, madam, I assure you," retorted the imperturbable Hook. "It has been, I am aware, so reported in the country, but without the least foundation; in fact those rascally newspapers will say *anything*."

"The good gentlewoman," says Hook, "appeared thunderstruck, opened her eyes to the full, gasped like a dying carp, and seizing a daughter in each hand hurried from the spot."

That the famous jester must be a lunatic at large was no doubt the confirmed opinion of the lady from Rye.

It is eleven miles from Rye by road across the centre of the marsh to Lydd and about eight as the crow flies. The lofty tower of Lydd Church springing high out of what appears like an island of dark woods on the far verge of a level grassy plain, is a familiar enough sight from here in clear weather. As you gradually approach it, mile by mile, on a bright afternoon, its old grey walls and pinnacles take on a strange white light in the westering sun, while the sombre-seeming foliage of the tall elms that enclose and flank it, begins to glow in all the radiancy of their native green. But Lydd, measured by these pages, is as yet some way off, though it may be noted in passing that it can be reached by a by-road a little shorter in mileage, and shorter still if taken up at the golf links by way of the light railroad. From thence it hugs the shore behind the sand dunes and the great sea wall which protects the Marsh as far as the coastguard station at Jury's Gap, where some large reedy pools recall, as is supposed, the great inundations of the thirteenth century. On the way here a few scattered buildings with a small new church and schools, behind and beneath the constantly battered sea defences represent the modern Broomhill, successor to that place of ancient fame and "fifty taverns" which it will be remembered shared the fate of the earlier Winchelsea, and was wiped out by the same inundations, though subsequently recovered. Traces of the original church may still be seen in a neighbouring field. In the mackerel season this stretch of otherwise secluded sea-front has lively interludes. The staked Kettle or Keddle nets, which account for so much of the catch, are visible every half-mile or so in the summer season, running far out into the shallow waters, and during the month or more when mackerel fishing is at its best, glittering heaps of these most graceful and radiant of sea-fish may be seen dumped upon the sand, with busy companies of men, women, and children packing them into baskets, and carrying them up to the carts which are in wait to hurry off with their loads to Rye station. In normal times mackerel, straight out of the sea, can be had almost for the asking at the height of the season in Rye Bay, and no fish, as every one is or should be aware, so well repays a quick transfer from the nets to the pot, or so suffers from undue delay.

At Jury's Gap all passage along the shore, save on foot, comes to an end. For soon after this begins that great projecting wilderness of ever gathering shingle which cranes away out to Dungeness Point, where it drops so abruptly into deep water that a good-sized ship can skirt it, as the saying goes, within " biscuit throw." Long before the war, however, big guns had begun to thunder over these desert spaces, and the artillery camp between Lydd and the seashore was already a recognized institution. Needless to dwell on the extensions that have taken place since then, or the greater importance the camp has assumed, and the infinitely greater significance of the tenfold thundering that booms over the Marsh and shakes betimes the windows of Rye town. The road, or rather the trail, for it is henceforth little more, to Lydd, now leaves the sea and wanders there informally over sandy commons, sprinkled with furze and rushes, or poor pastures just petering out in despair upon the shingle wilderness, and finally enters Lydd at the Camp end of the little town.

Though you but skirt the Marsh on this shorter road to Lydd, it affords throughout, perhaps, as characteristic a near view over this its wildest and least inhabited portion, as any. Here and there, just within its edge, as if to emphasize the miles of green and grey solitude that stretch away behind them, is a snug farm with stacks and barns and a big gabled house and maybe a dash of foliage. But from their back gates away out to a far horizon, without a hillock, but the vague tracery of the dyke banks, without a tree but a lone group of willows or some solitary thorn, without a house but a stray shepherd's cottage, but more thickly sprinkled with sheep than any other hill or plain in England, the interminable green pastures forge eastwards. For us, however, the heart of the Marsh and the ways which traverse it will be the more

ON THE MARSH.

illuminating route, though before dropping down on to it beneath the old Landgate, I feel that some brief and general sketch of how this famous and ancient triumph of reclamation with its 62,000 acres of mostly rich soil was achieved.

I would shirk any attempt at this physical part of the business if I dare. It will be much better, however, to say too little, than to get entangled in the intricacies of a struggle with a capricious sea that began with the Romans and in the sense of defending territory is going on still. Its complexities are infinite, the earlier records often conflicting, and the source of no little friction among modern investigators and of wonderful theories among the earlier historians. I should be sorry to have to get up the subject for an examination even with the aid of Mr. Holloway's not wholly reliable work upon it. For that ever-to-be-held-in-pious-memory gentleman, as the Germans would say, laid an ungrateful posterity under further obligations by a second work, *The History of Romney Marsh*, which is rather scarce. I read it over twice (it is only two hundred pages) some years ago, not for its fascination of style, but in an endeavour to get some order into the events of a thousand and odd years, which the author throws pell-mell at your head, together with a good deal of superfluous disquisition, leaving the reader to piece them together like a modern picture puzzle. That the futility of a single perusal so soon becomes apparent is probably the reason why only one person known to me personally has read the book through. A few others own copies, but will not commit themselves by any definite claim to have read them! The various town records too have of course a good deal to say about the Marsh, for there was a constant struggle between graziers coveting more land and sea-going people requiring more depth of water, and the two interests were generally incompatible.

Now the whole Marsh tilts slightly inwards. The land beneath the old cliff-line, at Appledore for instance, is actually lower by several feet than that near the sea-front. It is not surprising then that the first land which thrust itself up in the great bay was that on or about where New Romney now stands. Whether the Romans occupied the island and did any walling and dyking from it as a base, can be little more than guessed at, though Samian ware and such like has been unearthed in the neighbourhood. But as they possessed a well known port at the north-east end of the Marsh, guarded by a castle whose massive, uncouth, mortared fragments still stand or lie upon the hillside of Lympne, it is probable they did a good deal of reclamation. But through the earlier centuries of recorded history following the nebulous Roman period, the great church of Canterbury, the virtual owner and indeed by proxy the chief reclaimer of the Marsh, possesses the main story, buried in its archives, and dug out from time to time in fragments by zealous antiquaries. The Saxons were characteristically industrious in reclaiming what in their day was most likely a vast waterlogged expanse of mud and marsh, submerged at high tide, rather than a free-running sea, though in parts no doubt already embanked. It was intersected with deep and probably wide channels by which the waters from the Weald found their way to the open sea. Apparently, large islands of reclaimed land lay about in this watery space in the mid-Saxon period, gradually extending themselves into mutual contact, while like strips pushed their

GULDEFORD CHURCH, FROM THE VILLAGE.

way out from the mainland. Most of it was rich alluvial soil formed by the age-long deposits of the inflowing rivers and was well worth the labour of reclaiming.

It may be said at once, however, that most of this land-winning in Saxon, and indeed in the earlier Norman times, took place on the further or eastern half of the tract which alone is Romney Marsh in the proper sense of the term, though the whole is commonly so called. All upon the Rye side, from a line roughly drawn from Appledore to the Romneys was reclaimed at rather later dates and is known technically, and by sections as Walland Marsh, Denge Marsh, and Guildeforе Marsh. The local term both now and always for reclamation is " inning " and the several plots of land which grew into Manors and parishes, under Canterbury for the most part, were severally known as " innings." Throughout all this nearer and later inned half of the Marsh, there is to-day only one village and that one near to its further limits. There are few farmhouses away from its edges, and the only sign of man is the thinly scattered cottages of the shepherds here known as " lookers."

The whole Marsh indeed is striking in its abiding sense of peace, space and solitude. But this Sussex end, reckoning from the Lydd and Appledore branch railway which bisects it, is for this reason the more inspiring to those who respond to this manner of appeal. Most people who feel anything at all are I think thus susceptible. But there are others who are not, and it honestly depresses them. A clever young graduate of Edinburgh University who had never before been out of Scotland wrote recently to his people from Lydd, where he was camped with his battery, that this was the most Godforsaken country he had ever seen, or that he ever could have imagined. I was standing in the modest garden of the lad's home in the Border country when his scathing and uncompromising verdict was read aloud to me in delightful ignorance that I was actually an inhabitant of this far-away abomination of desolation. Mountain streams were flashing upon both sides of it, wild woods rose sharply upon every hand and purple heather flared everywhere along the sky-line ; one could see Romney Marsh from his point of view with singular clarity !

The term marsh, by the way, may give a false impression. For it has been admirably drained by deep dykes these hundreds of years past and forms a gigantic chessboard of watercourses, impassable save by the bridges which connect field with field, and though in very wet weather water lies freely about in places the land generally is quite dry. Within the easy memory of elderly men ague was universal ; most of them had it themselves in their youth. To-day it is practically unknown, a transformation which no one seems able to account for. No physical change whatever has taken place in that short time, nor indeed within a much longer one. There may once conceivably have been more mosquitoes, but there are still what people who have never lived in mosquito countries would call quite enough. Yet malaria has disappeared, or virtually so, within forty years. In olden times, even as late as the Georges, the Marsh had a shocking reputation as a place of abode; all sorts of opprobrious epithets are lavished on it by the old writers. The big landowners, with a rare exception or two, never resided there, but always in the up-country, and the same seems to have been the case with some of the larger farmers. A popular prescription for the ague, among the unlettered, was a live spider wrapped up in a gingerbread nut, washed down by a cup of tea.

The Marsh is now quite sweet, and swept by the fresh sea winds, as salubrious a place of residence as any other. But outside its two little towns of Lydd and Romney, and their outskirts, no one lives upon it to-day, save farmers and parsons. "Thomas Ingoldsby" said that the world consisted of Europe, Asia, Africa, America and Romney Marsh. Lambarde, writing in 1570, says of it, that as a place of abode it is " evil in winter, grievous in summer, but never good." He describes the county of Kent as consisting of three upward steps from the shore; the first (Romney Marsh) as *Wealth without health*, the second (up the hills into the Weald) as *Wealth and health*, the third (nearer London and the Thames) as *Health without wealth*. "*Fames in agro lapidoso*, a good stomach (hunger ?) in a stony field." " Romney Marsh," he goes on to say, " is famous throughout the realm, as well for the fertilitie and quantitie of the soil as for the ancient and wholesome ordinances there used for the preservation and maintenance of the banks and walls against the rage of the sea. It is at this day governed by certain laws of Sewers that were made by one Henry de Bath in the time of King Henry the Third. These are now become a patterne and examplar to all the like places of the whole realme whereby to be governed." Henry de Bath's ordinances are virtually those of to-day.

The Marsh has its mystery if you approach it properly, and most emphatically its beauty for those who love wide-open unencumbered plains, which sun gleams and cloud shadows touch so responsively with flying feet. It has its history, heaven knows, centuries of it, in which reckless lawbreakers, midnight rides, fierce encounters and the grim gallows-tree are the outstanding features. Above all these intangible attributes Romney Marsh has its sheep, and of that famous breed which has carried its name all over the world—thousands and thousands of them. A good-sized, white-faced sheep carrying an ample fleece, the *Romney* or *Kent* ought to be among the most profitable in the world, as unlike other heavy breeds its winter requirements are almost nil. On its own rich level pastures it has almost the hardy habit of a mountain sheep, which sounds paradoxical. Romney with its small sister marshes of Pevensey and the Stour on either side is the finest sheep land in Great Britain. The fact that much of it carries six to twelve big sheep to the acre will be sufficiently conclusive to the reader with the least pastoral knowledge, though it will not mean much to the artist. Nor anywhere can so many sheep be seen at a single *coup-d'œil* as from any height above the Marsh, particularly between Lydd and Rye, where there has been very little tillage. For elsewhere there is always a moderate acreage under the plough and there will almost certainly be more. But the wholesale breaking up of the finest old pasture land is not calculated to bring about the millennium of all-round productiveness that the Cockney who instructs the farmer through letters to the papers so ingenuously imagines. Unless, that is to say, half the industrial population of the towns are going to forsake them, a most improbable proposition, and turn market-gardeners, or small holders, for which last they are less adapted by temperament, habit and tradition than probably any people in Europe.

The month of June, when the gleaming white of the freshly shorn sheep, which like ten thousand mushrooms dimple the radiant green of the early summer grass is the time to look down over the Marsh from some commanding height, such as Playden hill or even Rye town. I remember a prominent Scottish agriculturist, familiar with most of Great Britain, saying to me, when a hopeless invalid at the close of his life, that one of the things he always regretted having missed, was a sight of Romney Marsh in June, as there could be nothing like it, he thought, to the seeing eye, in the whole world— nor in all probability is there. An even distribution of some 150,000 sheep in so small an area is to be seen nowhere else. For those whom such things interest, it may be noted that all the lambs are removed from the Marsh in autumn to back-lying upland farms and brought back in April as tegs. This relieves the pressure when the grass is not growing and gives the young sheep a better chance to mature.

May is an anxious month on the Marsh with big sheep farmers, who have of course to stock up their pastures on the estimate of a normal season. If the rains hold off, as they occasionally do in this region of rather dry summers, for the very weeks when they are most wanted, the feebly growing young grasses get bitten down so close that they cannot properly respond to the refreshing showers when these eventually fall. The Romney Marsh sheep are sometimes crossed with the Southdown, but to nothing like the extent that crossing goes on nowadays in most parts of Britain. They have made great way too of late in South America and the Colonies, particularly in New Zealand, whose graziers come frequently back to the Marsh for breeding stock. The origin of the breed is lost in the mists of time, though a theory exists upon the Marsh that, owing to their amphibious qualities, Noah shipped a pair upon the Ark as more likely to survive the voyage than any other sort. The present type, however, seems little older than the last century, and the Leicester had no doubt something to do with improving and stereotyping it. But in early days cattle and pigs (the latter only as summer grazers before the mast in the upland woods) shared the Marsh with the sheep in relatively larger numbers than now. The polite palate professes a distaste for Romney Marsh mutton as too coarse, classing it with Lincoln, Leicester and the like. With the craze for small mutton and lamb which became universal in the 'eighties, large mutton fell out of demand. The local gourmet, however, will tell you that

GULDEFORD CHURCH ON THE MARSH.

Marsh mutton in the summer and autumn is the primest of meats. After all, these are salt marshes, and it is the *mouton de pré-salé*, that the Briton abroad welcomes or is expected to welcome on a *table d'hôte* menu. Furthermore all this mutton is grass-fed, and unlike other heavy breeds the fattening sheep get practically no turnips and not much cake at any time. They also lamb nearly as late as hill sheep, in April that is to say.

The farms upon the Marsh are large—five hundred, a thousand, even two thousand acres—though some are smaller. The land is curiously patchy, as one would expect from a country submerged within recorded history, but the better quality on the whole prevails, and that, whether in grass or in tillage, as are some parts where fine wheat is grown, is very good. In the great old days of the 'sixties and 'seventies, £4 an acre was not an unusual rent, though it had been pushed up that high by competition beyond a doubt. About half, or less than half, that figure is the present standard, and I will undertake to say that in the tillage districts such hearing would make a visiting Lothian farmer's mouth water. A chronic theory of the Scottish farmer that the whole South is under-rented and enterprise thereby discouraged, would find here (in his eyes) an apotheosis of justification. But I shall get into trouble if I pursue so cryptic a subject any further. Most people are ready to tell the British farmer exactly what he ought to do, but few are interested in crops save vaguely as a feature in the landscape or as covert for partridges.

A mile out of Rye by the Rother bridge is the hamlet of Guldeford, on the section of the Marsh known by that name. A curious rude old sixteenth-century church (served from Playden) without tower, and covered by a double gable roof, stands solitary upon the Marsh, suggesting from a distance a glorified and venerable barn till the pointed windows with their worn mullions and tracery reveal themselves. There is nothing of interest in it but a small tablet on the wall bearing some carved models of armour associated with the Guldeford family. This tract of Marsh was about the latest of all recovered from the sea, an achievement which was the work of Sir John Guldeford, one of the great people of this neighbourhood, and aroused for the damage it caused to the harbours of Rye and Winchelsea no little clamour and official protest. The *inning* of this Marsh and the creation thereby of the parish of Guldeford to Sir John's great benefit was begun in 1532, and in three years' time " three great and huge creeks (shown by the way on a map in Camden's *Britannia*) were obliterated to the utter decay," declared a Rye jury, "of the Haven of Camber."

Till the eighteenth century nearly a mile width of water seems to have flowed between Rye and Guldeford. A regular ferry plied here for travellers from the Marsh villages and towns, as we noted in a former chapter, while looking at the old ferry house on the Rye shore. An old diary I read somewhere gives a harrowing picture of frenzied travellers on a stormy and windy night upon the Guldeford shore, to whose shouts and pistol shots the Rye ferryman turned a discreetly

ON THE WAY TO BROOKLAND.

deaf ear. But a notable fracas took place at this ferry in 1688. One Carter, an official of the Romney Marsh preventative service, had caught eight Owlers or wool smugglers *in flagrante delicto* at New Romney. When brought before the Mayor they were at once admitted to bail, whereat this zealous officer, being new to the ways of the Marsh smuggling Zolverein, seems to have been painfully surprised. He and his men, however, had cause for more than surprise. For the gentle owlers, now at liberty, raised the Marsh, and the troop of preventative men were driven out of the town. They next took refuge in Lydd, but were pursued by an ever-gathering mob of avengers and hunted from there right across the Marsh to Guldeford, where they had just time to fling themselves into boats and escape to Rye, abandoning their horses to the mob at their heels. About 25,000 packs of " free wool " were at this time being shipped every year to France from the Marsh. No wonder people put up with malaria! The Guldefords descended upon the Ports from the upland country about the third Edward's time under the name of Gilford which represents the usual pronunciation in vogue to-day. So the local purist who complains of this as a modern lapse, which he often does, may consider himself as hoisted with his own petard.

Guldeford, generally called Gilford, Church, though architecturally a pariah and an outcast among the churches of the Marsh, has its own romance, mainly connected with smugglers. One story runs that the parson on a certain occasion gave out that as the roof was dangerous there would be no service next Sunday and locked up the church.. The parson's anxiety was not for the safety of the congregation but for a cargo of brandy which he had been persuaded on the usual commission terms to store there. The ten miles of road from Guldeford to Lydd is the loneliest on the Marsh. For half the way it is the only one that traverses this six-mile belt of solitude, since for lanes and cross-roads there is here no need. It bends and twists at times before the frequent obstacles of a bedyked country, or again for a mile it romps away in a straight line to be suddenly brought up short to an uncompromising right angle and forced once more into a devious course. It is a little sad in winter, but then it ought to be or it wouldn't be the Marsh! The dark water ruffles coldly in the full dykes beside the road, the flowering reeds that whisper soothingly along their fringes in summer days rattle their dead stems together like dry bones in the winter wind. Here and there a row of giant willows, their warped trunks bulging beneath the surface of some brimming stream, strikes a note of contrast in the foreground of this wide waste. The moorhens, which

S

in summer mock at you with raucous note, from their safe harbourage of reed or alder, of willow bush or briar, are now surprised in the open and dash for safety on nimble feet or fluttering wing. The green pastures are everywhere patched with the tawny hue of the withered summer herbage. The sheep are no longer white but carry fleeces almost as dark from the salt sea mists as those of the smoke-stained specimens that roam the London Parks. The peewit too is everywhere abroad ; that really cheerful and not unsociable bird, who in spite of

BETWEEN RYE AND BROOKLAND.

himself gives forth a cry more calculated than almost any wild-bird note to announce the pathos of the waste, be it moor or marsh, mountain or downland. Seagulls always gregarious, whether upon the earth or in the air, scream in discordant chorus far away. A "looker" will probably be somewhere within sight, his shaggy dogs working in the leisurely manner that a flat country, heavy sheep and comparatively small enclosures permit. Indeed the dogs hereabouts have an easy time, save in very hard weather when the dykes freeze and the sheep range over the whole country. They do not run their hearts to a standstill in six or seven years like the collies of North Wales and Cumberland.

RYE TO BROOKLAND AND LYDD

This, too, is the season on the Marsh when all the old crew of smugglers, owlers, wreckers and the rest of them might well be seen with the eye of fancy, galloping in shadowy troops with their wool packs and brandy kegs, their pistols, cutlasses and blunderbusses, through the winter twilight. They would come out for no man's fancy in summer time I am quite sure. There is nothing creepy about the Marsh when bright suns are shining and warm airs breathing: when the Marsh flowers are blazing along the dyke edges, and the larks are singing,

THE WOOLPACK INN.

bees humming, and lambs bleating, and the little homesteads of the lookers, whether by the roadsides or away in the wilds, are bright with leaf and blossom. There is an ancient and solitary inn by the Lydd road, bearing the sign of *The Woolpack*, and one more significant of Marsh traditions one could not wish for.

But the road at this point, like the trunk of a tree, begins to put out branches that run all over the Kentish and larger half of the Marsh—for the county line, the Kent ditch cuts through it hereabouts to the sea. The village of Brookland is in Kent and the last parish in Walland Marsh. It clusters round a rugged but striking old church, which has the further claim of possessing the most curious detached wooden belfry in all England. I know its only possible rival well, that of Pembridge in Herefordshire. But the Brookland campanile is much more fantastic, suggesting a three-storied Chinese pagoda, or more aptly perhaps a three-flounced bell-shaped Victorian skirt, with so decided a tilt towards the church that a stranger catching his first sight of it, nearly a mile away, must inevitably approach it in a state of bewilderment

BROOKLAND CHURCH.

and curiosity. The structure is octagonal and roofed or walled, whichever you will, with boards. There are several legends accounting for its position, though throwing no light on its eccentric design. The most unkind of them has it that the disregard of the marriage ceremony was so prevalent of yore in the parish that on a couple putting in an appearance with that object, the steeple fell off the church in astonishment.

The church itself is sufficiently quaint, with its long externally barn-like nave, and in the absence of a west tower, what looks like a Liliputian substitute for one, on its north front. It was erected in the thirteenth century by the monks of Canterbury, and dedicated to their patron saint St. Augustine. The old high pews still adorn, or as some would say mar the interior. At any rate they give it that particular flavour of bygone rather than of ancient days which has a secular appeal to some, suggestive of wigs and ruffles and three-cornered hats, of William and Mary, or the good Queen Anne, of fiddle-playing choirs and interminable somniferous sermons, and last but not least of the pencil of Hogarth. If the visitor were aware that part of the church was formerly used as a cock-pit a further thrill might be experienced. There is also a wonderful old circular leaden font of the Norman period with figures on the panels illustrating the signs of the Zodiac. There is nothing very notable in the arcades or windows save that the former in the chancel are of the horse-shoe pattern, and the latter are rather good specimens of the Decorated style. But all the same there is an air of undisturbed antiquity, or perhaps rather of general quaintness, about Brookland Church, inside and out. Persons with some sense of the past but with no interest in the technicalities of architecture would probably feel more pleasantly stirred by Brookland than by some of the finer and older churches of the Marsh. Rye visitors come much to see it and rarely see any of the others to their great loss. It contains also a tombstone of Betherstone marble, date 1615, to John Plomer, a worthy who was Mayor and M.P. for New Romney and one of the canopy bearers to James the First. Betherstone marble is a Kentish product often met with hereabouts in memorial slabs, and would probably perplex most strangers on first encountering it. There is a cheerful-looking roadside inn handy to the church where in the bad old days the parson and clerk no doubt made merry between the services.

The Manor of Brookland, long since obliterated, belonged to our old friend de Passelye, of the moated house in Iden. There were few resident squires of broad acres in any of the twenty-two parishes of the Marsh, for reasons already given. Though even in sight of Brookland there are roomy old farmhouses which might easily have filled in that capacity the less exacting demands of a bygone day. The Derings, now of Surrenden, one of the oldest of the greater Kent families, were large owners hereabouts and still I think retain a little of their ancient domain. The Septuans or Septvans were the other great mediaeval family and disappeared before Tudor times. Seavans Court, marked on eighteenth century maps close to Scotneys Court, a farm still extant between Lydd and Jury's Gap, preserve their name. The Derings were the last of that type to have a residence on the Marsh, though not a stone is left of it.

BROOKLAND BELL TOWER.

Here and there in a village churchyard some tombstones bear the term "generosus" and a coat of arms with the name of a local landowner, in a small way, mixed up no doubt with one or other of the old burgess families of Lydd, New Romney or Hythe. But the Marsh had a strong democratic flavour, as might be expected, and its working class still exhibit the independent bearing of a community that have led an isolated and adventurous existence by land and sea.

There is a weird old residence at the end of the Brookland village, lurking behind much sombre foliage. I once inspected it by request of a military friend in Devonshire contemplating retirement, who had seen it advertised but had never seen

Romney Marsh! I do not think its history is remarkable, but if it hasn't got a ghost it ought to have. It may be noted, too, in passing that the pack of harriers which hunt the Marsh, abounding as it does in hares, have their kennels and stables at Brookland. The village and much of the parish stands a trifle higher than the surrounding country. Hence more evidence of timber and hedgerows, while some of the land has a high agricultural value, and grows fine crops of grain. Some years ago I noticed in passing a field of wheat near the village which struck me as of abnormal promise. A little later I passed it again when it was ready to cut and felt almost sure I had never in England, Scotland or North America seen quite the like of it. A week or two afterwards I saw it in the shock and felt yet more convinced that my eyes had not deceived me; nor had they. For the said field threshed out nine quarters to the acre, just a quarter more than the best I had ever seen on the famous Dunbar red lands of East Lothian, the cream of the earth for heavy grain averages, as well as for potatoes. The farm that produced that in 1882 then let and still lets for £5 an acre (250 acres). The Brookland farm I am told stands at thirty-five shillings, I believe about half its rent in the seventies!

A mile or more inland towards the hills, the quaint little church of St. Thomas à Beckett at Fairfield stands in bleak unsheltered isolation upon a hillock of the Marsh, a familiar sight to passengers on the railroad between Ashford and Rye. The smallest church on the Marsh, with a simple nave and chancel, it is an early wooden building encased in brick and has recently been well restored. The land about is low and wet seasons convert it into an island. The historian of a century ago describes its small congregation as almost always going to church by boat. But it is not so bad as that now. The depressions round it are thought to be due to the digging of sea walls made necessary by the thirteenth-century inundations which threw the Rother back on to the dry land here-

Lydd.

abouts, and of which another word presently. The branch railroad from Appledore to Lydd and New Romney, beyond Brookland village, roughly marks the division between Walland Marsh and that of Romney proper, though the road beyond it is the actual line. The thick grove that hides Brenzett Church and the tall grey tower of Ivychurch now stand up as landmarks ahead of us. We shall see something of them in the next chapter, so must return in this one to *The Woolpeck* and thence pass quickly over the half-dozen miles to Lydd, for they do not differ materially from those already traversed.

The pride and ornament of Lydd; next to its church, is the great wealth of noble elms that gird it about and press right up into its streets. The contrast offered by this upstanding island of lofty mantling foliage, rising above the miles of level treeless marsh, as one approaches it by the Rye road, has been already touched upon ; so also has the fine pose of the church tower which rises high above it. The old homestead of Westbroke, pleasantly embowered in timber, fronts the road a little before entering Lydd. It is noteworthy now and for a long time past as the stronghold of a family who between them are not only the largest sheep owners on the Marsh, but among the most conspicuous breeders and exporters of its particular stock. Westbroke was one of the three tseats of the Dering family when they lived on the Marsh, before acquiring Surrenden by marriage in the fifteenth century, but the original house stood a little distance away from the present one. Nodd, their earlier seat near Lydd, has long disappeared, even its site being uncertain. But besides Westbroke, Dengemarsh Hall, another old place of the Derings' still exists at the edge of the shingle wastes towards Dungeness, though represented by a modern farmhouse. Dengemarsh, it should be said, lies all about the south and east side of Lydd, and with that of Walland covers nearly the whole western portion of Romney Marsh as known in current speech. It was from Dengemarsh Hall, near the close of the fifteenth century, that Richard

Dering was carried off to France for the sake of a ransom, which moreover had to be paid. However it was probably but a small portion of what his ancestors, fighting under Edward the Third and Henry the Fifth, had wrung from the French.

The Rectory too, just beyond Westbroke, and embowered among more big trees, looks snug enough. And then comes the great church, with the original High Street of the little town stretching from its tower to a not very distant termination in the sandy shingle waste where stands the modern camp. There are enough old houses and shops in the tolerably wide and straight thoroughfare, to give it the air one would look for in a little old borough on Romney Marsh, with a past population of some fifteen hundred souls, now much increased. The adjacent thoroughfares, save for a building here and there, are not precisely engaging. The demands of the camp, some dozen or more years old, upon the shore side of the town and now vastly increased, are not conducive to æsthetic effect.

But the church of All Saints is very fine indeed. It consists of an embattled west tower 132 feet high, a nave with side aisles, and a chancel with a north and south chapel. The style varies from late Norman to Early English and Perpendicular. The double arcade of the nave, seven bays with pointed arches, has much dignity. Though at the first glance they look uniform, the three western bays are actually much later than the others, whose pointed arches stand on Norman piers as at Rye, and terminate in carved heads, most of which appear to be grotesques. There are fine perpendicular windows too in the east end, both of the chancel and its chapels, the latter being so short as to leave space for three plain lancets on either side of the high chancel, which on the inside are surmounted by curious trefoil-headed hoods. The windows of both nave aisles are Perpendicular or Decorated, the bases of their drip-stones on the exterior of the south wall being ornamented with the masks of kings, queens and ecclesiastics. There is a handsome exposed oak roof in the chancel, that of the nave being plastered but showing king-posts and tie-beams. A lofty pointed arch opens out the tower space, the ceiling of which is vaulted. There are two west doors to the tower, one of only three like instances in England, and in perfect symmetry with the great west window above them. In the north-west corner of the nave are the outlines of three arches that have been pronounced Saxon by a distinguished authority, and in any case point to the existence of a small building prior to the

LYDD.

present church. Many inscribed brasses that have been rescued from obscurity or from damaged tombs are now displayed along either wall of the nave on new oak panels, and a cross-legged effigy of a knight, Sir Walter Merel, 1333, is still *in situ* in the north chapel.

The top of the tower, as can be well understood, did constant service as a beacon and look-out post. The town records make mention of one particular occasion in the fifteenth century when men were kept up there for days and weeks together watching for the French. It was the custom of the various Ports to warn one another at once on scenting danger;

"fourpence pd. to a man from Hastings for tythings that Frenshmen were on the sea," is another entry in the records. A most spacious graveyard spreads around the church on the south side, more quaintly than artistically bordered by the fronts of houses, some of which redeem the situation by their respectable antiquity, while others do not. Curiously enough the church at one time belonged to Tintern Abbey and was thus connected with the Welsh Marcher-lordship of Striguil, otherwise Chepstow. It is supposed that one of the Clares acquired it and transferred it to the great Cistercian House which his family had founded. At the Dissolution Lydd came back through the Crown to the Archbishop, while among its vicars about this time it boasts no less a person than Wolsey, who is said to have raised the tower by a stage. There is a rugged weather-beaten old gravestone on the north side of the churchyard, on which the name Thomas Striguil, still just decipherable, marks, with some other headstones of the same family, a curious and sole surviving link between the far-away Anglo-Welsh Abbey on the Wye, the most beautiful ruin in England and this typical old Kentish church. They are believed to be among the oldest outdoor inscribed gravestones in existence. Near them is another, a head-stone to the memory of one Edgar who entered the Navy at ten years old, fought in "Admiral Hawke's *Victory*," sailed round the world with Captain Cook and was finally killed by Indians on the Island of Owhyhee. Then follow some lines in quaint nautical phraseology telling how the gallant seaman piloted his way to Paradise.

The great physical incident in the past, not merely of Lydd and Romney, but of the whole district was the almost sudden diversion of the course of their common river. Till the great storms of the thirteenth century, culminating in apparently the worst, that of 1287, the Rother, still often called, as it had always been in earlier days, the Limene or Lymne, found its entry to the sea between Lydd and the Romneys, New Romney being up till then a flourishing Cinque-Port town with Lydd as a "limb." The rage of the sea, however, on this occasion, as described in an earlier chapter, flooded this whole coast, carrying with it such masses of sand and shingle as permanently to choke the mouth of the Rother. Despite all the efforts of the Portsmen, who saw the source of their very existence cut off and receding from them, the stream of the river, baffled in its efforts to reach the sea, fell gradually back, and turning to the right at Appledore cut out a new channel along the edge of the old cliff line—the same, in fact, that it has followed from that day to this—all of which things happened within a comparatively short period.

But the Rother, in turning towards Rye as it came out of the hills at Appledore, below the Isle of Oxney, had not in those days to cut through much, if any, drained pasture land. For much of Walland and the whole of Guldeford Marsh was at that time water, swamp, or tide-washed sand-banks. So the current, once turned, encountered probably small resistance, particularly when it is remembered that the Marsh is tilted slightly inland towards the old cliffs. Anyway the fact remains that a considerable river which had flowed very nearly eastward to the sea through a ten-mile channel, that by the thirteenth century seems to have been well defined and bordered mostly by drained lands, suddenly altered its course to slightly south of west and ran at right angles for seven miles to Rye and its harbour. Many strange things were done all round the coasts of England by the fearful inundations of that period. But nothing anywhere I fancy quite so fateful as this sudden *volte-face* of a big river which turned two seaports, Lydd and Romney, into inland towns, and a century or two later proved the saving of another, Rye, from a like fate.

A deed of Offa, King of Mercia, granting a tract of land at Lydd in 774 to the Archbishop of Canterbury, seems to be the first mention of the place by name. This last is thought to be derived from the Latin *Litus* (shore) and applied by the

Romans to the scantily occupied coast fringe they probably found here, and with equal probability made a base for their own operations. The Saxon name of Lydd seems to have been Hilda, and its people with other men of Kent fought the Danes successfully on more than one occasion, at the Wick and Holmestone near Jury's Gap. Tradition says that the east and west rype, lands now adjoining the town, were granted to the barons of Lydd by the Archbishop for their valour against the Danes. The seal of this same Prelate is still used by the corporation in dealings with this particular tract. The gradual changes that took place around Lydd, between the date, say, of Offa's grant and the great inundations five centuries later, even if they were not a matter of some disagreement among those stimulated by local knowledge and associations to grapple seriously with the subject, make further elaboration here out of the question. To readers with no acquaintance, or but a cursory one with the district concerned, such discourse would be meaningless and indeed intolerable. But two other salient facts may be appropriately recorded. First, that the Rhee wall raised of old across the Marsh, east of the ancient course of the Rother, and roughly on the line of the modern highway from Appledore to New Romney, saved Romney Marsh proper, or most of it, from those inundations of the thirteenth century which wrought such havoc on Walland and Denge Marshes. Secondly, that prior to these inundations, Lydd and Romney may safely be pictured as confronting one another across an estuary, the widening mouth, that is to say, of the old Rother, as it flowed into the sea. Those, indeed, were the halcyon days of both towns, Lydd, the lesser, contributing its quota of ships, men and service to Romney, the greater, then in its full tide of Cinque-Port honours.

It is conceivable that there may be reflecting persons who imagine the ancient records of a little town to consist of a series of well-bound volumes, setting forth in due sequence and legible fashion the events of five or six centuries. In short, that their perusal is much the same thing as running one's eye over a church register in a vestry. As a matter of fact it is a big job in itself. Torn or discoloured pages, their ink faded sometimes to an obscurity that nothing but chemicals will restore; others again gnawed by mice and in some cases written in Norman-French, a tongue requiring some special mastery, are only some of the difficulties. Frequently whole volumes are missing; always too, such as there may be of the more legible Tudor or Jacobean periods are subject to the vagaries of ever-changing provincial caligraphy. Such extracts from them, both grave and gay, as seem to be of sufficient interest or that bear directly on the past life of the place have been transcribed during the last fifty years by the Historical MS. Commission. All the Cinque-Ports, and some of the boroughs associated with them, have been thus dealt with, Lydd among them, though in this case, as is perhaps natural, rather sparingly. But Mr. Arthur Finn of Westbroke has rendered his native place a service that is all too rare, and published in a well-printed volume running to four hundred pages the Chamberlain's accounts for part of the fifteenth century, that of the Wars of the Roses, and the churchwardens' accounts from about the middle of Henry the Eighth to the first of Elizabeth; and though figures may sound dull, the doings connected with them are constantly instructive and sometimes entertaining.

Edward the First seems to have given Lydd its first Charter, which is lost, but a confirmatory one of Edward the Third, quoting in full his grandfather's Charter to the Barons and men of Lydd and Ingemarsh (Dengemarsh), is reproduced in photogravure in Mr. Finn's volume. The town was granted all the privileges of the Cinque-Ports, as it had become a "limb" of Romney about the time of Henry the First. But in the fifteenth century, when the last-named town was left high and dry, Lydd seems to have grown sick of the connection, which included the overlordship of the Archbishop, and wanted to shake it off. His Grace of Canterbury in these times marched with the Abbot of Battle, who had lands running towards Lydd from the direction of Rye, and there were often heated passages between these distinguished clerics and the Lyddites, in respect of their various claims upon a constantly shifting foreshore. The incomes of these old towns were derived from *Scots* (rates levied), *Fines*, *Maltots* (sums paid on goods for sale), *Lyvelode* (a form of income tax), tolls on the sale of fish, and the hated poll tax which will be remembered as the cause of Wat Tyler's Insurrection. The bailiff and Jurats were elected annually in the church up till 1884, when, like similar towns, Lydd became a municipal corporation of the modern type.

After the shifting of the course of the Rother, Lydd had its fishing station a couple of miles or so to the south, at a spot now covered by the artillery ranges, and known as Dengemarsh. It was recognized as a subsidiary village to the town, enjoying certain rights. The rate at which land has been made by the shingle accumulations and the constantly out-thrusting headland of Dungeness has now left this site, together with the old Manor of the Derings, far inland. Among the records of the town recovered and published by Mr. Finn or the Historical Commission are innumerable entries suggestive of the life led by the people in olden days. Among the church records are several allusions to one John Bate, the hermit of Lydd, who rented church land, had a chapel thereon and was active in all church doings. Now a hermit, strictly speaking, was not a recluse; it was the Anchorite who shut himself up and devoted his life to prayer, fasting and flagellation, a devout megalomaniac in short. The Hermit was virtually a free-lance of the church and was formally inducted to his self-made cell, or chapel, by his monastery and with much ceremonial. He was very often an extraordinarily useful person, preaching and teaching in the open air, reclaiming wastrels, and even land, skilled in healing and frequently in farming, besides repairing fords and bridges.

This particular hermit came of a family prominent in Lydd, we are told, for three hundred years, and may have partly atoned perhaps for the misdeeds of his ancestor, a plutocratic and over-bearing butcher. The career of this butchering Andrew Bate may be traced from the time he was an apparently humble and inoffensive Jurat, proud no doubt of the honour, to that when he became a large and tyrannical landholder in Dengemarsh under the Abbot of Battle. He victimised the western fishermen drying their nets on his foreshore, drove away the inhabitants by the unchecked raids of his cattle on their crops, and bore himself generally with all the proverbial arrogance of the upstart. It was complained that he "wasted and put away from Dengemarsh seventy households, and not eight men left to defend it against the King's enemies." But he was so rich that all the powers of Lydd and its clients could make little headway against him. It is interesting too to find that a prominent town clerk of Lydd in the fifteenth century was Thomas Caxton, as is supposed, a brother of the famous William of printing press celebrity.

Though this corner was little affected by the Wars of the Roses, Lydd was compelled or induced to supply men to both sides at different periods. There are accounts of brawls of soldiers in the town, only noteworthy because the method of suppressing them was to bribe the officers to take them away! Wrestling matches appear frequently in the entries, Brookland being a favourite scene of operations. These took place on Sundays and were attended by the Bailiff and Jurats bearing gifts for the victors. There were frequent proclamations by the Crown, here as elsewhere, against tennis and dice, and in favour of archery, which suggests a sort of parallel in recent days between football and rifle-shooting. Tennis was no doubt the rude fives played against the church wall, which was common all over England and Wales, and in the seventeenth and eighteenth centuries was encouraged as a kind of protest against Puritans and Nonconformists, and an outward sign of

T

staunch Churchmanship. Jack Cade had of course a great following in this part of the country. But Lydd and Romney, unlike many of the villages we have passed through, and others we have yet to see, do not appear to have contributed more than a single individual apiece who had the courage of his opinions. Lydd however dispatched John Hayes with a letter to "the Captain at London," giving its excuses. It followed this with a porpoise, which cost the town six shillings and a good deal more in the horse hire for three men, who were apparently required for conveying and presenting it to Cade, "the Captain of the Ost." But even the porpoise must have been a pleasanter burden on a saddle-bow than "the quarter of a man," which as a warning to the rebellious was brought to Lydd soon after by a horseman who received two shillings for the grisly job. For this must surely have been for exhibition purposes after the fashion of the day, though the customary city gate to which these pleasant relics were habitually affixed was here lacking.

Bates are still living in the neighbourhood, as also I believe are Cobbs, Godfreys, Rolfes, and Allens, all prominent Lydd families as early as the fifteenth century. It is quite touching the number of entries, both in the Lydd and Romney records, of presents sent to various powerful people at the expense of the town, "to have their friendship," as it was candidly recorded in the account books. Porpoises and wine, with an occasional "grampus," were the favourite mediums for gaining the hearts of these exalted souls, Archbishops, Lord Wardens and the like. Nor is the roar of artillery altogether a new thing at Lydd, for the entries of these old days constantly tell of the dragging of cannon, cast in Sussex no doubt, to the seashore for practice in shooting. One great gun, "the Serpentine," was assuredly made at Lydd itself, the iron being fetched from Winchelsea and Hastings by boat and the brass also purchased in that country. They seem to have fired stones, children being employed to convey them. They were useful weapons, no doubt, though prior to the Tudor times they always burst sooner or later, so that the final damage they inflicted was on their friends.

Just after the making of the great Serpentine gun at Lydd, a letter came from the Earl of Warwick at Calais, warning the people to expect the French shortly, and a man is paid a penny, " to make a cry to muster at Romney," and a further penny for " making another cry " in Lydd, to the effect that every man in the town should keep watch in three parties and that no man should play at tennis ! Of lighter amusements there was good store in both towns ; each had its troupe of players, which toured the neighbourhood, some of the neighbouring villages repaying such visits with exhibitions of their own talent. Wild animals were constantly led about England on show, the eyes of the Lyddites being gratified with the sight of a dromedary and an ape on one occasion, while on another the King's bears paid them a visit. Music too had its votaries, and bands of minstrels belonging to great people, and even to the King, frequently gave performances, for which the town rewarded them with money and refreshments. " The Lord of Misrule " was also much abroad at Christmas and seems to have collected money for worthy objects with perhaps a little gentle pressure.

In the churchwardens' accounts epitomized by Mr. Hussey in Mr. Finn's volume, it is interesting to note the stirring up of things in Lydd church in 1553 when Bloody Mary came on the scene, the purchase of a mass book being naturally prominent. Regarding Church matters there is a curious note of a man being fined for " opening the parson's love letter." Another is hauled up before the magistrates for knocking the Vicar down. The impression made by Lydd, or Lid, on the topographers of the sixteenth, seventeenth and eighteenth centuries, such as Leland, Camden and Hasted is perhaps worth half a dozen lines. The first in his delightfully quaint English and spelling says : " The town is of a prety quantitie and the tounesey men use Botes to the se, the which at this time is a myle of." Camden calls it " a pretty populous town, whither the inhabitants of Bromhill betook themselves after the inundation." Hasted gives it a thousand inhabitants, " some few in a better situation in life but the generality of them are such as follow a contraband trade with France, or fishermen who have cabins on the shore with a common dining-room, where they spend the summer months."

George the First visited Lydd, as he did Rye, by accident. Indeed it seems almost certain that it was part of that same adventure related in an earlier chapter which landed him in any case at Lamb House. His ship, it will be remembered, was blown on to the Camber shore which may easily have meant the neighbourhood of Jury's Gap—to which spot Lydd would be more accessible than Rye. The Rye tradition that he walked to that town in a snowstorm may be at fault only in his objective point. For he not only went to Lydd but his approach was heralded in time for flags to be hung out, bells rung, and a coach prepared, as well as a parson to read him a loyal address, of great length it is said, while he sat in it. That most ungracious of monarchs, who must have been in a hurry to get to Rye *en route* for London, seems to have grunted out some sort of recognition of the Vicar's homily, though as we know he could not understand a word of English, and hated a country altogether beyond the scope of his limited training and understanding. On this particular occasion, however, we may sympathize with him.

Dungeness (Denge-ness), the actual point, that is to say, where the lighthouse stands, is nearly four miles from Lydd, and a branch line runs there from the station. For what purpose? the stranger travelling by it on to the great waste of shingle to which Dengemarsh itself soon gives way, is pretty sure to ask. But he will find there are a good many inhabitants of the waste, besides the lighthouse people, and coastguards scattered about in small and quaint abodes—fishermen and the like, besides two or three primitive inns and a lifeboat station. The natives often go about their business with boards strapped on to their feet, on the snow-shoe principle. And when you have paid one or two visits to this interesting wilderness and scuffled around on the loose shingle for two or three hours in ordinary footgear it will be easily realized that such going would become intolerable as an everyday business. The Ness has been pushing out to sea for ages, ever gathering to it the shingle drift that sweeps perpetually along the coast from the west, and making at the rate of about twenty feet a year. It forms a sure shelter for ships, and in bad weather quite a fleet may be seen upon its leeward side waiting till the storm abates. As already mentioned the shingle banks drop sheer into deep water, and big ships can come close in shore. The great feature of the spot, though, is its imposing lighthouse. It is well worth ascending, which can be done in company with the keeper. The present tower was erected in 1842 on the destruction of a former one put up just fifty years earlier. For centuries prior to that a quite primitive system of lighting the point with ordinary pitch, coal or wood beacons, set upon a platform, had obtained. The depth of the water at the shore makes this a favourite haunt of such sea-anglers as can manage to get out here. It is interesting too to watch the gulls, but a few yards from the shore, diving with rapid, hawk-like darts, into the water after fish. A Government meteorological post, maintained here, shows Dungeness to have almost, if not quite, the lowest rainfall in England, as low sometimes as nineteen inches. A road has recently been made out here from Lydd, by private enterprise, quite good enough for ordinary travel on wheels, to say nothing of the pedestrian. It is a curious, uncanny sort of outpost of civilization this. I know nothing quite like it anywhere else upon our coasts. On the southern flank of the broad promontory towards the Wicks and Jury's Gap are the scant remains of an ancient wood of holly trees, known as the

Holme. In olden days it was a great breeding ground of herons—a bird which to-day, as one would expect, is a common feature on the Marsh, though as a mere visitant from neighbouring heronries in the surrounding country. But a good authority on these, as on other local matters, who has frequented this particular bit of the Marsh all his life, tells me that herons from all over the country have an extraordinary liking for this one

ON THE MARSH.

waste spot where their remote ancestors bred, and that in former days, before the advent of the artillery ranges, he has seen as many as two hundred standing in long rows upon the edge of the shingle near the shore and presenting a most uncanny sight. The Marsh is naturally, over its whole extent, a great resort of ducks and other wildfowl, particularly in hard winter weather, when everybody who has a gun, and the opportunity to use it, seizes these not too frequent occasions.

CHAPTER THE NINTH

New Romney

A WELL-KEPT and, for the most part, straight road covers the four miles between Lydd and New Romney. There are few habitations upon it, but as the main route between Lydd and Hythe (twelve miles) it is a good deal used. It is not interesting, except for the fact that it crosses the now fertile bed of what was once the Rother estuary. The railway line from Lydd to its terminus at New Romney is really more so, as it takes a wide sweep, for obvious reasons of economy in construction, along the edge of, and at times within, the shingle desert of the Dungeness headland, and gives the traveller quite a good idea of this really weird waste. In view, however, of a glance at some of the more inland villages, we must here take a little circuit, returning to New Romney a few pages later in this chapter. One rather shrinks from quoting the points of the compass too literally in writing of the Marsh, for they might well mislead, owing to its queer shape. Even as a resident one is inclined to forget that its length runs nearly north and south, not east and west as one is apt insensibly to visualize a seaboard strip upon the south coast. Omitting the narrow strip from Rye to Fairlight cliffs, the Marsh is almost precisely the shape of the traditional fool's cap, with the bending back and pointed top, tilted slightly over by the weight of the bell. Rye marks the back of the crown. Dungeness the front in a west to east line, while the coast thence turning north to Hythe represents the slightly concave forepart of the cap, and Hythe itself the pointed crest. The old cliff line along the rear of the Marsh may stand for the back and complete the analogy.

Taking a twisting road then from Lydd towards the heart of the Marsh and Old Romney, after crossing the railway, the scant ruins of Midley Church at once come into view. A gable end showing a ragged window space with a few other fragments perched on a mound is all that remains of it, and it would seem to have been in this same condition over a century ago. As a Manor mentioned in Domesday, Midley must have been " inned " by that date and have become a parish then or later, with always no doubt a microscopic population. This now amounts to some fifty souls who are ecclesiastically attached to New Romney, though they still possess an absentee rector of their own. We will leave it at that, as no doubt matters have been adapted to fit the case, as in other similar ones.

Old Romney stands a mile and a half to the west of New Romney, near that broad, straight and admirable road which bisects the Marsh, following the trail of the old Roman embankment, the Rhee wall to Appledore. It has been insisted by many past writers that the present hamlet represents an ancient town and port on the Rother or Limene estuary, which in the Saxon period silted up and gave way to a " New " Romney nearer the sea. There is no foundation for the theory and present opinion rejects it. If such were indeed the case, there would be pathos enough in its present aspect. For a many-gabled, small Gothic church with shingle spire standing solitary upon a knoll in the meadows, and a large, well-timbered homestead a hundred yards away, showing glimpses of warm-tinted tile roofs and mellow brick walls, is about all there is of it.

But this combination, in the forefront of the far-spreading, sheep-flecked plain, presents upon a sunny day a truly charming picture. These larger farmhouses upon the Marsh, of which north of the Rhee wall there are a good few, are eloquent of the money that has been made here in past days. Unlike some other monuments of prosperity, they preserve the memory of substantial bank balances in its most engaging form. The echo of bleating flocks, of wool-laden wagons, of busy flails upon the old barn floors seems still in the air, to say nothing of high adventures upon sea and shore, of which in truth little was ever said. If there was abundance of fever and ague there must have been great compensations to offset these distressing maladies. Ample good living, lashings of meat and drink, were going forward, we may be sure, in these snug strongholds of yeomen and squireens, of Mayors and Jurats, and all the rest of the little autocracy that dominated this back-of-beyond country between Romney and Appledore, Hythe and Rye. Anyway they stand up with no little dignity, these Georgian houses behind their tall trees, often concealing much older interiors and generally covering ancient sites ; islands of foliage and quiet existence on the dyke-laced plain of greensward, with its interludes of tillage, its faint grey strips of willows, its dim inconsequent clumps of ash or thorn, its eloquent solitude.

A noble old yew tree stands conspicuous in the otherwise unshaded churchyard, but the interior of the church behind is a dream. Possibly the Vicar does not think so, for the clerical aversion to square pews is invincible. But these are no ordinary pews ; if the liberty may be pardoned, they are noble loose boxes and are overlooked, as they should be, by a two-decker pulpit— a three-decker would complete the picture, but one cannot have everything ! The nave is rather short, to be sure, which the length of the chancel more than counter-balances. But there are only two of these wonderful compartments at either side of it, and they fill the whole space from the pulpit to the gallery which most appropriately, together with the Royal escutcheon, looks down from the west end of the little church on this scene of ancient peace. One forgets the Early English features of the old building in this quite precious survival of Georgian or maybe Jacobean furniture. Two pointed arches divide off a small south aisle, while a very handsome old oak roof with moulded tie beams and curious king posts covers the nave.

A couple of miles along the Appledore road, and hidden but for its shingle spire amid thick trees, stands the parish church of Brenzett, which we noted from Brookland and, incidentally, from the cross-roads just here we may return the compliment.

OLD ROMNEY.

The latter amid its elms and cornfields lies without the Rhee wall on which we are travelling, while Brenzett is just within it. Church and vicarage lie picturesquely together, the one within its dark grove of elm and ash trees, the other encircled by its brighter garden foliage. The patron saint of Brenzett is a lady I never heard of, St. Eanswythe. But I find that she was the first head of Folkestone Priory, founded by her father, Eadbalde, King of Kent, and possessed miraculous powers. She made water run uphill to her oratory, she successfully banished certain ravenous birds from the country, restored the blind, cast out devils, cured diseases and thoroughly earned her saintship.

It is a pretty little Early English church of the pattern imprinted by the monks of Canterbury in their less ambitious efforts throughout their whole sphere of influence. There are three bays of pointed arches dividing the nave from a north aisle and some rather curious decorated windows and a good south porch. But the greatest surprise of all, particularly in a small church upon the Marsh, is the spectacle of a fine altar tomb, carrying two recumbent marble effigies. These represent, as inscribed below, John Fagge of Rye and Brenzett Place, and his son, of date 1639. They are both in the armour of the period, the elder in an unusual position, leaning on his elbow and contemplating his offspring with apparently a good deal of interest. Brenzett Place, now a farmhouse, is a few hundred yards beyond the church, on the road leading to Ivychurch, whither we are bound. The Fagges had held it since the reign of Elizabeth, succeeding the Edulphs, apparently an old Saxon family seated here for the two or three preceding centuries—Ralphe Edulph of Brenzett appears in the Heralds' Visitation of Kent, striking an almost prehistoric note among the ordinary English names of the Elizabethan gentry. The Fagges, who seem to have resided at Brenzett, failed in the male line about 1740, and their heiresses carried the property by marriage elsewhere. They had been great men upon the Marsh and in the Marsh towns, including Rye, as we know.

From Brenzett Church, still looking inland towards Appledore, another little island of timber, a mile away, rises above the bare Marsh, criss-crossed hereabouts by water dykes even more abundantly than elsewhere. Above this patch of thick wood shoots up the tower of Snargate church. This was the cure held by the Rev. Richard Barham, " *Thomas Ingoldsby*," the author of the immortal *Legends*, of whom something will be said later on. There is nothing worth calling a village round Brenzett Church, and in a mile we are at Ivychurch, where there is none at all. A cheery-looking roadside inn, a couple of homesteads, a modern rectory and a cottage or two, support, as it were, one of the most interesting, largest and, partly for that very reason, one of the most pathetic looking churches on the Marsh. Some years ago I noted on the west door that the rector and his churchwarden bore the same name, a fact which might, to be sure, have meant nothing, but happening to mention the matter to a local, I was informed that it was the Rector's wife who held the office. Now this was an interesting situation. I had never encountered the like in all my wanderings. Was it, or rather I believe I should say is it, unique in England? There is no earthly reason why a lady should not be churchwarden. Indeed I know of at least one instance of such a thing, though not a rector's wife, but the inference here is that the parish of Ivychurch, which in acreage is very large and in population very small, could not produce a second male qualified for so exalted a post.

Turning to the church itself, it was built of sandstone and dedicated to the patron saint of England in the second quarter of the fourteenth century, the surrounding land having been " inned " apparently in Henry the Second's time. It may be noted too in passing that when Canterbury granted tracts of land—in this case it was to the family of de la More—the tenants were bound over to keep out the sea by all those recognized methods, now this long time known as " the customal of the Marsh." The " inning " of Ivychurch must therefore have been rather belated. The de la Mores, with a brief interlude, gave way to the well-known Godfrey family of Lydd, who held the Manor from Henry the Eighth's time to the middle of the eighteenth century. A lofty and heavily buttressed embattled tower of three stages makes Ivychurch a landmark far and wide over the Marsh. A newel staircase on the north side terminates in a hexagonal beacon turret, now surmounted by a leaden cap. A nave and chancel covered by the same roof supported by a continuous arcade of pointed arches, gives the building, which is a hundred and forty feet in length, the impression of being even larger than it is. A wide north aisle under a separate gable roof with a battlemented parapet lit by many large decorated windows and flanked by a curious circular tower would help to fasten this church of St. George on the memory after the briefest acquaintance with it. Over the south porch is a parvise or priest's chamber reached by a newel staircase. The body of the church is profusely buttressed, and the decorated tracery that fills most of the pointed windows on either side is much worn on the exterior.

IVYCHURCH.

Indeed the whole church has an even more than commonly weather-beaten surface, which emphasizes the rather melancholy aspect inseparable from so large a building in so lonely a land. But within, this sense of pathos becomes accentuated. A stranger unacquainted with the Marsh would expect monuments and memories, chapels, stained glass, altar tombs, effigies, brasses, and mural inscriptions. But in all this vast interior there is nothing, or practically nothing, but what the builders left here centuries ago, save an early fifteenth-century oak screen and a short length of panelled seating in the chancel, but, if this seems rather lost amid the waste, the work is very good. There are not even any pews; a dozen or two chairs with kneeling mats in the middle of the nave represents the Anglican requirements of the sparsely peopled parish of a church the size of a Welsh cathedral. Twenty odd years ago a traveller writes of it as harbouring the wildfowl of the Marsh and reeking with its penetrating storms. A story runs that the Archdeacon on paying a surprise visit of curiosity or inspection, was startled on entering the nave by the fall of a dead owl on to his head. On lifting his astonished eyes, the first thing they lit upon was the fragment of a text upon the wall, "*How dreadful is this place,*" which must have provided

IVYCHURCH.

an admirable story for the next archidiaconal meeting. All this, however, has been put right by renovation. There is nothing the matter with the church in a structural way. It is a fine building, but looks as if it had spent six hundred unappreciated years here, and been starved for lack of sympathy! Even if some of the wealthy yeomen who lie amid their families and their ancestors within railed enclosures in the green graveyard had left memorials of themselves inside, it would have helped at any rate to save the forlornness of the situation.

NEW ROMNEY

If laymen of might and leading have somehow passed Ivychurch by, many of its rectors have been distinguished persons : Alexander Burnet particularly, an Aberdonian too, and here on the Marsh ! But he became Archbishop of Glasgow, in the early seventeenth century, when Scotland was all ablaze with sectarian fires, and fell upon the western Covenanters with such heavy hand that he is credited with stirring up the first of their fierce insurrections. In 1530 John Stokesley, Rector of Ivychurch, was transferred directly to the See of London, and while there caused "the most virulent tirade against the Reformation yet written," to be read in church by every curate in his diocese. His successor at Ivychurch became the first Dean of Canterbury.

A clerestory runs the whole length of the church, consisting in the nave of small quatrefoil windows deeply splayed, though most of them are sealed up, but their character is changed on the south side of the chancel to double trefoil headed lights. The oak roof covering both nave and chancel rests on king posts, springing from stone corbels. It is plastered in the nave and north aisle and open over the chancel and south aisle. There is also an old sundial in the churchyard, and the stranger would assuredly notice there, as indeed everywhere throughout this district, the local predilection for those long, circular, mummy-looking gravestones that take the place of the usual turf mounds beneath the headstone. A delightful old farmstead adjoins the churchyard and faces the road where it leaves the village for its three-mile journey through a thinly peopled country to New Romney.

Hereabouts and in all those parts of the Marsh where the plough finds favour, there are occasional fields of lucerne to be seen, a grass virtually identical with the alfalfa that in the irrigated dry belts of both North and South America give the farmer four or five crops of hay a year, and give him more than consolation for the interminable droughts. This however, with its one annual cutting, is a common enough grass in England, but the crops of turnip seed raised upon the Marsh over considerable acreages will be a novel sight to most people, whether farmers or laymen. I can fancy the latter being altogether at a loss, even on a near inspection of such a field in the flowering period. And this would not be surprising, as I believe turnip seed is grown for market nowhere else in England but in parts of the fen country, the article being one of those with which the Continent has in the main supplied the British farmer. Indeed the output of the Marsh has declined a good deal within the past decade, through low priced foreign competition, I believe. The changed situation will no doubt alter this among so many other things agricultural.

A mile short of New Romney the ruins of a small church are visible from the road ; this is Hope All Saints, one of those many foundations with which the borough was originally provided. The noble tower of New Romney Church, like that of Lydd, but having the greater distinction of its Norman origin and features, overlooks the Marsh for miles in all directions. For that matter it has been conspicuous in the picture ever since we left Lydd. The entry to the little town by the Ivychurch road, if you know your final turn, makes it easy to avoid a long string of new villas which offer a most depressing welcome to the incomer, and to approach the High Street by what might be called a flank move. By this manœuvre the first impression of New Romney from the outside is all that it should be, one of irregular lichen-tinted tiled roofs, of gable ends and old brick walls rising out of paddocks and gardens. The High Street is open and countrified, for New Romney is a very little town, claiming only about thirteen hundred souls within and without, about the number in fact that it is computed to have held just a hundred years after the disaster of 1287 that ruined it as a Cinque-Port. Its High Street, which is nearly all that matters for us here, is not very unlike that of Lydd, but better. For though its old buildings are mostly Georgian-fronted the town seems to hold the spirit of their common and peculiar past more tenaciously. Like Lydd it has a modern neighbour between it and the sea ; in this case not a military camp, but widely scattered villas, and a sea-front terrace that have grown out of the Littlestone golf links. All this, however, is quite removed from the town and merely disfigures the seaward outlook to a remarkable extent.

Early antiquaries have run rather wild over the origin of the name Romney, frequently attributing it to the Roman occupation. Moderns, and indeed some ancients, have rejected this entirely, deriving it from a Celtic word, *Rum* or *Rumin*, a *marsh*, and we know how frequently the Saxons retained the place names that they found here. The first mention of Romney—for the prefix " New " seems to have been a sixteenth-century innovation to distinguish it from old Romney—occurs in the grant of a fishery at the mouth of the Limene (Rother), to Christ Church, Canterbury, in 749 by King Eadbright. It thus appears in Domesday : " in Romnel there are four times twenty and five Burgesses which belong to the Archbishops' Manor of Aldington." After a further enumeration the entry continues, " but the King has all service from them and they have all custom and other forfeitures for service of the sea and they are in the King's hands." This last merely identifies the place as one of the Cinque-Ports, which it will be remembered are thought to have had recognition in the time of Edward the Confessor and in some form or other long before that. There is no doubt that Romney at the Conquest was a flourishing port with a fine harbour and that it contributed ships to Harold's fleet, which under the King in the Isle of Wight lay watching the Normans the whole summer before William's invasion. But its patience, and still more its commissariat, gave out, and Harold was forced to withdraw it to the Thames. No large fleet with a large army, says Freeman, had ever before been held together for four months in peace time, and this one, under the urgent calls of domestic duties and lack of provision broke under the strain in September and left the Channel clear for the disaster of October.

During William's crossing two or three of his ships seemed to have straggled towards Romney and had a disastrous encounter with the men of that town, which upon that account claims to have had its own little fight with the Normans just before the great battle, and with a different result. Freeman endorses the claim and tells how the soothsayer who had encouraged William by foretelling his success, lost his life in this Romney skirmish, and how the Conqueror rather ungratefully remarked on hearing it, that in correctly anticipating his master's fortunes, yet incapable of foreseeing his own death, the prophet must have been something of a fool. William, however, took it out of Romney on his March to Dover later on.

The life of Romney as a Cinque-Port till the disaster of 1287 which greatly damaged the town as well as the harbour and reduced it to more or less decay, need not detain us here, as it partook in all of those collective exploits sufficiently described in earlier chapters. Less than a century afterwards, though some sort of a channel to the sea seems to have been kept open, the old bed of the Rother from Appledore had become so dry as to be fit for cultivation, and sharp disputes about ownership arose. In its palmy days the town had generally contributed five ships to the royal fleet, but its central situation among the Ports made it both then and in later years a popular meeting-place for the brotherhood of the Cinque-Ports. A Brotherhood and Guestling, the last term denoting those occasions on which the " limbs " of the Ports were represented as consulting guests, was generally held after Easter and again in the early autumn. The seven Ports took it in turn to provide a President, who was addressed as " Mr. Speaker." These dates enabled the Court among other things to appoint delegates at the last-named to Yarmouth Fair and at the Easter meeting to hear their reports of it.

It was a very sorry tale they had to listen to at the Easter sitting of 1589, by which time the attendance of the Ports' officials at this function was beginning to be looked upon with a jealous eye by the Yarmouth magistrates, as something of an intrusion. As it was the number had been reduced from the self-confident half-score who in the thirteenth century rather lorded it over the Yarmouth officials, to a lone pair, whose object was to maintain in the teeth of many disagreeables the ancient rights and dignities of the Cinque-Ports upon the Yarmouth bench, rather than to prove themselves of any very practical service. Mr. Lake of Hastings and Mr. Lennarde of Dover, Jurats of their respective towns and " Bayliffs of the Barons of the Cinque-Ports to the towne of Great Yarmouth " found their job that year a very disagreeable one indeed. Fortunately " Bayliffe Lake " kept a journal of these agitating weeks which was printed some sixty years ago in the Sussex Archaeological proceedings. It runs to many pages and is both instructive and in parts immensely, though not intentionally, entertaining. The writer was also M.P. for Hastings at the time, and may possibly on that account have felt the smart of neglect and rebuff in his personal as well as in his Cinque-Ports official capacity. The two gentlemen, according to time-honoured custom, were accompanied on their mission by " their learned counsel, town clerk, two sergeants bearing white rods and a brazen horn, a gaoler and one carrying a banner of the arms of the Ports." The banner, of green silk, with the arms painted on it, bound with a fringe of green and gold and tassels, though much decayed, is still in a chest at New Romney.

Trouble indeed seems to have been anticipated, but the little cavalcade were cheered by the good reception they met with as they rode into the town along its quaint Dutch-like harbour front, by " a great store of people." But this was all very well ; the crowd probably did not know that Messrs. Lake and Lennarde had come to pluck a crow with their superiors. The portentous question to be settled, or apparently the recent wrong to be righted, was that of sitting equally with the like number of Yarmouth magistrates exactly under the Royal Arms, both in church and in court. It was extremely important to the dignity of either that a vertical line drawn from the escutcheon should fall precisely between the Cinque-Port and the Yarmouth magistrate who formed the right and left of their respective rows. This was now the crux of the matter for the two Ports' representatives, as Yarmouth had of late manifested intentions of putting in a Chairman of its own. The Yarmouth Bailiffs too had ventured to take Cinque-Port prisoners out of the temporary Cinque-Port prison and deal with them themselves, contrary to law, which would seem even a more heinous offence ; but this came second in the list of grievances.

The Yarmouth notables probably felt trouble was brewing, and so shirked the usual courtesy of visiting the Portsmen the evening of their arrival, in spite of the fact that eighteen hogsheads of beer had been sent by sea to support the month's hospitality expected of the Ports' Barons. So the latter sent for them, to which they responded in person and excused themselves courteously, under the rather thin plea of pressing business, for not having taken the initiative. The two Ports' Barons then " took them by the handes and placed them at a syde bourde " after which sittingd own themselves they " with great reverence " unfolded their past grievances, particularly the Royal Escutcheon business, and politely expressed a hope that they themselves would not be asked to submit to such slights. The two Yarmouth men then retired, promising to confer with their brethren. The next day was Sunday, and the critical question of place in that most spacious of English parish churches was right upon them. Before service, however, Bailiff Bennett, on behalf of the Yarmouth Corporation, came to them, and then they knew the worst, though it was plausibly put. For in regard to the Court-house, said Bailiff

Bennett, " they had always been accustomed to have their learned Steward, Mr. Stubbes, to sit in the middle under the Queen's arms, being a very wise and grave gent whom they were loth to displace, etc. etc.," but that they, Messrs. Lake and Lennarde, " should have all that by right or courteseye they before ever had." They did not ask that, replied the Ports' Barons curtly, for in former days they had taken precedence, and now they only craved equality. As for Mr. Stubbes, they had no use for him at all, he was not even a " Justiciar." Two of each town upon the bench " sitting indifferently " under the Queen's arms, that was their claim. If this were not conceded, as well as the same honours in church, they would at once return and the Cinque-Ports would then begin to talk to Yarmouth. Bailiffe Bennett, being in doubt what to answer, " somewhat smilingly took his leave " ; the smile must have been significant, as it moved the others to grave suspicion of his sincerity.

When they arrived at the church, the Yarmouth Bailiffs were all seated under and on each side of the canopy, and showed no intention whatever of budging, so the Ports' Barons in high dudgeon had to drop into seats many removes from " the place of honour where they were wont to sit next unto the ould bayliffe." The next business after the service was that of the toll-house or Court, our two outraged friends waiting at their quarters, as was customary, till the local cases had been dealt with and a summons sent them that the Port concerns in the Court of the Herring Fair were coming on. But they waited in vain, so leaving their lodgings and pushing their way through a great multitude of people about the Court doors, they entered the chamber and did reverence to the row of scarlet gowns upon the bench. But there in the very midst, and right under the Royal arms, sat that wretched outsider the learned steward, Mr. Stubbes. Bailiff Lake now read his commission according to form, to which the irrepressible Mr. Stubbes, vile intruder, took upon himself the business of replying, " bidding them hartily welcome " and asking them to step up to the bench, the dissembling rogue. For when they got there Stubbes sat tight with two bailiffs, one on each side, filling up the whole space under the canopy.

Then Bailiff Lake again up and spoke, and with much circumlocution and some acerbity told the " learned steward " that they were not going to sit there dealing with the Ports' cases, while he, a complete outsider and two Yarmouth bailiffs filled the whole space under the Royal arms. Mr. Stubbes nearly choked, but when he had bridled his choler and was calm enough to speak, he said a great deal, which may here be reduced to the statement that so far as the Ports' bailiffs were concerned, he would see them hanged before he would move an inch, but if his own bailiffs said the word he would vacate the seat of honour in less than no time. The Yarmouth bailiffs, having put him there for the express purpose of snubbing the Cinque-Ports visitors, had of course no intention of saying any such word. They merely repeated the request that their visitors should take their places on the bench, that is at its extremity, while the latter for their part having taken, so they declared, " a Royal oath to maintain the privileges and dignities of the Ports " would do nothing of the kind. The quarrel as to place in church and on the bench continued for a week or so, and a great deal of forcible, as well as some very quaint, language was handed about. So Messrs. Lake and Lennarde went home unappeased, and with sore heads and with, no doubt, a rather fiery report to make at the next court of the Brotherhood at New Romney. It must not, however, be supposed that this sort of thing was chronic, it was merely one of the frequent outbreaks inevitable to a once useful custom that proved ever more irritating to the Yarmouth Corporation as its utility declined with changing circumstances. The sort of cases that resulted from the fair may be gathered from the complaints at this one of some Dover man against a Yarmouth crew who had " insulted them at sea and on shore." On inquiry, the Yarmouth lot proved to have instigated the wrangle, and were condemned to pay the others a barrel of beer " so all we're made friends " and no doubt with equal unanimity got royally drunk together.

The Parish Church of New Romney, dedicated to St. Nicholas, so naturally popular a saint upon this coast, is conspicuous for its fine tower of five stages, the two lower of which are late Norman, the middle transition, and the two upper of rather later date. It is lit upon the west side by many fine windows, effectively marking the period to which each stage belongs, and is entered by a recessed and finely moulded Norman door, while a singular feature of this noble tower is the narrow lean-to aisles upon both its north and south sides. It is surmounted by pinnacles with a stair turret at the north-west angle, but is without battlements, for the sufficient reason that it still carries the base of a long fallen stone spire, resembling in shape a shallow inverted bowl, and thereby providing a second characteristic, rare if not unique. The nave is Norman, but of older date than the Norman tower, which ranges from the middle to the close of the twelfth century. It is part of the original church which had no tower. Some remarkable round-headed lancet windows, which are thought to have lighted its west end, now look into the tower space above the arch opening into the nave. The latter consists of an arcade of six Norman arches on massive piers alternately round and octagonal, another rather uncommon feature. The arches show both billet, and embattled or crenelated moulding, and spring from scolloped capitals. The Norman clerestory remains and consists of deeply splayed quatrefoil windows, though now only opening out into the aisles, which were added later.

The chancel, of three bays, was erected in the early fourteenth century and its pointed arches rest on slender octagonal columns. Three parallel gable roofs after the usual style of the country, cover in this case both nave and chancels respectively. The latter and its two chapels are conterminous, each of them having a spacious east window of the Decorated period, that of the main chancel containing five lights and terminating in a profuse display of reticulated tracery. Each

NEW ROMNEY CHURCH.

of the side chapels, where altars once stood, contain sedilia which is rare, and a piscina which is not, and also hagioscopes for providing a view of the high altar. In the north wall is a recess beneath an arch with floral decorations, and now containing a stone coffin. The bones of a man were discovered here eighty years ago when the masonry was removed. The escutcheons of the Furnese family still hang upon the north wall, and recall the fact that Sir Henry and his son, in 1712–13, with the best intentions boarded in the oak roof of the high chancel and decorated it with one of those conventional gilded suns of the fierce kind that one may thank Heaven never shine upon Romney Marsh, accompanied by Hebrew lettering. Poor gentlemen! they little dreamed that the tearing down of this sublime composition and the exposing of their condemned oak roof would one day be accounted to the credit of a future Vicar, as an act of reparation to the outraged building.

There are many old mortuary slabs on the church pavement, some obviously those of priests, and upon several the brasses still remain. One of 1574 is to Thomas Lambarde, a relative of the famous Kent historian, so often quoted in these pages. Another tomb is that of a Huguenot doctor, who fled from France in 1689, and practised for years in the town. But the most interesting of all these memorials is a large altar tomb in the south chancel, of date 1526, to Richard Stuppeny, covered with a marble slab. It was renovated by his great-grandson as described on a brass affixed to it in 1622. The chief interest, however, lies in the fact that the Jurats of the town held their meetings here, using the tomb no doubt as a table. This continued till modern times, and the Mayor is still elected at Richard Stuppeny's tomb, though the family commemorated by it was nothing like so prominent as that of the Godfreys, Cobbs, Southlands and other bygone magnates of the little town who lie buried here. The above-mentioned great-grandson Stuppeny is himself commemorated in a very similar tomb in much the same situation in Lydd Church, where it was used by the Corporation for the same purpose.

But from a purely dramatic point of view, nothing in the church appears to me so moving as the conspicuous marks of the great flood of 1287, which destroyed the town's naval importance and overwhelmed the whole reclaimed country to the west and south of it. There is no occasion to hunt about for this. The pillars of the nave for about four feet up show a dark discoloration, marking with a generally abrupt line the surface of the water mixed with mud, sand and beach, that no doubt remained here a long time, before removal was possible in the chaos of such a catastrophe. The church stands to-day several feet below the surrounding ground, showing the latter, in part at least, to be the deposit of that terrific inundation. In olden times there were two other churches in the town and two chapels. The former were those of St. Martin and St. Laurence, and they were both removed by order in the sixteenth century, for the two excellent reasons that they were tumbling down of themselves, and further that the size of the town under the new Reformation ideas did not warrant rebuilding them. The sites of both are within the town, while many walls and buildings preserve their stones. Of the two chapels considerable remains of that belonging to the Priory of St. John, now enclose a rose garden, attached to a private residence on the High Street. The exterior fronting a side road would give instant pause to almost every one. For at some no very distant day a general collection of ancient remains has been gathered about or affixed to this old chapel wall with rather startling effect ; portions of the original building, however, are evidently *in situ*.

Other inundations seem to have followed the great one of 1287. Lambarde writes : " Both the town of Rumney and the Marshe receaved great harme in the 8 yeare of the reegn of King Edward Third by an hydeous tempest that threw down many steeples and trees and above 300 mills and Housings there." One or two others mention this, but in the matter of details it is open to question whether there may not be some confusion with earlier floods. These disasters together with its insanitary condition made it necessary to offer great inducements to people to live on the Marsh. The Court of Romney Marsh with its bailiff and twenty-four elected Jurats, " has benefit of all fines, forfaits and amercements, the privileges of leet, lawday, and towne, and exemption from tolle and taxe, Scot and lot, fifteens and subsidies and from so many other charges as I suppose no one within the Realme hath." Cryptic as this enumeration of privileges will probably sound to the reader, he will no doubt have guessed enough of it to come to the same conclusion as Lambarde.

It is a wonderful thing that there should never have been a recurrence of these catastrophes on anything like the same scale. What caused them? It can hardly have been the mere bursting of artificial barriers, for the seas apparently broke over everywhere. There is a theory that the rush of water up Channel was so great as to be unable to get away through the Straits of Dover quick enough in the teeth of adverse tides from the North Sea or possibly a sudden change of wind, and was consequently dammed up to overflowing. If such were indeed the case it might happen again, should those occult influences which govern the ocean currents take a notion some day to combine with untimely hurricanes and some untoward state of the moon! For obvious personal reasons I prefer myself to belong to the optimistic majority!

New Romney was never a regular port for France like Dover, Sandwich, Rye and Winchelsea, nor did pilgrims ever take ship there. It was hardly more than a Port and capital of the Marsh, catching fish, importing a little wine, supplying its few ships to the Navy and doing a roaring trade in " owling " and later an equally active and illicit one in spirits and silks. One illustrious passenger, however, took ship here for the Continent, though he did not reach it, and this was Thomas à Becket. For having angered the King the Archbishop set out to interest the Pope in favour of himself, but taking ship at Romney he was driven back by contrary winds, and compelled to disembark again. The Records of the Cinque-Ports were always kept here, and what remains are still, with a few exceptions, in safe keeping in the Town Hall. The Brotherhood and Guestling was also generally held at New Romney as the central port of the Seven. The last recorded meeting was in 1865. The Corporation of Romney Marsh held and still holds its now much more serious meetings at Dymchurch in its old Court House at that place. Never surely was a thinly peopled region so full as this of barons, combarons, mayors, bailiffs, jurats, commissioners and such like dignitaries.

The Historical MSS. Commission delved some fifty years ago in the Cinque-Port records at New Romney, but their transcriptions contain little that would interest here. Their efforts on the town records are rather more illuminating, and curiously enough some of these had fallen into the hands of St. Catherine's College, Cambridge, and are there yet. The most interesting perhaps of the borough's old relics is the long curved brazen horn, which among other civic uses was taken by the representatives of the Ports to Great Yarmouth, and blown at the opening of the Herring Fair. It was produced at our present King's coronation and two sergeants were sent round the town with it to announce the Proclamation, and the other functions of the day. But the gladness of the moment was too much for these thirsty heralds, and they failed to get a single toot out of it. After handling the said horn, I am inclined to think that it would require something more than a merely sober man to blow it with effect.

During the long seigneury of the Archbishop, Romney chafed no little at his domination, for helpful as this had been during the period of church building and land reclamation, by the time of the Tudors the boot was on the other leg, and the Romney men found themselves merely tributaries to the church at Canterbury, without, in their opinion, receiving any *quid pro quo*. They were continually sending dolphins, grampuses, porpoises, congers and other products of the vasty deep to successive Archbishops " to gain their friendship." They never had been able to persuade their spiritual Lord to grant them a Mayor. But in the turmoil of the Wars of the Roses, when Richard the Third put on his guilt-stained crown, the time seemed propitious for taking the matter into their own hands, as the new King had formerly been Lord Warden. So sending a " grampus " or some other sea-monster to the Lieutenant of the Tower, they proceeded to elect a Mayor on their own account. But the Battle of Bosworth, with the accession of Henry the Seventh, upset their game, and it was not till Queen Elizabeth, for a good round sum of money, gave them the desired charter, that John Cheseman in 1563 was elected the first Mayor.

For a century after the great inundation, the Romney men had struggled to keep some sort of a channel open to the sea. But by the early fifteenth century its already dried-up bed was let for pasture. Leland casts in passing some quaint compassionate words on the place : " Rumency is one of the five ports and hath been a netely good haven insomuch that within remembrance of men shyppes have come hard up to the town, and cast anchors in one of the churchyards. The se is now a ii myles from the town so sore thereby now decayed that wher ther wher iii grate paroches, for sumtyme is now scant one wel mayteined." In the New Romney Records, as in those of the other Marsh towns, there is of course a great deal to say concerning the constant struggle between land and water. Sometimes the sea is the enemy, at others it plays the treacherous friend, forsaking ports, harbours and villages that had depended upon it more or less for a livelihood and leaving them high and dry. And this is much more serious, being incurable, whereas the other business was only a matter of care, labour and expense. I have refrained from any attempt at a precise relation here of the gradual reclamation of the

Marsh, with all the setbacks and difficulties which attended the agelong process. Considerable and precise acquaintance with the lie of the land would be essential to following its intricacies, and not a dozen readers of this book are likely to be thus equipped, while of these a majority will probably be familiar with all there is to be known on the subject.

The Romney barons took their place of course among the Cinque-Port canopy-bearers at the coronations. After that of Edward the Third, it is related in the records, that the canopy with all the spears and accessories were handed over to New Romney. There is also an entry of expenditure in 1398, for three gowns and hoods of scarlet for the Romney canopy-bearers at the coronation of Henry the Fourth. Following that of Charles the Second, there was a most unseemly fracas over the possession of the canopy in Westminster Hall, degenerating into something between a tug-of-war and a Rugby football match. Bishop Kennett in the third volume of his history has left a most entertaining account of it. It seems that so soon as the barons bearing the canopy had brought the King back to the foot of the stairs in Westminster Hall and were turning towards their particular and specially arranged table, set for the State Banquet, the royal footmen insolently and violently fell upon the canopy to carry it off. The barons, however, " though scant in numbers and strength did their utmost to defend it " as one may well imagine. But being overweighted by the mob of lackeys, they were dragged with much uproar and clutching desperately at their property, the whole length of the hall to the door. Happily this was slammed at the critical moment, with much presence of mind, by the York Herald, Mr. Owen, or the pampered rogues would assuredly have got away with the spoil. When the turmoil, or the news of it, reached the King's ear, he ordered the prompt dismissal of his outrageous domestics. But a rough-and-tumble fight in their gala clothes was not all that the Cinque-Port Barons had to put up with on this unfortunate occasion. For in the meantime the Bishops and Judges had taken possession of their table, the Barons' own special table set in the exact position, next to that of the King which the ancient dignities and traditions of the Cinque-Ports on these occasions absolutely demanded. The Bishops would not budge, and the Judges, possession as we know being nine-tenths of the law, of course would not stir. So after vain expostulations and some strong language, the canopy-bearers had to " edge in " and take their seats at a lower table among a crowd of barristers and suchlike.

There is an item of expenditure in the town books, concerning men and ships for Henry the Fifth's expedition to France, which produced the Battle of Agincourt, and another " for victuals for divers good men and mariners for going to see against our enemies off the coast." In later days there are frequent references to the " players " not only of Romney who were famous, but of the neighbouring places who came there " to crie their plaie." Scriptural performances were of course popular after the Reformation, and often took place within the church, while the various troupes of minstrels together with their pay or refreshments are duly noticed. One party of visiting players is alluded to as " that of our lord Prince Henry the Seventh which came with a baboon." Another item " given to Dr Scot who preached here 10*d.* in drink " (perhaps five shillings of our money) would not look quite seemly nowadays ! They understood too how to " celebrate " occasions in those times. The churching of Lady Beaumont, wife of the Lord Warden at Dover, would not seem an epoch-making event, but the " best men of Romney " all went to Dover, and had a great feast. And with regard to feasting, cider and perry seemed to have been freely stocked in all these towns in the Middle Ages, besides their French wines.

English prose strikes one as being backward and incoherent, even for Henry the Eighth's time, among the parsons of the

Marsh. The rector of Snargate at any rate was not a stylist, and he is funnier even than Leland. " Ryht worshepfulli Masterys," he writes to the Romney Jurats. " I understand that my neybere Wylliam Lambarde shall have amatted (admitted) afore yow as to morover masterys J. Herde, Wylliam Colman grante hym iiis, and iiii*d*. This I will testefey. No more tho (to) yow this tyme, but Gode kepe yow. By your Syr Gorge Schantton, Preste at Snargate." Perhaps the town clerk was an expert at interpreting these masterpieces. It is a big jump from this one to the lucid English of the " Wylliam Lambarde " named in it if as seems probable he is the historian.

We noticed the popular names for females at Winchelsea in the Middle Ages, Agatha having an easy lead. Here is an abstract which lies before me from the Hythe Records, and would no doubt apply equally to New Romney. Out of 130 female names, Joan appears thirty-two times, Alice nineteen, Isabel eighteen, Agnes twelve, Christina eleven, Margery ten. Less popular are Phillipa, Lucy, Magota, Margaret, Cecily, Juliana, Lettice, Lore, Mabilia, Matilda, Dionysea, Avycia, Beatricia, Elena, and Elizabeth. Martha, Agatha and Petronilla curiously enough are not in it, and Mary had not yet appeared. Among men " John," as all over England and Wales, immensely preponderated. Hence the avalanche of Joneses that deluged tribal Wales, when almost every family in that unfortunate country was suddenly saddled for ever and a day with the Christian name of its father or grandsire after surnames became imperative. There is an entry in the New Romney Records to the effect that a Henry Percy of Alnwick, a son of the Earl, became a resident freeman of the town in 1476, a curious migration for so conspicuous a member of that famous Border breed.

In the plot to murder William the Third, Captain Barclay, the chief agent in it from St. Germains, landed near New Romney. Macaulay tells us of a certain smuggler named

Hunt, who lived on a desolate part of the shore and for years had found smuggling Jacobites in and out of the country more profitable than even lace and spirits. Scores of men of condition had found refuge in his shanty, on their transit back and forth, and many packets of despatches he kept by him wrapped round with lace and temporarily concealed as if smuggled goods, till he found means to get them away in a French ship. Barclay landed in 1696 under the protection of Hunt to lead the forty accomplices who were to murder William at Turnham Green as he returned from hunting in Richmond Park. The King was warned in the nick of time. The leaders were caught and hung, save Barclay, who escaped abroad, probably via Romney and through Hunt's assistance. The latter's descendants still live in Old Romney. In comparatively recent times, a woman and her daughter, living near the shore in this neighbourhood, became notable as receivers and distributors of smuggled goods, particularly lace and silks. The preventative officers on one occasion paid them a surprise visit, furnished as they thought with clear proof that goods were in the house. The women, however, sighted them in the distance and though without hope of getting the stuff away, their fertility of resource was equal to the occasion ; the elder woman undressed and bound her body round and round with all the silks in her possession, put her night-clothes on and got into bed. On the arrival of the officers, she was groaning in the pangs of severe illness, and the daughter, sitting at her bedside on the only keg of brandy in the house, covered with a cloth, was absorbed in filial ministrations to her suffering parent. The officers of course searched the house in vain, but were quite disarmed of all further suspicion by the well simulated groans of the old lady and the feigned distress of her daughter.

The sea, in the shape of a shallow bay covered only at high tide and known as Romney Hoy, came up within half a mile of the west end of the town fifteen to twenty years ago.

Smacks or small freighters occasionally drifted up on the tide and landed a cargo near where the present railway station stands, while a mile or so of good road now runs across well grassed pastures to Littlestone, where the waters rolled so lately. Living people can easily remember seeing ships by the churchyard such as Leland speaks of. But this did not mean such access to the sea as was of any real value. All that went in the fourteenth century. No inland waters, when the Rother had withdrawn itself to the old cliff edge, and its present course, could be persuaded to flow into the sea at Romney with sufficient force to keep a navigable channel open. A long cut was made to Appledore, but in course of time all attempts to keep it open were abandoned. All kinds of schemes for damming up and storing waters had been mooted, but proved either impracticable or too expensive. But this is all very ancient history. Romney, I take it, has found more solid consolation in the ugly inconsequent blocks of buildings that at Littlestone loom along its distant sea-front than in its old attempts to regain such sea traffic as could hardly hope to equal even that of Rye.

Echoes of the social splendour of Romney in Georgian times may still be found upon the lips of the oldest inhabitants, gathered from their fathers and grandfathers; the string of carriages which filled the High Street from end to end when a Miss Cobb was married, or the resounding convivialities which cheered the place when a Master Godfrey was born. The old houses where these magnates of the Marsh, this amphibious fifth continent of the earth, in its great days ate and drank and danced, the world forgetting and by the world forgot, look rather seedy now. The Cobb mansion is the workhouse and the lines of its once ample gardens may still be seen far out in the fields. Some of the others are week-end houses of London members of the Littlestone Golf Club, and retain their external characters, their one-time owners being nothing now but names graven upon worn slabs in the pavement of the church aisles. The sole survivor of one conspicuous old Romney family died not long ago, I believe, as a barber in Folkestone! *Sic transit gloria Mundi!*

The *New Inn* on the quiet High Street, though Georgian fronted, is mainly fifteenth and sixteenth century within. It contains a panelled room on the ground floor and a great deal of very curious old work upstairs, and again under the roof where most of its beams and rafters are original. The back view from the meadows shows its antiquity to advantage, and indeed does as much for all the other old buildings in the street. It is in appreciative hands as regards its present owners, and in matters material, the hotel is very popular with visitors to the town and to Littlestone. The *New Inn* seems a strange designation for so ancient a house, recalling that of its greater and more famous namesake in Gloucester, the most complete survival of an ancient hostelry in all England. Many current stories, too, are rife of the ingenuous self-importance of the Marsh folk in former days. One of them is said to have accosted a policeman in London and asked him if he had seen Mr. B—— pass by. The constable replied curtly that he knew no such man " What! " cried the indignant Romneyite or Lyddite, " not know Mr. B——! Why, he is a bailiff of Romney Marsh! "

There are primitive people still about. Some friends of mine up the country quite recently imported two Marsh maidens of about eighteen and twenty as house servants. They were daughters of a " looker " in a particularly desolate part of the Marsh and unsophisticated to a degree. They employed their " hours out " in killing rabbits and suchlike harmless but masculine pursuits rather than in decorating themselves and promenading with the village swains. In course of time they asked if they might both go home for a day or two. On being reminded that it would be more convenient for one to go at a time, they pleaded that this would not serve the purpose as there was to be a " christening up " in their family which apparently ran downwards into double figures. My friends not taking their meaning, the maidens gave them to understand that it was customary to have a family christening in batches to save trouble. In their case the parents had postponed or overlooked the troublesome occasion till the presumably final infant had arrived, and so the " christening up " included the lot and was naturally a tremendous affair. It is needless to say the astonished mistress had no further objection to urge.

The old town mill upon the mound at the seaward extremity of New Romney, lifting its sails above the foliage strikes a very effective note as one approaches the little town. It used to be let out by the Corporation, I believe, every year by tender. This end of the Marsh has the merit in summer of being more bracing than Rye bay, and a glance at the map will suggest the cause. When exposed to the full blast of a fierce March east wind this merit is not so obvious. We consider ourselves in Rye to be more than ordinary victims of that pestilent visitor from the Steppes of Russia. But the difference between Rye and New Romney on such occasions might almost be likened to that of being in the trenches or under fire in the open, so pitilessly is the latter raked by an east wind when it really means business. Littlestone, like St. Leonards its climatic antithesis, was in inception at any rate a one-man enterprise. I have already described it, and if this left no impression on the reader's mind, which is more than likely, I can only repeat that I have nothing more to add, except that the Golf Links, running north up the coast, are admirable and have been established about thirty years, a little longer than those of Rye. But the course does not rank quite in the same class as Rye and Sandwich in the eyes of the tip-top players. Moreover, though a sand course in the main, a few holes are of a meadowy or semi-inland nature. To the average player indifferent to this partial blemish and not ambitious of being put to the uttermost test, Littlestone offers all the other exhilarating qualities of a good seaside sand course, quite another thing by the way from playing on chalk downs or rolling pastures overlooking the sea!

CHAPTER THE TENTH

Dymchurch—by Lympne—to Bilsington

BY the coast road, which now runs almost due north, Dymchurch is about four miles from New Romney and Littlestone. The Golf Links extend for some distance upon the right, between road and sea till they meet the former, while a mile away on the left, the old church of St. Mary stands out effectively upon the Marsh ; Norman in origin, but mainly

THE MILITARY CANAL.

Early English in style and of no great size : sheltered by a screen of old trees with its massive, part-Norman tower, its shingle spire and long lancet windows in both nave and chancel, it is a good example of a simple and ancient church

DYMCHURCH—BY LYMPNE—TO BILSINGTON

set peacefully apart from the haunts of men. Its parish covers nearly 2,000 acres, and its population is a hundred and seventy, a fair type of Marsh figures generally. Dymchurch with its ancient church and Court House, just to the west of it, still the headquarters of the Corporation of Romney Marsh, is a very old village recently developed into a small watering-place. It has no very particular history, but has been for centuries of great importance in all that concerns the drainage of the Marsh. For ages past the magistrates of the Liberty of Romney Marsh have dispensed justice in the New Hall, the old Court House here. It is now the headquarters of the Lords, Bailiff and Jurats of the Level of Romney Marsh. It is also the headquarters of the Ancient Corporation of the Marsh, which in days gone by held considerable powers, but whose business now is limited to electing every year their own magistrates for the Liberty, and to taking charge of wrecks.

Nearly all that vast labyrinth of waterways which interlace Romney Marsh proper "sewer out" here, while Dymchurch wall, which confronts the sea for three miles at the most vulnerable part of the whole coast, is far and away the strongest and most elaborate of all these sea defences, having a slightly concave front of masonry twenty feet high. It is supposed to have had a Roman predecessor, as Roman remains have been found near about, and the ruins of Portus Limenus the base of Roman enterprise, are now not far away. At any rate, there has been a Dymchurch wall of some sort since the twelfth century, as the church was built just behind it on lower ground. Impregnable though it looks, the sea from time to time makes partial breaks in this stupendous and skilfully devised rampart. If it did much more, I fancy the north quarter of Romney Marsh would be shouting for lifebelts! But I believe it is well looked after, though it costs a lot of money. The holiday houses and bungalows of the newer Dymchurch cower in rows behind the great wall, making it, however, their promenade and the ample sands beyond the sporting ground of their offspring, who even in normal Augusts seem the chief floating population of the place. Away to the right is the point and lighthouse of Dungeness, while to the left, the cliffs of Dover form the other horn of the bay. The church stands attractively within a grove of trees, but is not otherwise particularly inspiring. It is represented by a chancel, nave, and a partially contained tower. The interior includes a Norman chancel-arch and some lancet windows. The south door of the nave, too, is Norman, as well as some lower portions of the tower. The Benefice includes three of those neighbouring churches of the Marsh, that like Midley and Hope, near Romney, have long fallen into melancholy ruin, or become mere heaps of stones. Blackmanstone, Orgarswick and Eastbridge are vanished rectories and sinecures, now merged in Dymchurch, and stand by lonely roadsides like shadows of a populous past, which of course they are not.

The monks of Canterbury and their tenants did not build for congregations, present or future, but partly to the Honour and Glory of God, and partly under certain obligations of tenure to do so. When Ivychurch, for example, was first erected, there were fifteen people in the parish! In *Ellis' Letters* there is a curious address or petition to the Council from the parishioners of Dymchurch, in Henry the Eighth's reign. Their parson had refused, according to Royal order, to dispense with the Popish ritual, so in the meantime, awaiting the pleasure of the authorities they had laid him by the heels in gaol. Besides the Court House a few other old buildings survive in Dymchurch, but what may be called its business portion is ugly and mostly modern. Fortunately there is not much of it. There is a useful looking hotel, too, *The Ship*, facing the sea, in the watering-place part of the town near the church, and as Hythe is only a mile or so further than New Romney station, most traffic I fancy goes that way. The direct road to Hythe follows the sea wall till it is turned inland by the interminable rifle ranges that form the narrow point of the Marsh, giving way to the villas and modern developments that cluster round the older Cinque-Port town of Hythe. All the way from Dymchurch to the Hythe ranges, the Marsh, from four or five miles wide, is rapidly drawing to a point. The old cliffs behind it, too, are loftier at this end. The hill barrier of Bilsington, Aldington and Lympne, by which we shall return in this chapter, is more generally imposing than that which overlooks the Marsh from Winchelsea to Appledore and Orlestone. Moreover, this angle of the Marsh does not look quite so out of the world as most of it, and there is rather more timber about though the population is quite as scanty. As you draw towards the point, poor and sandy pastures, sprinkled here and there with stones, show themselves even towards the hills, as evidence of their submersion in Roman times beneath the estuary that made Hythe and West Hythe ports.

But of this later, for Newchurch, the heart of this North-Eastern angle of the Marsh, must not be overlooked. It is better approached, however, from Dymchurch by a choice of two roads running inland and each forming roughly two sides of a parallelogram, one passing the derelict churches of Orgarswick and Eastbridge, the other the less obvious pile of stones that represents what once was Blackmanstone. Otherwise the Marsh hereabouts is very much what it is in those other portions which we have traversed in more leisurely fashion. There is as good reason here as anywhere else to notice two typical products of the Marsh throughout its whole extent from Rye to Hythe, to wit the eels in its dykes and the hares on its pastures. Greyhounds have always had their share of the latter with the harriers, and coursing has been a prominent feature of Marsh life and sport. Eels have hardly a sporting side to them, though probably the long-handled spear with which the Marshman transfixes his elusive quarry in the muddy bottom of one or other of the innumerable dykes has its own cult of dexterity, besides its useful spoil. The latest authorities on this mysterious fish tell us that every eel in the country at seven-years-old finds its way to the deep water of the Atlantic, where it spawns and dies, the elva pushing their way back in shoals of myriads to their ancestral rivers and ditches. A seven-year-old Romney Marsh eel I have no doubt could find his way to salt water without fingerposts, though some of them must have a great many corners to turn.

Newchurch, a mere hamlet, has no distinction but its church, and this is large and one of the finest on the Marsh. It consists of a west tower, nave and chancel with three aisles running throughout, each aisle being covered with a gable roof supported by tie-beams and king-posts and in each case exposed. The tower is lofty and embattled and heavily buttressed like that of Ivychurch. It is conspicuous at a great distance and carried a beacon in ancient times and is probably of early fifteenth century date ; at any rate it is entered by a door suggestive of that period, a depressed pointed arch in a square frame, the spandrils filled with cusp ornamentation. The interior of the church is Early English to Perpendicular. The nave arcades of pointed arches rest on octagonal columns, while the windows are Decorated or Perpendicular. There is also a small and quaint window high up above the chancel arch. The church is in admirable order, but as everywhere else on the Marsh the population, about 250, is and always was absurdly inadequate to the size and dignity of the fabric.

Sauntering one summer day about the large churchyard, full of the recorded and unrecorded graves, both obliterated and legible, of generations of Marsh folk, I was struck with a sinister tale still readable on the panel of a large railed-in altar tomb. They were *armigers*, these people, and evidently, from their place of abode, small squires of the type that once lived on the Marsh. In this case the mother and the whole family, a large one, had died between the ages of fifteen and thirty-five. I wondered whether the malaria, the scourge of olden times, though not often directly fatal, caught some weaker families and wore them down one after the other, as in this case, before middle age? An antediluvian working on the road outside gave me some quite cheerful ague reminiscences of his youth. I asked him if there was any about in the parish nowadays. "No, sir, there ain't no ague. They calls it by another name now." This was pretty good for my octogenarian friend, who was not going to admit the passing of any fine old Marsh habit.

From here to Botolphs Bridge, virtually the end of the Marsh before it bids good-bye to solitude and merges into the military area of Hythe, with all its clamour and traffic, is about four miles. There is nothing upon the way to be seen or noted but the things of the Marsh that everywhere go to make up its quiet and characteristic existence, though the green and woody hills of the old coast line are now quite close upon one's left hand. They are higher too than at other points, and Lympne Castle stands perched upon the very brink of their summit with a pose, I feel sure, unmatched by any other feudal building in this soft southern country. The old military canal, overshadowed by its unbroken procession of elm avenues, has hugged the base of the hills through the whole length of the Marsh, and it wanders on from here, growing ever more picturesque, to Hythe, following always the old trail of the Rother or Limene, which in a sense has twice changed its course. Here, beneath these steep slopes, we are confronted by another of those great physical changes such as subsequently ruined Lydd and Romney. As late at least as the day of the Romans, the principal outflow of Romney Marsh, the gathered waters that is of the inland valleys of the modern Rother, went mainly out beneath these lofty and now landlocked cliffs to Hythe, where there was then a wide outflow. To use the term river, however, as generally understood, in connexion with the ancient conditions of the Marsh, then probably a mass of big islands and promontories with the sea washing at high tide among them, would be misleading. But it seems quite certain that navigators then on the way to Appledore and the inland rivers, whether traders or raiders, followed the large waterway along this eastern line of cliffs and the fringe of the Marsh. At the close of the Roman occupation it seems also certain that the seaway ran up as far as West Hythe, now a trifling hamlet at the hill foot, above which Lympne Castle and church rise so proudly, and met a channel of some sort running down from Appledore.

As if to set at rest all question of this having been the great

BRIDGE AT WAREHORNE.

Roman port and landing place, the remains of the towers and walls and bastions of a Roman fortress lie heaped about upon the hillside, as if some landslip had shifted it and left a portion suddenly fixed in all attitudes of a headlong glissade—some in the act of toppling over, some actually fallen. This seems indeed to have been the case, though a local superstition characteristically ascribes the chaos to an earthquake. The castrum covered ten acres and its remains to-day, rather confused and chaotic though they be, are among the more conspicuous ancient remains of Roman masonry in England, though comparatively unknown. They would assuredly astonish any one stumbling on them unawares, covering as they do, though in fragmentary fashion, such an extent of ground. For the merest tyro could see at once that this was no Norman work. It was in fact the Portus Limenus of the Romans, one of the three chief gateways into England during much of their occupation. A broad inflow of the sea, as already noted, then ran up here to the cliff foot, extending by means of a probably much narrower waterway to Appledore and the outflow of the inland waters. The towers and walls still extant are spread about the hillside at some little distance up the slope, but the traces of the port and harbour where now runs the military canal were obvious enough till comparatively recent times.

In 1852 some serious excavation was undertaken by Mr. Roach Smith, a well-known antiquary, with the assistance of other experts and the financial help of interested people, local and otherwise. The Government, then as ever the most lavish in Europe of pensions and sinecures, refused any serious assistance towards a better insight into those four enthrallingly mysterious centuries when Britain was to Rome in a measure what India is now to Britain. Millionaires again do not often appreciate these things, while those who do are generally poor men. At Wroxeter (Uniconium), near Shrewsbury, for example, 140 acres of a Roman-British city lie beneath the plough. Pathetic efforts, mainly by local people of intelligence, have exposed small sections of it here and there, as the antiquarian world well knows, but much of this had to be refilled in 1912 and 1913, so that a few pounds' worth of wheat or turnips might again be grown above the streets and villas and shops so tantalizingly displayed. For there was no money to avert this trifling business ! A cynic suggested at the time, and with quite admirable perspicacity, that a peerage should be offered to any wealthy man who would devote fifty or a hundred thousand pounds to exposing and *keeping* exposed such buried cities as this one at Wroxeter, " The White City," whose destruction in the sixth century by the pagan Saxons is so movingly described in the famous poem of Llywarch Hên who witnessed the debacle. As peerages were practically on sale, it was pointed out how infinitely worthier would be such a source of nobility than a big cheque paid to the Party funds ; how significantly honourable, too, not to say resounding, would be the title adopted from the scene itself, and what a boon the work to future generations! Limene then, or Lymne, was a port, not it may be supposed a place of residential importance. The excavators attributed its dislocated appearance to a landslip, a quite natural occurrence on a hill of this particular formation. For lack of means their work was of course very limited, but great numbers of Roman coins and all the usual ornaments and fragments of pottery were unearthed. From inscriptions on tiles and slabs, it seems almost certain that the *Classiarii Britannici*, the marines of the Roman-British fleet, were mainly quartered here. No light is thrown on the type of garrison by the *Notitia*, which has given us such ample details regarding the Roman wall, Caerleon and other places occupied by infantry and cavalry. Nor again in these southern Roman stations are there found many of those altars or dedicatory tablets to officers or their wives, or to the presiding deities of the various legions which seem to speak to us so intimately across the centuries, from a period wrapped as is this one in almost total gloom. These stray men and women alone seem to survive and, what is more, to live almost as near to us as those commemorated upon the eighteenth-century tablets in Rye or Romney churches. The young cavalry officer of this ala or the infantry centurion of this or that famous legion, with his years of service attached, is lamented by his wife or his parents. Or, again, a mother and a son unite in honouring a distinguished soldier father, while a regimental surgeon occasionally strikes from his memorial tablet an extraordinarily modern note. Lamented wives, who have followed the drum to Britain and succumbed to the

DYMCHURCH—BY LYMPNE—TO BILSINGTON

unaccustomed rigours of its climate, are invoked by sorrowing husbands, or sons, or both, while the regimental pride is constantly displayed in altars to this corps or to that, as well as to their commanders and to the presiding deity who from some Olympian height demands the votive offerings of his particular legion.

The marines of the Roman service who were quartered at Lympne, Richborough and Pevensey were not much addicted apparently to thus honouring either their departed relatives, their emperors or their gods. As regards the first they were perhaps enforced celibates, or as seafarers had "a wife in every port," and did not feel so acutely the obligation of a memorial stone. From an interesting report of the excavators of 1852, published at the time in a small book with plans and illustrations, it seems that the Turnacensians (from Tournay) were the only troops quartered here whose nationality can be verified, and that is by means of the *Notitia* in its only reference to the garrison at Portus Limenus. Only a single commander has left his identity behind him, one Aufidus Pantera, a prefect, or admiral of the British fleet, who took the precaution of erecting an altar to Neptune. But then the resources of these enthusiastic excavators were slender. Still they exposed the well-preserved foundations of a villa, probably an officer's house, and of another building, apparently soldiers' quarters. They also convinced themselves that there was only one entrance to the Castrum, whereas in those upon the Roman Wall, and I believe in the north generally, there are usually four. The two hundred and sixty coins discovered were nearly all later than the close of the third century, which, together with some other signs, points to the probability of the station, important though it became, as belonging to the last century or so of the occupation. At any rate, rarely in England is so much Roman masonry, in round tower and massive wall, to be seen lying or standing above ground in one spot as here.

The weird confusion of it too in a manner adds to the kind of awe with which one cannot help regarding the few works of this inscrutable epoch, that have weathered the storms of all these centuries ; that have sheltered birds and beasts and haymakers and shepherds and tramps and lifted up their grey walls upon the landscape like any other of the many ancient buildings or their ruins which are by comparison but things of yesterday, and the symbols of altogether another and a later world. No small amount of building still lies here just beneath the surface of the pasture. The strength of the

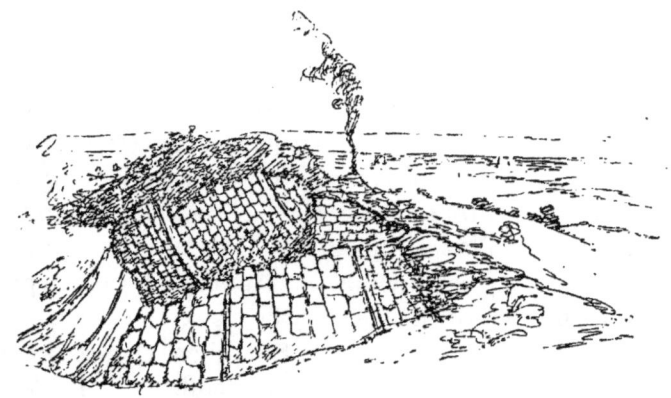

Roman Walls (*after an old Drawing*).

masonry is of course prodigious, the inside material being composed of the hard limestone of the district, while the facing stones are of the same, interspersed by courses of Roman tiles. The indestructible nature of Roman mortar is due, I believe, to the greater proportion of lime to sand than was used by subsequent generations. This, however, has not prevented the difficult task of breaking up the masonry and carrying off the stones, for hundreds of buildings in certain parts of England still contain them. Lympne Church, and probably the castle too, are in part built of this material.

Sir Victor Horsley did some later excavation here, discovering, among other things, a fine pavement under the gate tower and also the steps of the old quay at the foot of the hill. We have thought it well to reproduce here copies of the two sketches made at the time of the first excavations, as bearing more directly on the Roman work, since some slight changes have inevitably taken place during the past seventy years. The landslide which upset so much of Studfall Castle (the Saxon name) must have been very severe, as some of the buildings were turned completely over. But landslides are fairly common on this ridge; there was a bad one at Sandgate within recent years. Hasted, the Kentish historian, also tells what sounds a tallish story of a half-timbered house standing on the slope half a mile west of Lympne (the modern spelling). It was in 1726, he declares, that it slipped down from the brink of the hill some fifty feet in the night and so circum spectly that none of the inmates knew anything about it till they found a difficulty in opening the door in the morning! But the *Gentleman's Magazine* thirty years afterwards vouched for the fact, and I know myself of a barn in Shropshire that glissaded very much farther than that and seemed little the worse for it.

West Hythe lies some half a mile from Studfall Castle, at the foot of Lympne hill—on the military canal as a matter of fact. We should already have crossed the bridge there on our way to the Roman port if the licence of the printed page had not allowed us to take a shorter cut to it. West Hythe, however, though there is now nothing of it but a modern inn, a few cottages and a ruined church, could not possibly be overlooked, as for a long time it was practically a Cinque-Port. But the water, in part at least, deserting it, most of its inhabitants followed the shrinkage down to "New" Hythe, which became in due course one of the recognized Cinque-Ports, with " Old " or West Hythe as an unimportant " limb." Leland wrote of it : " It hath bene a very great towne in length and conteyned iiii paroches and chyrch yardes. The haven is a

LYMPNE AND ROMAN REMAINS.

praty rode and lieth meatly strayt for passage owt of Boloyn." There now remains only the ruins of the church of St. Mary the Virgin, of which the pointed chancel arch alone is in fair preservation, the remainder being greatly decayed. In 1380 two hundred houses in West Hythe were destroyed by the French, who went on and wreaked their vengeance in like manner on Appledore, so it must then have been a considerable place. It was not till Elizabeth's time that West Hythe finally lost the small channel which still connected it with the sea, and thus the harbour which had served the Romans vanished in its dwindled form only with the Elizabethans. And so, too, all that was left of the river Limene, which, with its two arms, or estuaries, here and at New Romney had existed in shifting forms since recorded history began, was utterly extinguished, in favour of the present Rother.

The road from West Hythe up to the main thoroughfare following the ridge of Lympne hill, represents a terrific climb. Near its junction with the other, once stood the ancient Cross of Shipway, where as late as Tudor times the Warden of the Cinque-Ports was sworn in, and many of the important gatherings of the Portsmen were held, till the more convenient shelter and situation of Romney became the common resort. We are not tied to roads here at any rate, and in such case the finest approach to the dominant feudal building now known as Lympne Castle, with the adjoining Norman church, is up the long green steep from the Roman works. Half-way up, a footpath continues the steep ascent by the course of a little woody stream that descends the hill and was once utilized as a water supply for the Roman fortress. Unfortunately the castle has been recently restored as a private residence, and though possibly with excellent taste, that is not the question. To keep such places from falling down and to save them as historic monuments is one thing, and till the war such worthy precautions would not have amounted to a fleabite in the wealth of the nation, but to adapt them to modern private dwellings, with all which that entails, is quite another, for many obvious reasons. Bamborough, on the Northumbrian coast, though altogether on a much greater scale, will recur to many as a case in point. Much however of the old work here remains, and the building is still worthy of its imposing site.

It was originally built by Lanfranc, William the Conqueror's Norman Archbishop of Canterbury, who rebuilt the Cathedral after the fire of 1067, and reconstituted the Church of England according to Norman ideas and interests. No doubt stones from the ruinous Roman castrum were freely used in the construction of both castle and church, some of the tiles being visible in the latter. The castle continued in possession of the See of Canterbury, and was enlarged and crenelated, probably in the late fourteenth century. It appears to have been utilized as the Archdeacon's residence, though archdeacons were much more important functionaries in the Norman period than in ours, as those familiar with the works of the greatest and most delightful of all archdeacons, Giraldus Cambrensis, well know. But even such as he, in an embattled baronial castle perched upon a steep and frowning over land and sea, would seem a little over-housed! At any rate it was always known in former times as the Archdeacon's House, and it was only in later and peaceful days that it became Lympne Castle. Prior to the time of its recent restoration, the middle portion seems to have been used as a farmhouse.

The church, which almost touches the castle, is very interesting and rather out of the prevalent local type. It consists of a Norman nave and chancel and a thirteenth-century north aisle and entrance porch. The first sight of the interior is a little bewildering. For one thing it seems almost encumbered with a superabundance of massive arches and pillars, though this is more of an impression than a reality. When the north aisle was added, early in the thirteenth century, the massive north wall of the nave was merely pierced into two pointed arches, a like arch being cut through the north side of the tower space. The east end of the nave opens into the tower space with a sharply pointed arch, showing by its Norman impost mouldings that there was probably a round arch prior to the alterations above alluded to. The eastern arch again, opening into the chancel, maintains its Norman character, which provides another rather curious feature, as one looks down the church from the west end. The west wall was entirely rebuilt in the last century. To speak, however, of the chancel beyond its entrance arch as Norman is not accurate. That the eastern portion of it is thirteenth-century is indisputable, but that the western part is Norman is by no means so certain, a difference in size of the lancet windows that light all three sides being about the only evidence. The alternative is that the Norman chancel was entirely pulled down during the thirteenth-century alterations. Save a small circular window over the three lancets which light the east end, all the rest are of the last named pattern, those in the north aisle being very small and deeply splayed. Over the pointed eastern arch of the nave are three more lancets, now blocked up, which once helped to light the tower, and go to prove that the roof of the original nave was at a lower elevation than the present one. Frescoes were discovered some years ago under the limewash on the pier of the west arch of the tower, but from one cause or another they have disappeared. A stone seat runs along both the north and south wall of the chancel, and just under the altar rails is a memorial slab to a Finche and his wife, who left considerable benefactions to the parish. In the north wall is a recess beneath a trefoil canopy of Edwardian date, which is supposed to have held the effigy of a Crusader. Many mortuary slabs lie on the pavements, their inscriptions often illegible from the age-long pressure of the rustic boot; among them a coffin lid, showing the floriated cross of an abbot or monk, will be noted at once.

The graveyard is spacious and well kept, and from that

portion of it on the sunny south side, or back of the church, you can best appreciate the rugged massive walls of the fabric and the full stature of the tower. Above all, you get a view over the Marsh from this eastern end of it that will be a novelty to those accustomed only to enjoying it from the heights above its westerly portion. I am inclined to think it surpasses even these, as regards the effect as a whole. You are lifted higher up, for one thing, and the churches of the Marsh with their spires and towers are more in evidence. That there is more foliage visible on this side than in the Lydd and Rye district may be taken either way, according to taste, but I think from Lympne Hill you can better command the fine curves of the coast so sharply accentuated by Dungeness. You can also see the heights of Folkestone and Dover at much closer quarters, while Fairlight is comparatively faint and far away. Furthermore, you may see the coast of France here upon ordinarily clear days, and with what different eyes now one looks upon that coast to-day as compared with a few years ago!

The perfervid local guide books will tell you that there is not a finer view in England. The writers probably mean—though they do not know it—the finest in the south-eastern counties, which I think it quite probably is. Innumerable persons who have not even a nodding acquaintance with more than a quarter of their own country make these sort of foolish statements in newspapers every week, quite often from some hilltop in Surrey, as if four or five hundred feet elevation in a gentle rolling country could conceivably provide such an outlook as a natural platform of three or four times the height! If you have lately stood, for instance, upon the familiar heights of Malvern and looked over twenty counties from Snowdon to Stratford-on-Avon, and from Exmoor to Leicestershire, Hindhead and Boxhill and the other notable week-end views of the Londoner will not do, or anything like do, not merely in extent but in inspiring detail. ‘How should they ? even if their relative limitations were not smirched, as Mr. Wells truly says, with modernity in every shape.

Here, at any rate, looking over Romney Marsh is the old, old England. There is no doubt about that, and furthermore we have the sea, from Dover to Fairlight, shining beyond, and yet more, that particular little bit of sea, with the coast of France lying low upon its further bounds, which of all the seas that wash the shores of England has been most pregnant with weal or woe for its people ; the unceasing danger point from age to age over which the sword of fate has hung continuously from the victorious Roman, Saxon and Norman, to the baffled Napoleon. Possibly it has now lost much of this significance. But two thousand years have all but passed since Julius Caesar landed, as some say here at Lympne, and that is time enough, with all its momentous burden of events, to consecrate this narrow bight, this historic danger spot of the silver streak.

Turning homewards from this eastern limit of our pilgrimage, the high ridge road above the Marsh gives us also on our right hand a fine outlook over the wide vale through which the continental expresses run their familiar course to Folkestone and Dover, with the Kent Downs rising high behind it. In less than two miles the one-sided village of Court-at-street, otherwise Court-op-street, or Court-of-street, calls for a halt. Leland found a wonderful yarn about a borough town with a mace and brazen horn to its credit, having once stood here. But Lambarde, a later and more knowledgable and critical authority, as a Kentish man, brushes it aside as relating in fact to Lympne and West Hythe. Its earlier name seems to have been Belcaise, or Belcastrum, but where the " Faire Castle " was I do not know, though Leland was shown some remains of it. But the *genius loci*—if the gender may be overlooked—of Court-at-Street is the Holy Maid of Kent, who in the seventeenth year of Henry the Eighth's reign created such a hubbub in the county, and even in London, and met such a cruel fate. For the ruins of the chapel which was the scene of these amazing doings still survive below the village, though the girl herself lived a mile or two further up the road in the parish of Aldington. Her name was Elizabeth Barton and she was but a servant to a member of the ancient and ubiquitous Kentish family of Cobb, whose departed glories we took note of, it may be remembered, at New Romney. The houses along the village street face south in cheerful and sensible fashion, and look down over the Marsh and sea unimpeded by any obstructing neighbours across the way. But at the further end the Manor farm in picturesque profusion of barns and outbuildings and rickyards is an exception. Threading your way through these, a deep sunk woody lane leads down the green slope and out into an open meadow, where upon on side is a tree-shaded pond and on the other three roofless walls of the chapel to which four hundred years ago people flocked in their thousands to hear the utterances of this poor demented, imposed-upon impostor.

As it was in Lambarde's own lifetime, though early in it, that these scenes took place, and as he was a sober, critical writer and a highly-educated man, as well as a Kentish one, it seems superfluous to quote any other authority on the Maid of Kent, plentiful as they are. Lambarde gives a long and precise account of the whole business. It seems that the Chapel of Our Lady at Court-of-Street was then in a ruinous condition. It was occupied by a hermit, one of the practical, active sort with an eye to the main chance. This pious soul, together with Mr. Masters, Priest of Aldington, saw an opportunity, either at once or later, of using an epileptic, hysterical peasant woman as a kind of side-show for raising money to rebuild his chapel and replenish, no doubt, his own and the Vicar's pockets. That it became, however, much more than a side-show we shall see. Now this all happened but a few years before the Reformation, when superstition was being everywhere exploited and turned into cash, not always expended in church restoration! Lambarde, in the quaint fashion of his day, and as a member of the Reformed Faith, ascribed the incident to the Devil in a very personal sense, who, struck with panic at the approach of the Reformation, engineered the whole thing. " Fearing that if he did not now bestirre himself busily he was in peril to lose infinite numbers of his subjects. So practising most carefully in all places he saw his opportunity at Court-at-Street, and set his monkes, friars, priests, nonnes and the whole rabblement of his army" to work up Mr. Cobbe's parlourmaid as a gigantic fake.

One cannot follow Lambarde through all the wonderful physical symptoms of this epileptic and hysterical girl, such as would no doubt be disposed of to-day in ten minutes by the local practitioner from Lympne. But she went frequently into long trances and related afterwards to her simple audience in what a wonderful manner and in what wonderful places she had spent these unconscious interludes. She had visited Heaven, Hell and Purgatory, and reported the present situation in one or the other of various local folks who had recently departed this earth. She brought messages from the upper world, commanding the strict ritual of the old Church, mass, confession and prayers to the Saints. Launching into prophecy and divination she amazed the locals that trooped to see her, even stating precisely what meat the hermit of the chapel two miles away was having for his supper, a fact no doubt previously imparted by that wily cleric. When feeling better (a miracle of course) she repaired to the chapel and drew crowds by her performances, physical and spiritual, together with all kinds of promises, in the character of special commissioner of the Virgin to all and sundry. She undertook to cure diseases, though she obviously could not cure her own. But that mattered nothing with these confiding crowds, and certainly not with the Hermit and his partner the Vicar of Aldington, who kept her up to the scratch in a masterly way. These performances went on for some time till " the fame of this marveylous maiden was so spreade abroade that it came to the eares of Warham, Archbishop of Canterbury, who directed thither Doctour Bocking, Master Hadleigh and Barnes (three monkes in Christchurch Canterbury), Father Lewes and his fellowe (two observants), his official of Canterbury and the Parson of Aldington, with commission to examine the matter, and to informe him of the truth."

These learned gentlemen, having examined the maid and found her sound on the old dogmas " waded no further in the discoverie of the frauds, but gave favourable countenance and joyned with her in setting foorth of the same." The consequence was that at her next visit to the chapel she entered it " with *Ave Regina Coelorum* in pricksong accompanied by these Commissioners, many ladies, gentlemen and gentlewomen of the best degree and three thousand besides." And so the mummery went on, hysterics apparently before the image and intermittent fits upon the ground, varied by metrical and rhyming speeches. The chief import of these seems to have been the better maintenance and endowment of the chapel, whose hermit must have been coining money, with a handsome commission no doubt to " the parson of Aldington." The Archbishop was properly humbugged by his Commission, and appointed the maid a nun of St. Sepulchre's in Canterbury. Here she continued her miracle frauds, in the interests of the doomed faith. She seems to have been regarded by the Church as of some possible assistance to it, as an object lesson in miracle-working in this its last kick. But the Holy Maid did not forget her Aldington patrons, as every one who wished to benefit by her professed cures had to " measure or vow themselves unto her at Court-of-Streete." " Thus," says Lambarde, " was Elizabeth Barton advanced, from the condition of a base servant to the estate of a glorious nonne. The Hermite of Court-of-Streete was enriched by daily offerings, St. Sepulchre's got possession of a holy Maiden, God was blasphemed, the holy Virgine, his mother, dishonoured ; the Silly people were miserably mocked ; the Bishops, Priests and monks, in the meantime with close eies winking, and the Devill and his Lymmes with open mouth laughing at it."

This farce was enacted for a long time, two or three years apparently. The chapel was rebuilt and handsome profits accrued to many people, and no doubt to St. Sepulchre's nunnery. It was only terminated by the folly of the poor girl herself, who whether her body was cured or not was naturally under such conditions suffering from a badly swollen head. For she began to prate about the King's personal affairs and told him to his face at Canterbury that if he divorced Catherine of Aragon and married Anne Boleyne " he should not be King of this realme one moneth after." Henry set another sort of Commission to work from that of Archbishop Warham. The maid confessed the whole thing a fraud, gave away her accomplices, or instigators rather, and there was a great hanging at Tyburn. The others ultimately attainted of high treason were Masters the Parson of Aldington, Bocking (her Confessor) and Dering, Monks of Christchurch, Golde a priest, Hugh Rich, warden of a Friars House in Canterbury, and Richard Risby. John Fisher, Bishop of Rochester, his chaplain, Thomas Golde and Edward Thwaites (gentlemen), Laurence, Registrar of Canterbury and Abel, a priest, were attainted of misprision. All of this later group were discharged. Of the former, the maid herself, Bocking and Dering, Golde and Risby were condemned to death. Probably the hermit was dead, as he is not included. But the Vicar of Aldington curiously enough goes scot free. Lambarde is silent on this, but according to Mr. Igglesden in one of his extremely pleasant Kentish sketches, a good many people have worked at the details of this extraordinary incident, without being able to throw any light on Masters' acquittal, but the act of it.

There is not really much mystery about the affair itself,

To what extent the maid humbugged the priests, or they her, is quite immaterial. Her delusions marched precisely with their interests. In the medical ignorance and rank superstition of those days one can practically visualize the whole sordid business. The doomed group were set upon a scaffold at St. Paul's Cross, and exposed to a prolonged harangue from the Bishop of Bangor. The hapless girl then delivered what purported to be her own confession, endeavouring rather pathetically to take all the blame upon herself, though even in this she was doubtless prompted by her wily fellow prisoners, anxious to save their own skins. They were then all shut up in the Tower till a special Act of Parliament could be passed for their execution, though why this formality, seeing that Henry made noble heads fly this way and that at will, I do not know! The maid was burned at Tyburn after making a speech in which she described how in her ignorance she had been made a dupe of, and in just such words as any one to-day who had read the story would put into her mouth. Her male accomplices and instigators were hung. The ruins of the chapel, with a Tudor doorway still remaining, are from their very peace and isolation well adapted to stir the fancy and quicken the interest in its strange tale which I have related here in but brief and sketchy fashion. Screened from the road by the buildings, gardens and surrounding paddocks of the Manor farm, it rests upon the sunny southern slope of the pasture looking out over the Marsh far below, as inconsequently as any ruinous old barn or cowshed till it reveals its character on a near acquaintance. A rather picturesque pool shaded with willows glimmers a few yards and may readily be converted into a charming foreground to the rude old building which centuries ago witnessed such uncanny doings and such brilliant pageants.

Still following the high road, Aldington Church with its fine tower stands up alone and with much distinction upon this broad lofty ridge, known as the Quarry Hills, between the

Marsh and the Ashford low country in and about the Stour valley. It is worth turning to the right and making something of a circuit for a glance at the church and village, though it is as a parish of importance, and incidentally rich in old homesteads, rather than as a village, that it stands out above all other places overlooking the Marsh. It was an old Manor of the Archbishop's for one thing, and in its now cultivated Chase, the Primate of England used to pursue the Archiepiscopal deer. Erasmus was vicar here for about a year in 1511, followed almost immediately by Masters of Holy Maid fame, whom he tells us was a young man well skilled in divinity, and further that he too was hung at Tyburn. Lambarde says the same thing, but unfortunately his death is registered at Aldington, of which he was still in possession ten years later, so there must have been reasons for pardoning him.

The church has a fine early sixteenth-century tower of considerable height which its conspicuous position, as I have said, makes the very most of. It was built by Archbishop Warham and is sometimes said to be the latest pre-Reformation work in England. But the last Prior of Evesham's glorious Campanile on the banks of the Avon has, I think, that honour, for it was not quite finished when the blow fell. Both nave and chancel have a south aisle, and the latter a fine Perpendicular east window, while a broad pointed arch opens nave and chancel to their respective south aisles, and there are also some good carved oak stalls. The churchyard is large, picturesque and well kept up. Sloping slightly to the north at that edge of the ridge, it well sets off the dignity of the church itself, which rising upon the lower side has for its background the wide sweep inland into Kent and away to the East downs.

Court Lodge speaks for itself in its name and, as a farmhouse, near the church, still preserves some of the old building which once sheltered the Archbishop's steward. Ruffins-hill, another old farmstead on a big scale, once apparently a squire's abode, stands at the corner where the branch road to the church leaves the highway. The ancient Kentish family of Deedes seem to have in past times purchased all the manors in the parish, and still remain in part possession. Following the main road to what is known as Aldington Corner, practically representing the village, Cobb Hall, whence emerged the Holy Maid, stands conspicuously above the road. It is a modest, half-timbered house, of the sixteenth-century manor house type in a plain way, and now divided into two tenements

OLD COURT LODGE, UDIMORE (p. 194).

for labouring people, but a good deal of the old work still remains inside. Aldington Corner, just beyond, stands well out upon the ridge top where four roads unite and consists of a good inn, and a few houses and cottages. It was a great smuggling depot in olden times, and the parish of Aldington was full of hiding holes for illicit goods run up from the Marsh. The cottages of long departed smuggling heroes are still pointed out by the older natives.

The long descent from Aldington Corner to the lower road,

DYMCHURCH—BY LYMPNE—TO BILSINGTON 341

which just above the Marsh undulates westward through many villages to Appledore, is delightful on a sunny day both in its foreground and distant views. A tufted height to the eastward is suggestive of the look-out spot of the whole neighbourhood, and so it is. For Aldington Knoll is in fact the only attempt of this protracted ridge between Lympne and Fairlight at what might be called individual enterprise. It is able to speak, therefore, to men at sea, and is said on that account to carry a shadowy garrison of drowned men ready to repel any agricultural efforts likely to alter the shape of its summit. So the farmer is said to leave it piously alone. That may be so, but even at the present moment it is hardly the spot that even a London land reformer would select to break up for grain or potatoes. Leaving Bonnington, a mere hamlet at the foot of Aldington Hill and in its turn looking down towards its own little church at the edge of the Marsh, at each dip of the road from now onward, the endless avenue that shadows the military canal is always present in the near foreground. *Tempora mutanta,* that this glorified and picturesque ditch behind the Marsh which was meant as much, I fancy, for protection as for transport, and the inverted flower-pots along the shore, should have been among our masterpieces of defence at the country's danger spot at a perilous moment, may well give one to think furiously. At such a rate of progress in destructive methods, what may a century hence have in store ? The arts of peace, thank Heaven, are not quite so revolutionary.

This old road, for instance, save for its surface, can have changed but little in the last hundred years. More people, I feel sure, travelled on it then ; fewer I think live beside it and in its villages than even of old. It is quiet enough now in all conscience, woody hills and solitary farms at long intervals upon the one side, the boundless silence and solitude of the Marsh upon the other. Approaching Bilsington, however, conspicuous on a neighbouring hill top, a modern country house and a very ancient priory stand almost side by side in startling contrast. The latter was restored, and I think converted to private uses, a dozen or so years ago, and would probably at this distance arouse no little curiosity as to its character on the part of the wayfarer. I never saw it in its former condition, and have never felt particularly moved to inspect in its present one, though I believe it was a question of restoration or extinction from decay, and that the restoration was very well done. Previously it did duty as a farm-house, and judging from sketches I have seen, it must have been singularly picturesque though probably not very comfortable. Bilsington Priory was a house of the Black Augustinians, founded in the thirteenth century by a Sir John Mansell, who made over to it the Manor, which must have been but a trifling item in the fabulous wealth he was supposed to possess.

A little further on, four roads meet and the few houses that gather round the *White Horse Inn* are known as Bilsington Cross, and constitute the village. An obelisk on the rise of a field close by which can be seen over half the Marsh, has always rather irritated me. It suggests so strongly those cloud-compelling, unsightly memorials, by means of which the later Georgians were so fond of advertising their filial piety to the country at large. Great statesmen, generals, admirals or even a beneficent Duke, thus set upon a hill top before the eyes of a grateful and adoring posterity is all very well. But a country squire of modest worth and no renown, looks rather absurd after a generation or two defying the lightning on the verge of a cliff, even to his descendants.

A family of my acquaintance in past days, seated about three hundred miles from Bilsington, used to say that they would gladly pay a good round sum, if decency allowed it, to any one who would stealthily place a charge of dynamite beneath their quite undistinguished Grandfather, who in the shape of a tall ugly round tower, exactly like a mine chimney, disfigured the summit of a shapely neighbouring ridge. And these disrespectful utterances were evoked partly because the spectacle irked their native modesty, as well as their sense of humour, to say nothing of their sense of art, and partly because it was embarrassing to be so often asked by ingenuous visitors if they had coal on the property! But this comparatively modest, though far seen obelisk at Bilsington, was erected to the memory of a former squire, killed in 1835 by a fall from his horse in London, as a retrospective thank-offering for his intention to vote for the Reform Bill if he got into Parliament, for which he had been nominated. One can imagine at that frenzied and critical period, a burst of local gratitude finding such expression. But even so, his very name, Cossway, means nothing I think now to the people of Bilsington.

The little parish church stands overlooking the Marsh, but has been very much restored. Its stumpy tower, hardly reaching to the gable point of the nave, is still quaint enough with its weather boarded upper stage and tiled cap. The church was connected with the Priory of Bilsington till the Dissolution. Within a moat which divides some leafy precincts from the churchyard, stands the ancient Court Lodge, recalling the old Manor of Bilsington and upon ground once covered by a large fortified mansion. The Manor of Bilsington has always held the right of presenting the last dish of the second course to the King at his Coronation dinner, and of offering him at the same time three maple cups. This may sound foolish, but it carried its reward in the shape of a Knighthood and occasionally something higher. Both George the Third and George the Fourth received the offer and conferred the honour. The gentleman commemorated in the adjoining field, who fell off his horse, just before getting into Parliament and voting for the Reform Bill, was the last to be knighted on account of this picturesque little attention. But the Manor, like most others hereabouts, has constantly changed hands. Lambarde has something to say about the above-

z

mentioned ancient custom, dating it at least to Henry the Fourth.

But he is much more interesting when speaking intimately of certain phases of country life, which few Elizabethan observers of it, save Owen of Henllys in his inimitable *Pembrokeshire*, touch upon. " The Kentish gentry," says Lambarde, for though himself one of them he knew other counties and was admirably well informed, " differ somewhat from others, they are not heere (throughout) of such auncient stockes as elsewhere especially in the partes neere to London from which citie (as it were from a certain riche and wealthy seedplot) courtiers lawyers and Merchants be continually translated and do become new plaints among them." Yet their revenues, he tells us, are greater than anywhere, not because of any superiority in extent and fertility of their land, but because of the situation of the country; good markets and high prices of produce being a great highway of trade, in short its ready access to the capital and the Continent. The Kent gentry too, he affirms, are well read and cultivated men as well as being generally familiar with legal matters. They look carefully after their estates too with an eye to the welfare of their families, and furthermore qualify their sons for entering the public service, which their position favours, or for success in other walks of life. Lastly, which is curiously significant, " they use hawking and other hunting, and other disports rather for their recreation than for occupation or pastime. The yeomanrie or common people is nowhere more free and jolly than in this shire. Besides they say themselves, in a clayme (made by them in the time of King Edward the First) that the commonaltie of Kent was never vanquished by the Conquerour, but yeelded itself by composition, and besides that the forward in all battels belongeth to them by a certain preeminence in right of their manhood; it is agreed by all men that there never were any bondmen or villains, as the law calleth them, in Kent." He then tells us that they never were in Kent so much " bounden to the gentrie by copyhold or custumarie tenures" as elsewhere, and belauds the Kentish custom of Gavelkind, which prevails to a certain extent to this day. In this sense of independence " they please themselves and joy exceedingly insomuch as a man may find sundry yeomen (although otherwise for wealth comparable with many of the gentle sort), yet for all that would not change their condition nor desire to be apparaited with the titles of gentrie. To be short, they be most commonly civil, just and bountiful, so that the estate of the old Franklyns and yeomen of England either yet liveth in Kent, or else is quite dead and departed out of this realm altogether."

CHAPTER THE ELEVENTH

Ruckinge to Rye

RUCKINGE, with the "g" soft, is the next village on the road. and of the whole lot I think, to all seeming, the most out of the world; a mere hamlet lifted just above the Marsh with the woodland course of the ever faithful canal making a pleasing background to its skirting meadows. A goodsized and ancient church stands by the road side aloof from and beyond the trifling village. Hasted calls Ruckinge " a mean

RUCKINGE.

little church." On the contrary it is a fairly large and very interesting building, of tower, nave with side aisles and a chancel with a south chapel. The tower is Norman, though its top stage is poor, of much later date and surmounted with a queer little pointed leaden spire. It has a beautiful, recessed and moulded Norman doorway, with star ornamentation on the capitals and imposts. Whether or no the south wall of the nave is a Norman survival it has at any rate a fine doorway of the period. The rest of the building is Early English, the octagonal columns of the nave arcade being much decayed. The south chapel of the chancel under its own steep gabled roof and of the same period has some good windows, a poor one at the east end of the main chancel and apparently a replacement. Some remains of a handsome fifteenth-century oak screen have been introduced into the chancel seats on one side and on the other is a long pew of plain oak of great age and thickness. An elaborately carved Tudor refectory table, as at Northiam, does duty as an altar. The efforts of present and past vicars have kept the large roof in good repair, no slight task in a squireless, friendless parish of 250 souls of a traditionally non-church-going type—except, I believe, on great occasions when some lingering conservative instincts seem to bring Marsh parishes in a body to the shrine of their ancestors. Chairs have replaced the old square pews, and though sentiment may sometimes regret their disappearance, when they stand gaping as it were for a congregation of 500—they must look much more disheartening to a zealous parson with a congregation of twenty than a judiciously arranged group of chairs in the centre of the church. The spiritual or egotistic pre-occupation of the monks could disregard these great empty spaces, while later on, when the whole parish was coralled into church by Tudor edicts of Puritan menaces, Sunday mornings must have been quite lively. But under the genial toleration of modern days, churches like this, even as is the case here, when well kept up, cannot avoid a touch of melancholy. No distinguished dead are commemorated within these long enduring walls, nor would you for a moment expect them to be. But the native will point out with alacrity the resting place in the churchyard of the local heroes of the past. For beneath a wooden slab supported by iron railings, the Rangeley family, of smuggling fame throughout the country, sleep their last sleep. Even Ruckinge, however, harboured for many years a future bishop in its vicarage, and curiously enough a Scotsman, as in the case of the neighbouring parish of Ivychurch. This was Dr. Porteus, who went to Chester and from thence to London. On turning up Hasted, I find the seclusion with which Ruckinge even now impresses one, struck the County Historian 140 years ago with even greater force, as is natural enough. " It is obscure," he writes, " and little known or frequented," while our now quite excellent road is described as " narrow, miry, as bad as any in the Weald and well nigh impassable."

RUCKINGE: WEST DOOR.

A mile or so beyond Ruckinge the transformed highway begins to show signs of emerging from the rural backwater it has traversed since Aldington and from the top of a steep pitch, Ham Street and Orlestone (one and the same) display their profusion of cherry orchards for which the spot is famous, their half-timbered houses and their new red villas, and we are for the time at any rate in the world again or relatively so. For we are also on the railroad and at the meeting of many highways. There are some snug houses here-about and one or two very ancient ones, notably the half-timbered post office, gathered about the four cross-roads and many orchards, whose fine display of blossom in the springtime is a familiar object of admiration to all habitual travellers on this section of the South-Eastern. The broad road to Ashford climbs the long hill from the Marsh edge, upon which the main village stands, past the red villas by the station and on to the top of the ridge, half a mile away, whence a turn up a by-road at the Rectory brings you in five minutes to Orlestone Church. It is worth the detour, and there is nothing sad about this little thirteenth-century building. The beauty of its peaceful situation overlooking the abundant woodlands that clothe the slopes of the hills beneath it, with the Marsh far outspread to the distant sea line and the yet more distant cliffs of Fairlight, would alone banish all thoughts of melancholy.

ORLESTONE.

Moreover it is a cheerful little Early English church in itself, restored not long ago, with a nave, chancel and shingle spire, decorated windows and a good oak roof, and from no point of view bespeaking the stranger's sympathy. Its uplifted little graveyard is better filled now than in Hasted's time, when it had " only one tombstone and that of no account." Orlestone in those days seem to have been a quite insignificant and obscure place with all its four roads " impassable save in fine weather." It shares its charming situation with the old Manor Court House, now a farm just across the church lane that ends here and serves them both. Part timber and part stone the older and sixteenth century portion of this ancient house contains among other things, a long, low oak-raftered groundfloor chamber, where the affairs of the Manor were conducted in olden times and those of the subsequent Court-leet which sat here later.

All manorial and estate accounts in the Middle Ages were surely meticulous to a degree! England was then a wild, woody and sparsely populated country. There are oversea countries or portions of them inhabited by Anglo-Saxons to-day, that bear much the same ratio of population to un-utilized or wooded area as old England, though in their case because they are more or less in their infancy. Whether rich or poor in individual bank accounts, the mere crude essentials of bare existence are so easily come by as to be of almost no consideration and for such obvious reasons. But in undeveloped wild England of ancient days, you find tiny patches of land subject to portentous documents—rights to the grazing of half a cow, or to the cutting of a few faggots in illimitable woods—reduced to precise figures in infinitesimal sums. Rivers teeming with common fish are dealt with as if a dense population were fearful of their food supply, and all this too in a country of which huge tracts of fertile woodland remained derelict under timber that in the bulk had no money value. Here in this vast Weald was a case in point. It was not, or at any rate only here and there, a hunting preserve, for these Royal or noble " Chases " were only patched about England. The nobles had no quarrel with land-development as such which would have greatly increased their revenues. It is difficult to understand this niggling and haggling and lawyer work over such trifles in the open spaces, when five-sixths of the country around was only waiting the axe and plough, and the clearing of English forests was child's play to what these same Englishmen later on in the seventeenth century faced in the woods of New England and Virginia. It is all rather puzzling even allowing for the cumbrous intricacies of feudalism. Here, for instance, is a contribution paid to the Lord of the Manor of Orlestone, no doubt in this very Court House or its predecessor, in Richard the Second's time, four cocks, twenty-one hens and the fourth part of one hen and 139 eggs and a half. *The fourth part of one hen and half an egg!* A pretty poor hen and a pretty poor egg to split up too, I'll warrant, under the primitive agricultural methods of 1394! No Buff Orpingtons or White Leghorns in those days! It would almost seem as if the lawyer, clerk and steward class, the only laymen who could read, write and cypher, were in a solid conspiracy to create grotesque intricacies for the better support and profit of their profession.

But enough of this, we are within a mile of Warehorne by pursuing the same road that brought us to the village below and continues its switchback course westward towards Appledore. And at Warehorne the Rev. Richard Barham, otherwise *Thomas Ingoldsby*, spent nearly five years of his earlier clerical life. We have, indeed, this long time been in what after a current literary fashion and in some cases a rather absurd one, would be called " the Ingoldsby country." *The Ingoldsby Legends*, however, if only in quotation, have established themselves as a classic, so the soil that inspired them must in a measure share the rather peculiar fame of their author. For this whimsical and entertaining person was a native of it ; not of Warehorne of course, but of this part of the county and very much so, as the scion of an ancient and well-known Kentish stock. He indulged to be sure in some poetic licence in regard to the splendours of *Tappington Hall* and its Washington Irving atmosphere, though legitimately enough as writing under a *nom de plume*. As a matter of fact his early home was in Canterbury, and the particular Barham who begot him was a scholarly humorous leisured person of twenty-seven stone weight. He derived part of a fair income from two farms which had once formed part of the old Barham estate, and had come back to a near ancestor through the accident of marriage. At the death of this genial and naturally not very enterprising heavyweight, in middle life, his son Richard with other moderate endowments became possessed of Tappington farm, with its picturesque modest house, and it was this that he endowed in fancy as *Tappington Hall*, with all the squirearchical glories of his ancestors, under the pseudonym of the *Ingoldsbys*.

About 1806 after being Captain of St. Paul's School, Barham went up to Brazenose as a gentleman commoner. Fairly well off, witty and popular he led the life at Oxford natural to such circumstances, though he lost a good portion of his property, soon afterwards, through the dishonesty of his lawyer. Eventually he took orders, though neither his losses nor his white tie interfered with his irrepressible gaiety and turn, or almost genius, for clever and humorous verse. He had made friends with Theodore Hook during the latter's brief sojourn at Brazenose, and it was not surprising that two such kindred souls, given the opportunity, as in this case, remained friends for life. In 1813 Barham became curate of Ashford, moving next year to Eastwell, when he married, and in 1817 he was appointed by the Archbishop to the charges of Warehorne and Snargate. Though curate of the first and Rector of the second, it was obvious enough why he took up his abode in Warehorne Parsonage rather than out on the drear and then malarious levels of the Marsh. Probably Warehorne, lifted just above its edge, was not ague-proof, still it is quite an attractive spot, with plenty of good timber round about it. The parsonage was rebuilt soon after Barham's time, in the same pleasant and roomy grounds, though not quite on the same spot as the one he had lived in. Furthermore at the corner where the by-way leaves the main road for the church, vicarage and small village, stands the handsome Queen Anne Mansion of *Leacon. Here dwelt Squire Hodges, whose company must have counted for a good deal to the Barhams, in what in those days of bad roads was virtually a social wilderness. Moreover, the Squire hunted the Marsh with a pack of harriers and the young parson was something of a sportsman himself.

To most men so genial and nimble-minded, Warehorne would have been exile indeed, but Barham's sense of humour and unrivalled facility in expressing it found plenty of material in the Marsh of those days. He was writing for Blackwood too at this time, as well as for other publishers ; children were appearing with their special interests and anxieties, and he seems to have done something to mitigate the utter spiritual neglect in which he found the whole district sunk. His portrait is that of a cheery, full-faced, rather pert, keen-looking man, with a mobile humorous mouth on the point of laughter. Like Macaulay, who in family letters, strange to say, did the same, Barham could write admirable serio-comic doggerel almost as quickly and as easily as he could write prose. His son, who published a long biography of the then world-famous *Thomas Ingoldsby* about fifty years ago, has produced some of these entertaining trifles. One of them is a note to Squire Hodges, whose hounds had driven a hare into the Rector's garden, where it squatted down exhausted and quivering within a yard of him. After several harrowing and pathetic verses, purporting to convict the hounds and their master of heartless persecution of an innocent beast, he winds up—

> Yet O in vain thy foes shall come,
> So cheer thee, trembling elf,
> These guardian arms shall bear thee home,
> *I'll eat thee up myself!*

Here again is an invitation to Dr. Wilmot of Ashford to come over and shoot with him—

> O Doctor! wilt thou dine with me,
> And drive on Tuesday morning down ?
> Can ribs of beef have charms for thee,
> The fat, the lean, the luscious brown ?

> No longer dressed in silken sheen,
>   Nor deck'd with rings and broaches rare,
> Say, wilt thou come in velveteen,
>   Or corduroys that never tear?
>
> O Doctor! when thou com'st away,
>   Wilt thou not bid John ride behind,
> On pony, clad in livery gay,
>   To mark the birds our pointers find?
> Let him a flask of darkest green
>   Replete with cherry brandy bear,
> That we may still, our toils between,
>   That fascinating fluid share!
>
> O Doctor! canst thou aim so true,
>   As we through briars and brambles go,
> To reach the partridge brown of hue,
>   And lay the mounting pheasant low?
> Or should, by chance, it so befall
>   Thy path be cross'd by timid hare,
> Say, wilt thou for a gamebag call
>   And place the fur-clad victim there?
>
> And when at last the dark'ning sky
>   Proclaims the hour of dinner near,
> Wilt thou repress each struggling sigh,
>   And quit thy sport for homely cheer?
> The cloth withdrawn, removed the tray—
>   Say, wilt thou, snug in elbow chair,
> The bottle's progress scorn to stay,
>   But fill, the fairest of the fair?

Among other things he wrote a couple of novels at Warehorne, while in *The Legends* are to be found of course a great deal of incident, associated with this part of Kent. He wrote more here perhaps than he would have otherwise done, having the bad luck to upset his gig and spill his family out of it driving to Ashford, a sufficient testimony of the state of the roads just a hundred years ago. He alone was damaged, however, breaking his arm and ankle and being more or less laid up for a year by it. He seems to have got on very well with the Marsh folk, though he did attempt interference with their wife-beating propensities. The smugglers too treated him with respect, though there is no evidence that, like many

Marsh parsons, he winked at the utilizing of either of his churches for storage purposes, though a large seizure of brandy had been made in Snargate tower not long before his arrival and an odd keg found under the vestry table. It is a lonely enough two miles of road even now, across the Marsh to Snargate. "Many a time," says his son, "was the genial Rector, on returning home at night, challenged by a half-seen horseman who looked in the heavy gloom like some misty condensation, a little more substantial than ordinary fog, but on making known his name and office he was invariably allowed to pass on with a 'Good-night, it's only parson,' while a long and shadowy line of mounted smugglers, each with a led horse laden with tubs, filed silently by." The nightly wages here as elsewhere, whether a cargo was run or not, was fifteen shillings for the armed and half that for the unarmed.

There was still a Marsh parson in Barham's time who, living at a distance from his church, used to come over on Sundays on top of a load of bricks, needed for repair of the chancel, which though humorous in the hearing, was at least a praiseworthy act in itself. Another clerical neighbour used to drive over to his church at any hour convenient to himself, send a boy to ring the bell and in the meantime smoke and drink with the landlord of the adjoining inn who was also the clerk. When the bell in their opinion had collected enough people, the jovial couple knocked the ashes out of their pipes and repaired to the church. On one awful occasion, however, which from its very nature seems to have been the last, the bell suddenly stopped. Parson and clerk looked at each other, with concern. It was the Rural Dean who like a bolt from the blue had descended upon the peaceful scene and the too patient congregation. The proceedings of this divine seem to have been notably indecorous. He had been known, in passing from the reading desk to the pulpit, to stop opposite his churchwarden's pew and, as if he had just concluded a long and laborious calculation, remark, " Well, Smithers, I'll have that pig." In 1821, however, Barham obtained a Minor Canonry at St. Paul's, though he might conceivably have remained at Warehorne all his days but for the merest accident, which was as follows :

He had gone up to London to consult Sir Astley Cooper about a sick daughter and happened to encounter an old friend in the Strand carrying a letter to the post office in his hand. Its purport was to ask a certain young clergyman to come and try for a vacant Minor Canonry at St. Paul's, in which election the writer had some special influence. In the excitement of this unexpected meeting and in the talk produced by it, the post office was inadvertently passed by, and indeed was never visited at all, for the letter was torn up and Barham substituted, with strong odds in his favour of election, for reasons immaterial here, as the nominee of his rediscovered friend. Barham asked for forty-eight hours' consideration so that he could return to Warehorne to consult his wife, and here is his acceptation of his friend's offer. Surely never was a Minor Canonry accepted, or what virtually amounted to such, in so unconventional and jocose a fashion.

> O, I'll be off! I will, by Jove!
> No more by purling streams I'll ramble.
> Through dirty lanes no longer rove,
> Bemired and scratched by briar and bramble
>
> I'll fly the pigstye for the parks,
> And Jack and Tom and Ned and Billy
> I'll quit for more enlighten'd sparks,
> And Romney Marsh for Piccadilly.
>
> Adieu, ye woods! adieu, ye groves!
> Ye wagon horses, ploughs and harrows!
> Ye capering lambs! ye cooing doves!
> Adieu, ye nightingales and sparrows!
>
> O, I'll begone! at once farewell
> To gooseberry wine and pear and codling!
> Farewell the sheep's harmonious bell!
> Farewell the gander's graceful waddling!

Farewell the compost's sweet perfume!
•Farewell rum-punch, nectareous liquor!
Farewell the pimples that illume
　The noses of the squire and vicar!

Adieu, my pipe! not that of old
　By swains Arcadian tuned so gaily,
But that of modern fame and mould,
　Invented by Sir Walter Raleigh.

And I'll renounce my dog and gun,
　And "bob" no more for eels in ditches,
The huntsman, horn, and hounds I'll shun
　And I'll cashier my leather breeches!

For me the fox may prowl secure,
　The partridge unmolested fly,
Whist, loo and cribbage I abjure,
　And e'en backgammon's lures defy.

The fair, its gingerbread and toys,
　Rough roads, deep ruts, and boist'rous weather,
Ye scenes of bliss, ye rural joys,
　Adieu! and, Bless ye, altogether.

Barham was duly elected, and soon afterwards became a Chaplain in Ordinary to the King and was presented by the

WAREHORNE.

Dean and Chapter of St. Paul's to the joint cure of St. Mary Magdalene and St. Gregory. A poor preacher oddly enough, he seems otherwise to have been a useful clergyman, though he mixed a good deal with the wits, wags and literate of the town and contributed freely to the journals and periodicals of the day.

Warehorne Church is a large and rather gloomy old building, though the last may be a mere impression from the amount of timber, yew trees, limes and elms, standing in and about its large graveyard, thickly strewn as it is with the mossy headstones of generations of farmers and smugglers. Among them are many to the Hodges of Leacon dating from the early eighteenth century, though they sit no longer in their ancient seats. A massive red-brick west tower, of not very much earlier date than Barham's incumbency, though it has taken on to its surface both age and ivy in that time, has an odd look attached to the old thirteenth-century stone fabric. It is a plain enough interior, comprising a nave with aisles and a chancel, but striking in the rather grim dignity of a large Gothic church in a quiet by-way that has not been tampered with for six hundred years. The nave arcade of five bays consists of pointed arches resting on slender circular columns, while the windows of both nave and chancel are mainly Decorated or Early English. In the head of a triple lancet window on the north side are set two small circles of stained glass, mainly red and yellow, with a figure in each armed with sword and shield, and facing one another in rather grotesque attitudes of attack and defence. This is supposed to represent a fight between Christ and Satan. The yellow shields held out at arm's length before the bodies of the two figures suggest footballs so strongly to all beholders as to detract no little from the sacred nature of the subject.

A large orchard spreads from the edge of the churchyard to the dip into the Marsh below, while on the other side the few houses that form the village are pleasantly distributed around an open green. It is a pretty enough spot in summer-time, but I rather suspect that a sense of the more tranquil beauties

WAREHORNE TO RYE

of nature formed no appreciable part of the otherwise abundant mental outfit of the Rev. Richard Barham.

Below the churchyard is the military canal and its everlasting but always fascinating wych elms, and a bridge over it carries the long lonely twisting by-road that leads across the Marsh to Snargate, which this whimsical parson used to traverse every Sunday. It is lonely enough to-day, you meet nobody on it, but a chance ploughman or looker, nor indeed is there any reason why you should. Green and rushy pastures, not here so clean as in many parts of the Marsh, spread far around, covered thickly in winter with plover, gulls,

WAREHORNE.

rooks, and starlings and more sparsely than in summer with the heavy Marsh sheep. The dry tasselled reeds rattle in the deep cold dykes, that follow the betimes grass-grown road. An occasional looker's cottage with its protecting ash or willow trees, its clamorous sheep dogs and always abundant store of ducks and chickens, or "chicken" to be locally correct, is the only near sign of human life. Snargate Church (St. Dunstan's) is almost hidden in a dark grove of trees, its hoary grey tower, where the brandy was so often stored, just showing above them. The church is of very fine proportions, while the interior is of the same period and not unlike that of Warehorne, a trifle smaller perhaps, but with a nave arcade supported like the other by graceful and slender cylindrical columns. A good old oak roof is supported by fine king-posts and tie-beams, while a lofty pointed west arch into the tower shows the unusual feature hereabouts of moulded imposts, though they are much worn away. It may be noted too that Snargate and Snave have been recently united and attached to Brenzett. To revert, however, to Warehorne, the main road thence continues a more than undulating four-mile course to Appledore. Taking a considerable turn inland from the Marsh, it leaves the old church of Kenardington perched bleak and bare upon the crest of a high hill to the left, and one is hardly surprised to hear that it was once shattered by lightning, and oddly enough about the same time as its neighbour of Ebony suffered the same misfortune. Within a mile or so of Appledore a most attractive old brick and tile homestead with large outbuildings stands near the road. Approaching it from the other direction, it would arouse more than a passing interest, as an ancient building at the rear of the house is then visible which would provoke the curiosity of any one with eyes in their head. This is a stone chapel with a steep gabled roof, recognizable even at a distance as mediaeval work. Once known as Horne Place and now as Horne farm, the property was owned by a family of that name from the days of John till those of Elizabeth and occupied by them till near the close of that period, when they moved to a house on land they had purchased in the next parish of Kenardington, still known as Little Horne. Early in Elizabeth's reign Horne Place passed through an heiress to a Guldeford, who refusing the oath of supremacy had to fly abroad, when the estate was forfeited to the Crown and conferred on Philip Chute, captain and standard-bearer at Boulogne. The Chutes were here till 1721, when the owner, failing issue, left it to the Austen family notable for centuries in this part of the world. Horne is now a large farm, and the chapel in question, though converted into two storeys and used as a store-house, is duly cherished from the ancient monument point of view and as a fabric is fairly perfect. It is some twenty-four feet long by half that width, and is of late fourteenth century date. The timbers forming a succession of Gothic arches which support the roof are in excellent condition and rest on ornamented stone corbels with shields. There is a long pointed east window with the tracery nearly perfect, and the same may be said of a north and south window with cusped-ogee heads and hoods to match. The house itself, as well as being good to look upon externally, is within a most engaging example of a seventeenth-century Manor house, with oak fittings and raftered ceilings. Some of it is probably earlier, some of it perhaps a little later. The spiritual needs of the Hornes seem to have been well supported as they also possessed a chapel in the south chancel of Appledore Church, still called by their long vanished name, as we shall have cause to notice anon. Appledore is well known to travellers as the junction for Lydd and New Romney. But the station is a mile out on the Marsh, while the place itself stands above the banks of the military canal, which with its double row of elms forming a wide grassy avenue upon the north side, serves as a cheery foreground to the ancient village with its uplifted many-gabled and beautiful old church. The wide village street running back from its precincts, which enclose church, vicarage and well-kept graveyard in a ring fence, is at least good to look upon and still contains a few of its old houses. This is one of the historic places of the Marsh where big things happened. The flats running inland from it, now drained by " sewers," are those of the old Rother estuary, which encircled the Isle of Oxney, though the north channel was then the main one. Appledore stood at the entrance of these far-reaching inland waters when they flowed on to the sea, first at Lympne and West Hythe and again later to Romney after it had become the chief, if not the only outlet.

It was a natural point of attack and defence, and is first

definitely heard of in the Saxon Chronicle, when the Danes sailing from Boulogne in 893 brought 250 ships up the Rother from New Romney and found a rude castle at Appledore. From this, the chronicler says they expelled the natives and established themselves in a better fortress raised by themselves. But all these strongholds, Saxon or Danish, were mere stockades on mounds or behind earthworks. The eighteenth century local historians had naïve visions of these Pre-Norman

APPLEDORE.

" castles " as redoubtable fortresses of mortared stone like those of the Normans. In the six intervening centuries between the occupation of these two doughty invaders, unless a few church towers may count as such, there was probably not a serious defensive work of masonry erected in the whole of England, save two or three castles built on the Welsh Marches by a group of Edward the Confessor's Norman friends, and even this proceeding raised a storm that cost their builders dear. The occupation of "Apuldwr" by the Danes must have ceased the following year when Alfred marched into Kent and so unwisely listened to their overtures for a peace, which they of course broke when it suited them.

Men have dicussed the derivation of Appledore for centuries. It is pretty safe to say it has nothing to do with apples and probably a good deal to do with dore, i.e. the Celtic word "dwr" water, which generally accounts for this termination unless there are special reasons against it. There is a much larger Appledore of course at the mouth of the Torridge in North Devon. Holloway thinks it is an old Teutonic word *Poldor* or a wet place, so atte-Poulder, which may be so, but I don't think it. The erudite Lambarde is altogether too ingenuous and thought it meant Appletree, which is not worthy of him. As I have nothing to suggest, but the termination which, however, I would back rather strongly, we will leave it at this ; particularly as I have not so far pestered the reader with any problematical derivations in these pages. Most of the names we have been concerned with are either too obvious or too cryptic to linger over. It is not as in the westerly portions of the island where place names seem to invite and almost worry you to derive them. Perhaps this is only because I know a certain amount of Welsh, which flavours the place names of so much more than Wales and nothing at all of the old Anglo-Saxon, the south-Saxon at any rate, but *wick* and *ham*.

The voluminous painstaking and generally admirable Hasted is very funny on his churches. He refers to the altogether attractive and fair-sized edifice here, the same in his day as now, as " a mean little church." He says the same of Ruckinge, oblivious to its Early English character. He thinks that when Appledore Church was destroyed by the French in 1381 it was rebuilt from the foundations, on the site of a Danish castle, with the material from the same ! There is a tradition that the church stands on the site of an old fort, which is likely enough seeing the excellent position for defence it occupies, and that a former church probably of wood stood on a spot some distance away.

It is not often that a highly qualified archaeologist lives next door to a country church, and furthermore as in this case has placed his knowledge of it in a handy leaflet, accessible to any interested visitor. As Appledore Church is thus favoured I shall merely state here that it consists of a handsome massive little west tower, probably it is thought of the transitional period, with a Tudor doorway, an Early English nave of three aisles and a chancel of the same period with two chapels. The north chapel though is distinctive, "a church in itself," as Dr. Cock describes it, of earlier date than the main building and set at right angles in transept fashion to the high chancel. But looking at the north aisle of the nave, it will be seen at once that the north arcade is missing and the proportions of the church thus thrown out of the normal. Here, however, Appledore's historical claims come in again. For the French burnt this north aisle, and it was rebuilt without an arcade, though the bases of the old pillars still exist.

APPLEDORE.

The south chancel is the Horne Chapel associated with Horne Place and its ancient family, though no memorials of them remain in the church but a recessed tomb assumed to be one. The interior is cheerful and well lighted. There is nothing pathetic about it as in the case of so many of its neighbours. There is a population of five or six hundred souls; and Appledore is not out of the world, and indeed a few summer visitors frequent it. The exterior of the church with its well-kept precincts and its happy

WAREHORNE TO RYE

situation at the foot of the wide village street is altogether charming.

The old court lodge farm stands perched on a knoll above the village, but the present buildings are modern. Near them are the remains of a Roman camp, and those of another are visible upon the further side of the village; nor would one have expected the Romans at Lympne to have left this other gateway to the coast unnoticed. A little stream or sewer runs down the flat valley near whose mouth Appledore stands and so under the military canal into the Marsh. This is all there is left of the main estuary that once circled round the north of the Isle of Oxney and carried the little fleets of other days to Newenden and even Bodiam.

It is an extremely pretty walk of about eight miles from here to Rye upon the shady banks of the military canal, till it joins the Rother, three miles short of the town. What is known as the military road follows the canal. Its quality varies from year to year—I was going to say from day to day. It is not much used, but being on a dead flat and gravelly (to put it mildly), not muddy, people on wheels of any kind are often inclined to venture it if they have not done so for a long time and forgotten its deceptive appearance. I have cycled it several times in the last dozen years and always regretted it but once, when they must have been doing something to it. It was constructed from Appledore to Winchelsea as a link in the chain of military communications in the Napoleonic war. But I only allude here to the Appledore section which does well enough now for heavy lorries or even cars, but for a cycle of any kind is to be avoided. A hundred yards away it looks at any point an excellent road. The result is that you are always imagining that smooth water is visible just ahead and expecting in a few seconds to be out of the grinding, slithery, loose gravel and be happy, and so mile after mile continue labouring, with ever blasted hopes, till you emerge on to a decent surface near Rye, and are then confronted by a toll gate! I cannot imagine who pays toll there except people who don't know the country, or the road or the many alternatives of entering Rye, from that direction by fine roads on the upland above or on the Marsh beneath. There are not many old toll gates left in England, and this is the most humorous one I know.

But however you travel it this is a most engaging path from Appledore to Rye, particularly on foot with the big trees giving character and even beauty of a tranquil kind to the solitary and deserted old canal. The pike and bream and roach lead, I should imagine, tolerably care-free lives in its waters, which only move when the wind gets through and ruffles their surface. High on the other side and close at hand rises the southern point of the Isle of Oxney, with the fine old church of Stone perched not far from its summit, and this is well worth turning aside for and mounting the two or three hundred feet by the steep lane that leads up to it. Beautifully situated on the further slope of the hill it looks north and eastward, up the fertile valley of the old Rother estuary towards Tenterden and away out to the distant chalk downs beyond. Ashford Church, vicarage and a wonderful half-timbered farm-house with projecting upper storey stand in an isolated group together, the little village lying at the bottom of the hill. The church has a fine massive tower, a nave and chancel, each with three aisles and of a generally Perpendicular character. There is a lofty west arch into the tower space resembling that of Snargate alone, in this neighbourhood, and with the same moulded imposts, though terribly crumbled on

STONE CHURCH (FROM BELOW).

WAREHORNE TO RYE 367

the north side. Over the chancel arch are two splayed trefcil windows with ogee hoods. Some fine old tie-beams and king-posts support the roof of the nave, which is plastered in. But the eastern half of the exposed chancel roof, beyond an apparently restored portion, is of barrel shape overlaid with cross-bars showing roses carved at the intersections.

Returning to the road, again the valley of the Rother soon

STONE CHURCH (FROM ABOVE).

opens wide between the Isle of Oxney and the uplands of Iden and Playden, and a short three miles from Rye the river itself rolls out under a bridge to join the canal. Here where the waters unite is a spot that artists have long ago discovered not altogether for the sake of the meeting waters, but for the further fact that the long twenty-mile avenue ends here with the canal in a fine group of tall and stately elms confronting the

AN OLD GATE OF ENGLAND

bare Marsh which, spreading away for miles from their feet, provides one of those arresting contrasts in landscape that cannot fail to touch the fancy of anybody who has got one. The road from here to Rye, between the Rother and the old cliffs, now improving in quality, if that be of consequence, makes a good finish whether to a day, or to a book. The long green sweep of the Marsh, with all its shifting lights, forges

MARSH, FROM CEMETERY HILL.

seaward from one edge of the road to the distant gleam of the sand dunes far away upon the Camber shore ; while upon the other, rise the bosky slopes, with interludes of sandstone cliff, against which the sea broke, just here, but a few centuries ago, till Rye town upon its rocky perch, from this approach as from every other, stands out inimitable and unique.

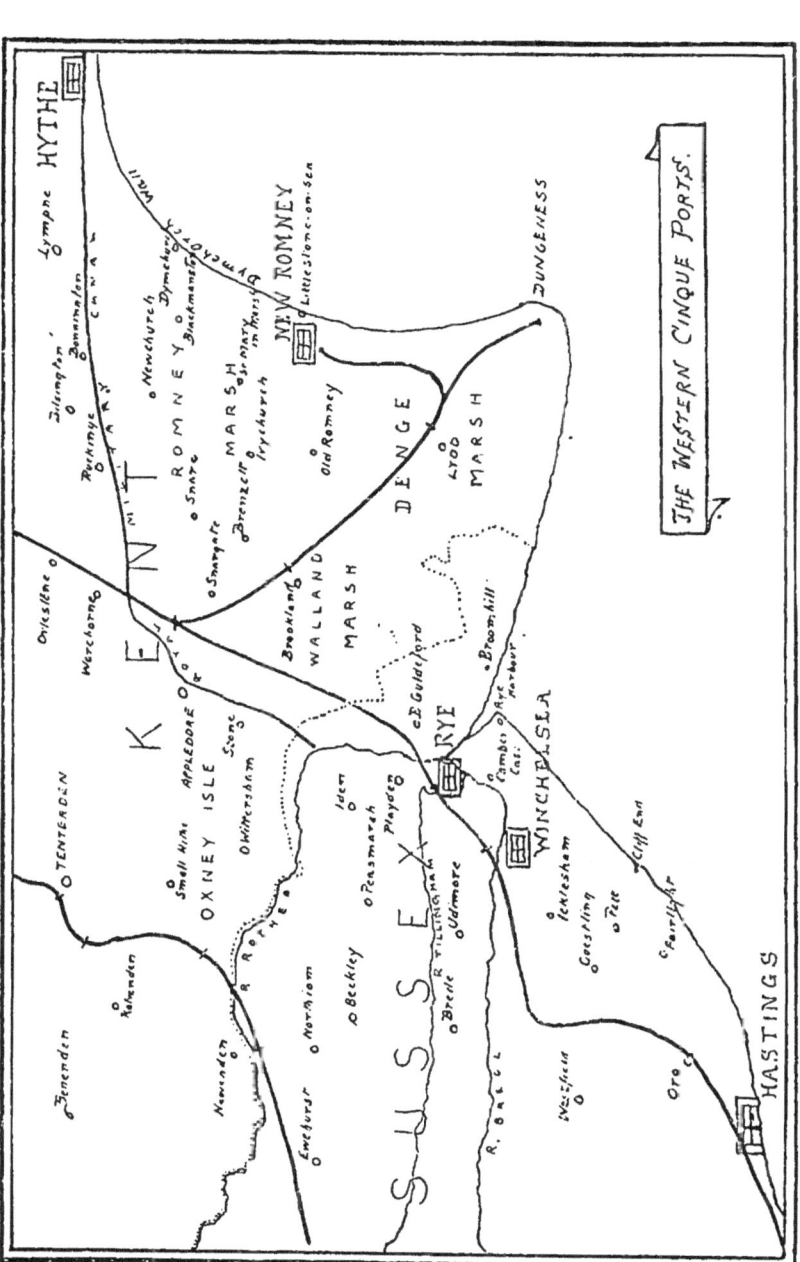

INDEX

ABINGTON, 86
Acton, 240
Agincourt, 125
Alards, The, 9, 119, 130, 131
Aldington, 334
,, Corner, 340
,, Knoll, 341
Allen family, 280
All Saints' Church, Hastings, 161, 162
Anderida, 216–219
,, Forest, 217
Appledore, 240, 254, 275, 296, 323, 361–365
Archbishops (Cantuar), 277
Ashburnham family, 186–189
Ashcombe, Lord, 223
Athelstane, King, 164
Aufidus Pantera, 325
Austen family, 360

BADDINGS GATE, Rye, 48
Bagot, Bishop, 80
Barclay, Capt., 310, 311
Barham [Thos. Ingoldsby], 351
Barons Grange, 244
Bate, Andrew, 274
Bate, Hermit, 278
Bathe de, 258
Battle, 187
Battle, Abbot of, 124, 125, 278, 279
Beachy Head, 161
Beauport, 177, 178
Beckley, 201, 225–228
Beuford, 215
Bexhill, 180
Bilsington, 341–343
,, Cross, 342
,, Priory, 342
Black death, 28
Blackmaston, 318, 319
Black Prince, The, 120
Bodiam castle, 220–224
Bonnington, 341

Botolphs bridge, 321
Bourne brook, 176
Boyne, Batte of, 87, 88
Boys, Miss, 158
Brede, 85, 201–206
,, Church, 203, 204
,, Place, 202
,, River, 22, 75, 109, 114, 116, 126, 142, 189, 192, 200
Brenzett, 271, 288, 289, 360
Brickwall, 208–211
Broad oak, 201
Brookland, 265–269
,, Church, 266, 277, 279
Broomfield, Thos., 195
Broomham, 186
Broomhill, 10, 106
Browne, 205
Buckhurst, Lord, 85
Bulverhythe, 175
Burdett, 195
Burnett, Bishop, 293
Burrows, Professor, 1, 3, 14
Burton, 182

CADBOROUGH, 120
Cade, Jack, 246, 280
Calais, 9
Camber, 100, 103, 105, 106, 126, 141, 142
,, Castle, 108, 109, 114, 127, 152
,, Sands, 98, 140, 144
Camden, 216, 228, 282
Carrier's farm, 212
Carter, 262
Castle tolls, 216
Caux, I. of, 124
Caxton, 279
Champneys, 55
Chapel bank, 240
Charles I, 85, 109, 127, 188
Charles II, 308
Cheseman, 307
Chute, 360

370

INDEX

Cinque Ports, 1-18
Clarendon, 188
Clifford, 143
Cobb family, 280, 334
Cobb Hall, 340
Cock, Dr., 365
Collier-Milward family, 176, 177, 178
Cooper, Durrant, 118, 125, 129, 152, 191, 203
Court-at-Street, 333-338
,, Hermit of, 334-338
Cousins, 175, 182
Cromwell, 127, 188
Cumberland, Duke of 64
Curteis family, 89, 246, 247

DALYNGRUGE, 222, 223
Damme, Battle of, 6
Deal, 10
Deedes family, 340
De la Mores, 290
Dengemarsh, 271
,, Hall, 271
De Montforts, The, 112, 113
Denis Duval, 38, 138
Dering family, 268, 271, 278
d'Eu Count, 166
Dieppe, 29, 85
Dodson, 91
Doleham, 205
Dover, 1, 2, 5, 10, 12, 170, 318
Drayton, The poet, 228
Dungeness, 141, 156, 252, 282, 283
Dymchurch, 306, 316-319
,, Wall, 317

EADBRIGHT, K., 295
Ealdbad, K., 288
Eanswythe, Saint, 288
Eastbourne, 161, 179
Eastbridge, 318, 319
East hill, Hastings, 160, 161
Ebony, 238
Ecclesbourne, 155, 160
Edgar gravestone, 274
Edulphs, The, 289
Edward the Confessor, 1, 2, 25
Edward I, 8, 9, 14, 112, 113, 115, 118, 193, 245, 277
Edward II, 9, 118
Edward III, 6, 9, 10, 25, 27, 39, 119

Edward IV, 193
Elizabeth, Q., 31, 34, 79, 128, 208, 210, 228, 307, 329
Ely, Bishop of, 113, 115
Erasmus, 339
Etaples, 48, 107
Etchingham, de, 117, 120, 193, 195
Etretington, 193, 195
Evans, Col., 93, 94
Eversfield, 182
Exden Valley, 216, 217, 218

FAGGE family, 289
Fairfield Church, 296
Fairlight Hd., 85, 103, 141, 143, 155, 156, 186
,, Church, 156
,, Glen, 157, 158
,, Place, 158
Faversham, 10, 11
Fecamp Abbey, 2, 26, 29, 113, 164, 166
Ferris, 160
Ferry Gate, Winchelsea, 114, 117
Finch, 119, 331
Finn, 277, 278
Fletcher (dramatist), 78
,, Bishop, 78-80
Folkestone, 10
Freebody, 195
Freeman, Professor, 296
Fresco Ho., Rye, 81
Frewen family, 203, 208-211
Froissart, 120
Furnese family, 303

GENEBELLE, 84
George Hotel, Rye, 37
George I, 64, 282
George IV, 93
Gibbon, 219
Gildas, 213
Godfrey family, 280, 290, 303
Godwin, Earl, 165
Gosley, Capt, 80
Grebell family, 64
Gris-nez, C., 48
Guestling, 155, 86, 99
Guldeford, 263
,, family, 261, 263
,, old ferry, 262
Gungarden, Rye, 48, 55

INDEX

HALL, 109
Halton, 161, 183
Ham Street, 349
Harold, K., 166, 295
Hasted, 282, 348, 363
Hastings, 1, 4, 5, 10, 11, 12, 85, 156, 190; account of, 160–184
  ,, Battle of, 165
  ,, Castle, 166, 167
Hawkhurst gang, 149–151
Henry I, 13
Henry II, 305
Henry III, 7, 29, 113, 131
Henry IV, 11, 308
Henry V, 12, 125
Henry VI, 23
Henry VII, 126
Henry VIII, 12, 18, 108, 109, 318, 333, 337
Hodges, 353
Holloway, 31, 51, 52, 53, 70, 80, 89, 216, 231, 246, 254
Holloway House, Rye, 52
Holmestone, 276
Holme, The, 284
Hook, Theodore, 249, 352
Hope, All Saints', 294
Horne Place, 360
Horsfield, 59, 92, 107, 194
Horsley, Sir V., 327
Huguenots, Rye, 32, 33
Hunt, 311
Hussey, 281
Hythe, 1, 5, 10, 11, 12, 110, 321
Hythe, West, 322, 327, 329, 333

ICKLESHAM, 113, 117, 155, 189
  ,, Church, 191
Iden, 243–246
Iden, Alexander de, 246
Igglesden, 337
Inderwick, 114, 130, 138
Iron industry, 226–231
Ivychurch, 271, 290

JAMES, Henry, 59–61
James I, 86
Jeake, 1, 31, 66–70, 87, 88, 128
John, K., 14
Jordon, 195
Jury's Gap, 251, 252, 282, 283

KENARDINGTON, 360
Kennett, 308
Kent ditch, 265
Knellstone, 194, 196, 198, 199
Knollys, 222, 223

LAKE, 297–300
Lambarde (historian), 257, 304, 333, 334, 335, 343, 344, 363
Lambarde, Thos., 303
Lamb, Capt., 158
Lamb family, 55, 61–64
Lamb House, 59–64
Landgate, Rye, 27, 40, 98, 99, 253
Lanfranc, Archbishop, 330
Leacon, 351
Leasam, 247
Leland, 124, 281, 333
Lennarde, 205, 297–300
Lewknor, 223
Littlestone, 312, 313–315
Liverpool, Lord, 96
Lord Warden, 2, 3, 10, 15, 33, 37, 82, 84, 87, 109, 115, 309, 329
Losenham, 220
Lovers' seat, 158
Lower Mark, 216
Luce, 124
Lydd, 10, 102, 251, 252, 258, 271–282
  ,, Church, 272, 234
Lympne, 321, 322, 329, 333

MAID of Kent, 333–338
Mansell, Sir John, 342
Masters, 333–339
Mathew of Paris, 105
Maytham, 219
Melville, Lord, 96
Merel, Sir W., 273
Mermaid Inn, Rye, 70–72
Mermaid Street, Rye, 65, 73
Meryon, 89
Midley, 286
Military road, 363
Millais, 137
Moat farm, 244–246
Monastery, Rye, 39, 56
Montfort de, 7
Monypenny, 219
Murray, Gen., 177

NEWCASTLE, Duke of, 89

INDEX

Newchurch, 319, 320
Newenden, 216, 217, 220
Newfoundland Fisheries, 18
New Inn (New Romney), 313
New Place, 191
New Romney, 1, 5, 10, 12, 14, 15, 280, 286, 294-315
  ,, ,, Church, 301-304
Norry, 85
Northiam 205-215
Noviadanum, 216

ODIARNE, 240
Offa, K., 164, 275
Old Hospital, Rye, 67
Ompteda, Baron, 181
Ore, 157, 159, 161, 181
Orgarswick, 318, 319
Orlestone, 348, 349, 350
Owlers, 148
Owlie, 240
Oxenbridge family, 202, 203, 204
Oxenbridge farm, 242

PALSTRE Court, 240
Parker, Archbishop, 228
Passelaye de, 245
Patmore, Coventry, 178
Pattison, Poet, 232, 233
Pay, 11
Peacocke's Grammar School, 38
Peasmarsh, 201, 231-233
Pelhams, The, 89, 177
Percy, 310
Pett, 103, 110, 155, 189
  ,, Level, 140, 141, 144, 146, 189
Pevensey, 10, 164, 165, 169, 218, 220, 325
Philippa, Q., 120, 131
Playden, 243, 246, 247
Plomer, 207
Portues, Bishop, 338
Portus Limenus, 317, 324
Pusey, 93

QUARRY hills, 338
Queen's Well, Rye, 32

RANGELY gang, 348
Rhee wall, 286, 287, 288
Richard I, 26, 27
Richard II, 10, 28, 124, 351

Richard III, 307
Richborough, 325
Robert of Winchelsea, 134
Rolfe family, 280
Rolvenden, 219
Romans on Romney Marsh, 254
Romney Hoy, 311
Romney Marsh, 21, 22, 100, 101, 107, 108, 141, 201, 249-329, 332, 333
Romney, Old, 286
Rother, river, 22, 48, 75, 99, 100, 105, 201, 215, 216, 217, 233, 237, 238, 241, 275, 278, 285, 286, 295, 296
Ruckinge, 346-348
Rudstone, Robt., 240
Ruffins hill, 339
Ruxley crew, 174
Rye, 1, 2, 4, 6, 10, 11, 12, 13; account of, 19-96, 99, 100, 101, 103, 105, 106, 112, 114, 118, 124, 125, 141, 189, 220, 251, 258, 275, 368
Rye bay, 252
Rye Golf Links, 101, 102
Rye harbour, 26, 98, 100

SACKVILLE, 205
Sandwich, 1, 5, 10, 12
Seaford, 10, 169
Selden, 216
Septuans, The, 268
Ship and Anchor Inn, Rye, 45
Shipway Cross, 329
Shipyard, Rye, 25
Shovel, Sir Cloudesly, 176
Sluys, Battle, 9
Smallhythe, 241
Smith, Roach, 323
Smuggling, 145-155
Snailham halt, 192
Snargate, 310, 355, 359, 360
Snave, 350
Spaniards, battle in Rye bay, 120-123
Spanish Armada, 6, 31, 50
St. Bartholomew, Massacre, 32
St. Clement's Church, Hastings, 161, 162, 195
St. Denis Abbey, 164
St. James of Compostella, 135
St. John's Priory, N. Romney, 304

INDEX

St. Lawrence Church, N. Romney, 304
St. Leonard, 134-136
St. Leonard's parish, Winchelsea, 134
St. Leonards (see Hastings)
St. Mahé, 9
St. Martin's Church, N. Romney, 304
St. Mary's Church, Romney Marsh, 316
St. Mary's Church, Rye, 53-59
Stocks farm, 239
Stokesly, Bishop, 293
Stone-in-Oxney, 238, 242, 366, 367
Striguils, The, 274
Studfall, Roman remains, 327
Stuppenny family, 303
Sweyn, 165

TENTERDEN, 10, 30
Thackeray, 138
Thanet, Earl of, 215, 233
Thomas à Beckett, 305
Tillingham river, 22, 75, 200, 205
Tintern Abbey, 274
Tufton, 215, 223
Tyler, Wat, 278

UDIMORE, 114, 117, 119, 120, 192-201
,, Court Lodge, 193

WALSINGHAM, Thos., 117, 119
Warehorne, 351-359
Warham, Archbishop, 336, 339
Watchbell Street, Rye, 42-45
Welland Marsh, 265, 271
Wellington, Duke of, 37, 183
Wesley, 70, 137
Westbroke, 271
White family, 209, 210
Wick, 276, 283
William the Conqueror, 1, 165, 166, 296
William III, 310, 311
William of Ypres, 48
Winchelsea, 1, 4, 5, 10, 12, 22, 25, 26, 27, 31, 84, 103, 105, 108; account of, 110-139
Winchelsea, beach, 142
Winchelsea, Old, 105, 106, 112, 131
Witches, 82, 83
Withers, 87
Wittersham, 233-241
Wolsey, Cardinal, 274
Woodhams, The, 195
Woolpack Inn, 265
Wyatts' rebellion, 240

YARMOUTH, 9, 13, 14, 15, 16
,, Herring Fair, 296-301
Ypres Tower, Rye, 28, 46, 78

www.ingramcontent.com/pod-product-compliance
Lightning Source LLC
Chambersburg PA
CBHW020828160426
43192CB00007B/560